ANTI-RACIST SCHOLAR-ACTIVISM

MANCHESTER
1824

Manchester University Press

'For the undercover guerrilla scholars, thieves for reparation, freedom-dreamers, and those pretending professional compliance while living another secret life, this is your book. Treasure it as a record, guide, and manifesto. Share it with your best-loved comrades and take heart. But don't show your boss.'
Gargi Bhattacharyya, author of *Rethinking Racial Capitalism: Questions of Reproduction and Survival*

'This is an excellent and welcome addition to literature on racism, activism, and higher education, and a unique resource for university students who are trying to navigate higher education institutions and think through the contradictions, tensions, and possibilities of being "in" the university, but not necessarily becoming "of" it, while committed to a politics of anti-racism. A necessary and compelling book.'
Aziz Choudry, editor of *The University and Social Justice* and *Activists and the Surveillance State*

'As a polemic on commitment and agency and an irreverent critique of the neoliberal university, *Anti-racist scholar-activism* is not just one book but many. A primer on the history of anti-racist thought, and a consideration of the epistemology and pedagogy of anti-racism. Expect to be provoked on this rollercoaster of a read.'
Liz Fekete, Director, Institute of Race Relations

'Including compelling readers to understand more fully the theories, meanings, and significance of the foundational organising concepts of the book – anti-racism and scholar-activism – Joseph-Salisbury and Connelly engage scholar-activist readers to reflect critically about our own work through the experiences of their study participants. Who among us has not faced situations described in the volume, but how can we better understand those, do better work, and become more authentic as we face dilemmas and contradictions as scholar-activists? These are the interventions the book makes into the readers' lives. Ending the book with "A manifesto for scholar-activism" challenges us to examine our praxes and is emblematic of the clarity of their own.'
Margo Okazawa-Rey, Professor Emerita, San Francisco State University

Anti-racist scholar-activism

Remi Joseph-Salisbury and Laura Connelly

Manchester University Press

The right of Remi Joseph-Salisbury and Laura Connelly to be identified as the authors of this work has been asserted by them in accordance with the Copyright, Designs and Patents Act 1988.

Published by Manchester University Press
Oxford Road, Manchester M13 9PL

www.manchesteruniversitypress.co.uk

British Library Cataloguing-in-Publication Data
A catalogue record for this book is available from the British Library

ISBN   978 1 5261 5795 9   hardback
ISBN   978 1 5261 5796 6   paperback

First published 2021

Typeset
by New Best-set Typesetters Ltd
Printed in Great Britain
by Bell & Bain Ltd, Glasgow

In memory of Aziz Choudry, whose fingerprints are all over this book; an outstanding scholar-activist, comrade, and inspiration to many!

Contents

Acknowledgements

This book was born out of our frustrations with academia: its institutional values and cultures, its harms, and its disconnect from the urgent issues of the real world. These frustrations have not gone away but we have learned from and alongside our participants, scholar-activist friends, and the many anti-racist scholar-activists that have gone before us, that there are contradictions in the university system that we can exploit in service to our communities of resistance. Researching and writing this book has stretched our thinking immensely and impacted upon our praxis for the better. There are many who have supported and inspired us along the way, and who have left an indelible mark on this book, hopefully transforming it beyond our initial rant to something more critical, and hopefully, more generative.

We owe our deepest gratitude to those academics and activists whom we have worked closely with in recent years. Patrick Williams and Becky Clarke in particular have been a great source of inspiration and friendship, providing examples of how to work in service to social justice. So many of our conversations with them have shaped this book in ways that are so fundamental as to be untraceable, with Patrick becoming particularly profound after several pints in Sandbar. Our dear friend Kerry Pimblott has also been an infinite source of wisdom and positivity, whose incredibly

Acknowledgements

incisive thought has shaped us both as scholar-activists, and who is someone for whom we have infinite admiration. Roxy Legane, too, has taught us so much about anti-racism, resistance, and organising, and has been unwavering in her support and friendship. Born out of a shared commitment to anti-racist social justice, but becoming much more, these friendships attest to the beauty and joy that can emerge out of resistance.

We are also grateful to those that we organise alongside as part of the Northern Police Monitoring Project and Resistance Lab where we have thought collectively about what it means to 'work in service', and to those involved in the No Police in Schools campaign who have shown us what it means for us each to 'struggle where you are'. We owe much to, and feel very lucky to be a part of, this powerful and growing social justice infrastructure in Greater Manchester and beyond.

We're deeply grateful to the many friends, colleagues, and comrades who read and commented on drafts of the book's chapters: Kerry Pimblott, Adam Elliott-Cooper, Karis Campion, Scarlet Harris, Becky Clarke, Patrick Williams, Bridget Byrne, Meghan Tinsley, Waqas Tufail, Tom Redshaw, Manny Madriaga, Carlos Frade, Chantelle Lewis, Suryia Nayak, Nadim Mirshak, Stephen Ashe, Katucha Bento, Derron Wallace, Daiga Kamerāde, and Aziz Choudry. As well as reviewing a chapter, Luke de Noronha has offered conversations that have had more impact than he might realise, and generously talked us through a crisis in confidence on the eve of submission. And thanks, too, to Ornette Clennon, who has offered guidance and mentorship throughout, and who inexplicably read a late draft of the whole book in a matter of days. This informal peer review process encapsulates much of the supportive and collegiate spirit that we suggest is integral to scholar-activism. The rigorous feedback pushed the book much further and – like our participants – challenged us on our idealised notion of scholar-activism. For this, we are incredibly thankful. And thanks to those colleagues who have supported us within our institutions, particularly Bridget Byrne, Claire Alexander, Meghan Tinsley, Karis Campion,

Acknowledgements

Dharmi Kapadia, Luke de Noronha, Gaynor Bagnall, Tina Patel, and to those working elsewhere, who have continually offered support, Nadena Doharty in particular.

Shout-out to Jas Nijjar, Tanzil Chowdhury, and Leon Sealey-Huggins who have all inspired and supported us. And thanks from Remi, to those at the Racial Justice Network, with whom he learnt lots about anti-racist activism. Thanks to Laura and Oliver for their precious friendship. And thank you to the many activists and scholars, unnamed here, but with whom we have shared comradeship along the way.

A huge thank you goes to our families: to our parents, Christiana, Gary, Dawn and Rob; to Granda Norman, Grandma Dot, Nanna Flo, and Nanna Mu; to India, Talia, Rach, Anna, Jamie, Damo, and Ian; and to Archie and Sunny who have made the last few years of our lives so special. It's difficult to put into words how much we owe, love, and value you all.

Thanks, ultimately, to our participants whose insights and wisdom have fundamentally shaped the book, and our praxis, and to those many anti-racist scholar-activists who have gone before us.

Introduction: anti-racist scholar-activism and the neoliberal-imperial-institutionally-racist university

The seeds for this book were planted back in 2015 as we were in the final stages of completing our PhDs. Our earnestness about the potential of academia and our role as would-be academics was quickly souring into cynicism. We were deeply frustrated by what we saw as a disconnect between the university and the urgent issues of the real world: between scholarship and activism. Perhaps most of all, we were frustrated by our inability to navigate academia in a way that bridged that gap and allowed us to put our scholarship to work in service to social justice generally, and anti-racism specifically. As we have come to know the university more intimately, much of our initial cynicism has not only endured but deepened. That said, we have become more attentive to the contradictions in the university system, the pockets of hope and possibility we might exploit. We have also become more aware of, and inspired by, the work and praxes of those who occupy the margins of the university, finding ways to combine scholarship and activism – that is, those who we might think of as scholar-activists.

It is the perspectives and experiences of twenty-nine such people that we centre in this book; a book that delves into the complexities, complicities, challenges, and possibilities associated with anti-racist scholar-activism. The book reflects growing interest in scholar-activism in recent years, as seen in the upswell of blogs, events, and conferences on this topic. This is not to say that the practice of anti-racist scholar-activism is new. Far from it, it has a long and rich lineage. Yet, while there are many academics involved in anti-racist activism 'on the ground' and activism has under-pinned the radical scholarship of anti-racist academics past and present, very few have taken the praxes of anti-racist scholar-activism itself as their substantive subject matter, particularly beyond the US context. We think it is time to take anti-racist scholar-activism seriously as a subject of intellectual inquiry, not simply to fill a gap in knowledge, for that alone is a poor reason to do research. Rather, the current national and inter-national higher education (HE) context demands our collective response. The advancing pace of neoliberalism; the imperial academy's long history of reproducing structural violence and its deepening commitment to its courtship with the State; its suffocating institutional racism, in particular – all mean it is time that anti-racist scholar-activism moves its resistance from the margins to the centre. We therefore build upon the global Black Lives Matter (BLM) mobilisations of 2020, and the wide-ranging activisms taking place on HE campuses across the world, to give renewed attention to the university as a site of, and space from which we can engage in, anti-racist struggle.

This book makes three key interrelated interventions. Firstly, building on rich traditions of anti-racist scholarship and activism, we offer a new empirically informed perspective on what anti-racist scholar-activism means today – one that pushes beyond simplistic common-sense understandings in order to problematise and complicate the term. We suggest that it is better to think of scholar-activism as a verb rather than scholar-activist as a noun – that is, as something we do, rather than something we are. We show that anti-racist scholar-activism is anchored by a counter-hegemonic notion of working *in service* to communities of resistance,[1] and to anti-racism more broadly. Secondly, in considering the institutional context in which university-based scholar-activism is situated, we critique what we refer to as the *neoliberal-imperial-institutionally-racist university* from the standpoint of anti-racist scholar-activism. We explore how, mediated by technologies of neoliberalism, the university imposes a range of barriers, challenges, and – what we conceive of as – forms of *backlash* upon those engaged in anti-racist scholar-activism. Our contention is that despite the hegemony of these forces, there remain pockets of contradiction and possibility within the contemporary university. Applying the little-known concept of *constructive complicity* to the neoliberal-imperial-institutionally-racist university context, we show how those engaged in scholar-activism seek to exploit these pockets of possibility to (partially) mitigate, offset, and utilise the complicities that arise from affiliating with institutional power for the benefit of anti-racism. Thirdly, and related to the last point, we consider the wide-ranging ways that anti-racist scholar-activists can and do exploit the contradictions of the university. These include but are not limited to: the redirecting of resources – a praxis we call *reparative theft*; the production of work *in service* to communities of resistance; and *struggling where we are*. The latter is a concept that we develop based on a passing comment from the Jamaican-born pre-eminent public intellectual Stuart Hall in order to explore critical pedagogy, the union, and campus agitation.[2] Along the way, and with extensive reference to wider literatures (which we encourage the reader to follow),[3] we delineate some key principles that we argue guide anti-racist scholar-activism: we return to them in our manifesto for anti-racist scholar-activism.

Despite advancing a trenchant critique of contemporary HE, this book is written with a cautious optimism about the opportunities it presents for anti-racist resistance, and specifically for anti-racist scholar-activism. We follow Stuart Hall in practising 'pessimism of the intelligence, optimism of the will'.[4] We are deeply frustrated by the state of the world and of our universities. Yet, we are committed to finding the openings that we can exploit; to fighting back; to putting our resources, status, and privileges to work in service to anti-racism. In this respect, we draw influence from what the American historian Robin D.G. Kelley refers to as *freedom dreaming*.[5] To freedom dream is to embrace a politics which has 'more to do with imagining a different future than being pissed off about the present', though the latter certainly holds strong. This dreaming of a better world is not entirely abstract, but rather is built out of a long history of Black resistance. It is a recovery of the scraps and fragmentary visions left behind by revolutionaries. In this book, we combine the insights of our participants with the lessons of activists, intellectuals, and movements that have gone before us, as well as some of our own reflections forged through practice. In doing so, we seek to intersperse our more despondent arguments with the piecing together of shards of hope that map out a vision for anti-racist scholar-activism in the contemporary moment.

Although we want this book to have utility outside of academia, we recognise that it will likely be of interest to academics and students primarily. In the first instance, we hope that the ideas we present will resonate with those already involved in anti-racism, as well as other forms of radical activism. Remembering that we are all always developing, we hope the participants' accounts that we feature will encourage reflexivity and collective considerations of how we might all refine our praxes. This process of learning and refining has certainly been (and will continue to be) part of our journey. We also hope the book will be of interest to those who may not consider themselves to practise scholar-activism but nonetheless engage in, or are open to, academic approaches that cross-cut with some of the praxes we explore in this book: public intellectuals, critical pedagogues, and those involved in critical, engaged, and applied approaches to research, for example. There may be other readers who adopt more traditional approaches within academia, for whom this book may be discomforting. We only hope that it will be read with an open mind and in the good spirit with which it is intended – that is, with a view to encouraging more academics to adopt praxes that serve anti-racism, but also recognising and appreciating the small acts of good practice that many academics – not just scholar-activists – are already engaged in. Throughout the book, we offer small examples of this good practice to show that all of us can embed scholar-activist principles into our praxis, even those of us who have until now been compelled to invest energy in simply surviving in a racist, sexist, classist, ableist, and heteronormative academia,[6] or have had our horizons narrowed by the metric culture that is becoming omnipresent in universities across much of the world.[7] In this regard, *Anti-racist scholar-activism* is not intended merely to demarcate and divide but to foster a spirit of collectivity that urges readers to 'resurrect a language of resistance and possibility'.[8]

Whilst this book should be informative for those thinking about how to practise scholar-activism, we should be clear that this is not a simple 'how to' manual: it is not intended to be prescriptive. Although we offer some glimpses of praxes, we are deliberate in avoiding a descent into overly specific and particularised examples, or case studies. We want to resist overdetermining scholar-activism. That said, we endeavour to provide a broad set of ideas, principles, and frameworks that can be taken up, interpreted, and applied by different people, in different contexts, and in different ways. We delineate these principles throughout the book, before returning to them in our manifesto for anti-racist scholar-activism, the book's final chapter. We are sure that some ideas and praxes will resonate with some readers more than others because there is no one way to do scholar-activism. We also recognise that some of what we map out will be up for debate. With this in mind, we look forward to seeing the ideas advanced and refined, and challenged (in good faith, of course) elsewhere.

In the following pages of this chapter, we identify three key coordinates within which we locate and contextualise anti-racist scholar-activism – that is, anti-racism, scholar-activism, and the neoliberal-imperial-institutionally-racist university. These coordinates provide the backdrop for the exploration of anti-racist scholar-activism that we go on to articulate in this book.

We will take each in turn, and then afterwards briefly discuss the research underpinning the book and provide an overview of its structure.

Anti-racism in Britain

Anti-racism, as Scarlet Harris explains, has rarely been regarded as a subject of 'serious intellectual interest',[9] despite the existence of a sizable and growing body of scholarship on race, ethnicity, and racism. It is, therefore, an ill-defined, as well as fluid concept.[10] Common-sense definitions tend to construct anti-racism as the inverse of racism. Yet, despite their seductive simplicity,[11] these definitions are, as Alastair Bonnett notes, inadequate.[12] Such definitions narrow the scope of the complex and diverse forms of resistance that have emerged under the name of anti-racism, whilst also obscuring the loaded and contested nature of the term. Adam Elliott-Cooper points to some of the messiness of anti-racism when he notes how anti-racist academics and activists grapple with the tension that exists between confronting racial inequities on the one hand, and avoiding the reproduction or essentialising of race on the other.[13]

Anti-racist resistance in Britain has a vast and complex history, which makes it impossible to speak about anti-racism 'as a unitary or unproblematic phenomenon'.[14] What is referred to as anti-racism is characterised by heterogeneity. Alana Lentin highlights three key strands that have been formative in the development of British anti-racism. Firstly, emerging in the 1960s, was a 'solidaristic anti-racism' tied closely to trade unions and Left-wing movements. The concerns and foci of this strand of anti-racism were largely confined to opposing far-Right groups. Secondly, in the 1970s, came forms of anti-racism inspired by Black Power. Insistent on the self-organisation of people of colour, or *politically Black* communities,[15] this form of anti-racism was key to the development of a vocabulary and framework that understands racism as an *institutional* problem that is driven and perpetuated by the State.[16] John Narayan has shown how the anti-racism of British Black Power not only sought to unite African, Caribbean, and Asian people in Britain but also 'conjoined explanations of domestic racism with issues of imperialism and global inequality'.[17]

A third key form of anti-racism emerged in the 1980s, particularly through local Labour Party administrations. This tradition, referred to by Paul Gilroy as 'municipal anti-racism',[18] reified ethnic groups in ways that undermined the solidarity of political Blackness and pitted different ethnic groups against one another. It also advanced depoliticised, individualistic, and psychologically based understandings of racism – that is, racism as individual prejudice. Such understandings marked a stark divergence from the institutional understandings advanced in the Black Power tradition but were perhaps more compatible (in a relative sense) with the far-Right focused anti-racism of the 'white Left'.[19] As Jenny Bourne articulates, in this period '[t]he anti-racist struggle moved from the streets to the town halls where it became detached from the larger struggle for social justice and, under the heavy hand of management, froze into a series of techniques to achieve "equal opportunity"'.[20] In doing so, municipal anti-racism created 'a cadre of anti-racism professionals'[21] and fed a booming race relations industry.[22]

Despite emerging at different moments, these three forms of anti-racism have not been discrete or isolated. Indeed, it is the coalescence and antagonisms of these traditions that make the history (and present) of British anti-racism so complex and heterogeneous. Shaped by this history, there are at least two overlapping elements that lie at the heart of contemporary British anti-racism that are worth (re)highlighting here. The first concerns proximity to the State and, relatedly, the extent to which the State is seen as part of the problem or the solution. In this regard, Alana Lentin has suggested that the key tensions in British anti-racism are perhaps not between activist groups (though there are, of course, many tensions) but between the versions of 'anti-racism' practised by State institutions on the one hand, and those practised by activist and community groups on the other.[23] The second element – relatedly – concerns understandings of racism, and specifically whether racism is understood as a problem of individual attitudes, prejudice, and bigotry, or as an institutional and structural issue. As Alana Lentin argues, 'British anti-racism can be said to be shaped by the split between the oppositional interpretations of racism as either institutionally engendered or as a set of behavioural attitudes.'[24] This question of understanding racism is fundamentally important not only in its own right but because it shapes the nature of anti-racist interventions.

Reflecting on the contemporary moment, Liz Fekete – director of the radical British think tank the *Institute of Race Relations* – makes observations reminiscent of Lentin's. She argues that whilst once established by grassroots groups, the anti-racist agenda is now largely set by a multi-agency 'professionalised' industry that responds to racism via hate-crime panels and anti-extremism bodies comprised of State, private, and voluntary sector organisations. This industry, like municipal anti-racism before it, operates to delegitimise 'social movements that take a more transformative, radical approach', and locks 'out from the discussion all those who campaign against structural racism'.[25] This marginalising of those engaged in the more radical, structural, and institutional-focused anti-racist traditions has occurred over several decades but surfaced particularly prominently as we write in 2021.

Commissioned in response to the BLM protests of 2020 and published in the Spring of 2021, the UK government's Commission on Race and Ethnic Disparities report (the Sewell Report) provoked strong criticism from anti-racist communities (and beyond) for, alongside other reasons,[26] its attack on the concept of institutional racism. It came as little surprise to many that the report reached conclusions that pushed strongly against the concept, and thus the thrust of the global BLM movement which, at least in part, centred on the persistence of institutional racism. After all, the report's author (Tony Sewell) and the influential Conservative tasked with setting up the Commission, Munira Mirza, had both previously downplayed, if not outright denied, the presence of institutional racism.[27] Though we are reluctant to give much attention to such a problematic report, the implications of its findings are instructive of the contemporary landscape for anti-racism. As the *Institute of Race Relations* notes, 'where racism in Britain is acknowledged in the report, the emphasis is placed on online abuse, which is very much in line with the wider drift in British politics and society away from understanding racism in terms of structural factors and locating it instead in prejudice and bigotry'.[28] The downplaying and denial of institutional racism diverges notably from the findings of the 1999 Macpherson Report, commissioned by the then UK Home Secretary Jack Straw into the police (mis)handling of the murder of Black teenager Stephen Lawrence. The Macpherson Report, limited as it was,[29] highlighted institutional racism in the investigation into the murder of Stephen Lawrence and, in doing so, brought institutional racism into the mainstream of political and popular discourse on race in Britain. The Sewell Report is but the latest example of a concerted effort to lash back against the findings of the Macpherson Report, the concept of institutional racism, and the radical anti-racist tradition.

To be clear, we are not suggesting here that the Sewell Report is an anti-racist report in even the more municipal anti-racist sense. Rather, we are suggesting that the report is instructive because, although it may represent an attack on anti-racism more broadly, it is an attack on more radical, institutionally focused forms of anti-racism in particular. It attempts, therefore, to confine the scope of anti-racism, if not absolutely, at least to its individual-focused forms. But whilst the report's symbolic (and the likely ensuing material and political) implications paint a pessimistic picture for the more radical institutionally focused anti-racist traditions, this is only a partial picture. The widespread opposition to and rejection of the report, particularly amongst anti-racist activists and organisations, is indicative of an enduring tradition that holds more critical (structural) understandings of racism, a tradition evident to a certain extent in the 2020 BLM protests. Our point here then is that although anti-racism is fraught and complex – and though more liberal, municipal anti-racism may be in the ascendency – the radical tradition forged through the Black Power era lives on.

Given the ascendency of municipal anti-racism in the 1980s, it is perhaps no surprise that Paul Gilroy, writing in the 1990s, decried 'the end of anti-racism'.[30] It was in a similar vein that the UK-based intellectual, activist, and once director (1973–2013) of the *Institute for Race Relations*, Amba-lavaner Sivanandan, urged us to take up Black Liberation as 'a richer and more long-term project of emancipation than that offered by what was perceived as the narrow confines of anti-racism'.[31] Despite these fervent critiques, and the complex history of anti-racism in Britain, we feel strongly that 'anti-racism' should not be abandoned as a term. It need not be reduced to its more narrowly defined and depoliticising incarnations, and there are a multitude of examples of activism and scholarship that continue in its radical spirit. Moreover, its declining use in municipal and institutional settings – often overridden instead by discourses of diversity, equality and inclusion, and unconscious bias – increases the opportunity for its reclamation.

As we will go on to demonstrate throughout the book, despite some nuanced differences in understandings of anti-racism, each of the twenty-nine participants situates their work in the radical, self-organising, and emancipatory traditions of anti-racism – that is, traditions that view racism as a structurally and institutionally embedded phenomenon that is State-driven, historically rooted, and intimately tied to legacies of imperialism and colonialism. Following our participants, the anti-racism to which we refer is also one that is inextricably linked to other resistance movements – a point we consider in more depth, and through a Black feminist lens, in the next section of this chapter. Like Fekete, we understand anti-racism to be most powerful when it is cross-community – when solidarity cuts across race and class divides, and is local, national, *and* international in nature – and to be most persuasive when it is 'tailored towards specific interventions'.[32] Our participants are involved in interventions focused on a range of issues and areas, including: policing; prisons; immigration and the hostile environment;[33] education; Islamophobia; legal frameworks such as the UK government's counter-terrorism strategy, Prevent;[34] housing; work and labour rights; and a range of others. Although we avoid descending too deeply into specific and particularised examples in this book, the nature of these interventions no doubt informs the perspectives of our participants and the arguments we set out in *Anti-racist scholar-activism*.

Anti-racist scholar-activism: tracing its foundations

In existing literature, (university-based) scholar-activism refers to the dual role occupied by academics who combine scholarship and activism in the pursuit of social justice.[35] In some respects, it describes an approach that is vastly different to, perhaps even antithetical to, traditional approaches within academia; one which seeks to harness the power and resources of universities for activist groups and/or communities,[36] and is embedded in and forged through involvement in resistance movements.[37] Yet in other ways, specific praxes of scholar-activism might overlap with other approaches within academia. With this in mind, we tread a fine line in the pages that follow between employing a definition of scholar-activism that is so narrow it draws upon idealised versions of activism and one that is so broad it overinflates the concept, making it vacuous and empty of definitional power.

We use the term scholar-activism in this book because it is both commonly used and widely understood. Moreover, despite its problematics – which we come to in the next chapter – scholar-activism was the term most favoured by our participants. We acknowledge, however, that what is invoked through the term scholar-activism, and what we have described above, overlaps significantly with a range of other terms in existing literature and discourse. As such, we adopt 'scholar-activism' in an expansive sense in order to capture something of the essence of a range of related terms, including Patricia Hill Collins's *intellectual activist*,[38] Walter Rodney's *guerrilla intellectual*,[39] Stefano Harney and Fred Moten's *subversive intellectual*,[40] and a range of variants including *activist scholar*,[41] *academic activist*,[42] and *activist academic*.[43] We use the expansive term scholar-activism to also capture the even more subtle distinctions that are drawn, often through punctuation, to signify different emphases.[44] Notwithstanding the nuances and different inflections of these terms, there are significant similarities in their defining characteristics and the forms of praxes they encourage. Furthermore, some of the conceptual work underpinning these other terms, as you will see, informs our theorisation of anti-racist scholar-activism in this book. Although this literature is instructive, our task in this book is to explicate more clearly the particular forms that *anti-racist* scholar-activism takes. In order to do this – and to locate the work of our participants in a longer genealogy that extends beyond those using related terms – here we want to touch upon some of the key tenets that underpin the radical scholarship and praxes of some of the seminal figures whose work has shaped the vision of anti-racist scholar-activism that we go on to capture in this book.

Whilst myths of objectivity and neutrality characterise traditional academic practice, more radical work, particularly within feminist and anti-racist traditions, has insisted on the importance of rejecting neutrality in favour of taking up the side of oppressed communities. This is the first tenet we want to highlight. The African American intellectual and activist W.E.B. Du Bois captured this orientation most powerfully when he reflected that 'one could not be a calm, cool, and detached scientist while Negroes were lynched, murdered, and starved'.[45] The message that Du Bois conveys is that there is simply too much at stake to engage in pretensions of neutrality. Moreover, such pretensions are ignorant (in the racial epistemological sense)[46] to the unequal nature of the status quo. It is this to which the US revolutionary Black activist and academic Angela Y. Davis refers, in her oft-cited words: 'in a racist society, it is not enough to be non-racist, we must be anti-racist'. As we go on to argue in this book, rather than undermining academic rigour, the explicitly political and partisan nature of anti-racist scholar-activism offers a higher level of integrity and honesty than scholarship that purports to be objective. It makes clear – rather than hides – the assumptions and positions that underpin scholarship. It represents a stronger conviction for 'fact finding, bearing witness and truth telling'[47] that is tested and refined through engagement in resistance. This brings us to our next point.

The relationship between theory and action is central to the tradition that we want to delineate here and is, therefore, the focus of our second tenet. As Sivanandan urged us, we must not simply think for thinking's sake, but think in order to do.[48] This emphasis on doing was similarly central to Frantz Fanon's assertion (referencing Marx) that 'what matters is not to know the world, but to change it',[49] as well as to the claim made by Fred Hampton – the former chairman of the Illinois chapter of the Black Panther Party – that 'theory with no practice ain't shit'. These statements should not be misread as disavowals of theory. Rather, they point to a particular approach to theorising. The work of the Black feminist intellectual bell hooks is particularly instructive in this regard: she reminds us of the importance of theory, pushing us towards a richer understanding of the liberatory purpose that theory can serve.[50] With the relationship between theory and action in mind, and drawing upon the Brazilian critical pedagogue Paulo Freire, we use the concept of *praxis* throughout this book in order to capture the dialectic between 'reflection and action'.[51] Always with a view to social transformation, the concept of praxis is underpinned by and informing of theorisation.

Related to the understanding that better scholarship is produced when it is informed by struggle, the third tenet we want to put forward pertains to embeddedness. As the Guyanese Pan-Africanist Walter Rodney insists, spending time outside of university campuses with those engaged in resistance is of fundamental importance: sitting down with, listening to, and learning from – that is, grounding with – one another.[52] Antonio Gramsci pushes this a little further in his vision of the *radical organic intellectual*.[53] Whilst the conservative intellectual acts as an agent of the status quo – identifying with 'the dominant relations of power' in society and in turn becoming 'propagators of its ideologies and values'[54] – the radical organic intellectual is directly involved in counter-hegemonic struggle on the side of the oppressed. Such involvement can lead to greater recognition that knowledge is produced by 'the people', as the Colombian early adopter of action research Orlando Fals-Borda insists.[55] Similar lessons can be drawn from Black feminism.[56] Central to scholar-activism, therefore, is theorisation 'from below'. In this regard, anti-racist scholar-activism should not involve doing work *on* oppressed communities. Rather, as we discuss in Chapter 2, it should entail meaningful engagement *with* and embeddedness *within* what Sivanandan calls communities of resistance.

A fourth tenet informing the vision of anti-racist scholar-activism that we are articulating relates back to some of the issues we noted earlier in relation to the history of anti-racism. Here, we advance an understanding of race as being internal to and intersecting with other structures of oppression. As Stuart Hall once said, 'I have never worked on race and ethnicity as a kind of subcategory. I have always worked on the whole social formation which is racialised.'[57] In this sense, race is better understood not as a 'thing' in and of itself, but rather as internal to all social processes.[58] Conceived of in this way, race ought not to be seen as a 'rival' variable to class. Indeed, as the Pan-African Marxist revolutionary C.L.R. James teaches us, race is not incidental to class any more than class is incidental to race.[59] Thus, just as Western Marxism should continue to be challenged for its failure to understand the struggle of Black people globally,[60] so too should the 'growing number of self-styled activist-intellectuals' who adopt 'racial politics that reduce the structure of the modern world to a single immutable antagonism: between blackness and anti-blackness.'[61]

A consideration of racism and its intersections is foundational to Black feminist thought, which points us towards more incisive forms of anti-racism that are better equipped to grapple with the complexities of the task at hand. Black feminism rejects 'additive approaches to oppression'[62] in favour of analysis that considers how race, gender, class, and other structuring forces form an 'overarching system of domination,'[63] in what Patricia Hill Collins refers to as the *matrix of domination*. This concept is integral to our arguments in this book. By rejecting the reduction of people to 'one category at a time', an intersectional lens engenders recognition of the relationality of social positions, as well as the power relations that are constituted by and are constituent of those positions.[64] This approach is essential in anti-racist movements since, as the radical thinker and activist Andaiye reminds us through her reflection on the Working People's Alliance in Guyana, too often our movements privilege male and middle-class leadership over women's and working-class leadership. This is despite the fact that, as contemporary work attests, anti-racist campaigns are often led by Black women.[65]

A fifth tenet that we want to spotlight here is the importance attributed within scholar-activist traditions to communicating knowledge outside of the academy. Once again, we can take our instruction from the late Stuart Hall who saw the 'communication of ideas to as wide an audience as possible' to be a paramount necessity.[66] Central to scholar-activism is a repudiation of the locking of knowledge into the university and the simultaneous mechanisms of exclusion that function to lock communities out. A similar level of attentiveness is paid to communication by Patricia Hill Collins, who, in her theorisation of intellectual activism, urges us to adopt two key strategies. The first relates to *speaking truth to power*, which requires us to use the power of knowledge to 'confront existing power relations' within society.[67] The second, *speaking truth to the people*, involves bypassing the powerful – and thus, conserving energy – to speak with those whom Collins calls 'the masses'.[68] Key here is the idea of operating on multiple registers – that is, of maintaining a focus on challenging the matrix of domination, without losing sight of how the greatest potential for social justice resides not with those occupying positions of (institutional) power but within communities of resistance.

The last tenet we want to draw upon here emerges from Black Studies, and particularly Stefano Harney and Fred Moten's formative work on *The Undercommons*.[69] Pointing to the contradictions and tensions associated with working in the university, Harney and Moten emphasise the importance of being 'in but not of' the institution. As they do so, they nod to the possibilities brought about through our affiliation with the university,[70] whilst more forcefully urging the *subversive intellectual* to remain critical of the university as a neoliberal-imperial-institutionally-racist space. We are to remember not only that our priorities lie outside of the university, but that they are often oppositional to those of the university. With this in mind, the task of the subversive intellectual is to undermine the university or, in Harney and Moten's terms, to 'spite its mission'.[71] As the US sociologist Steven Osuna implores, we should 'exploit the contradictions of the system in order to … organise against it';[72] we should put our affiliation with institutional power to good use.

Although these tenets are non-exhaustive, and there are others that we draw out as the book progresses, they offer an insight into some of the key influences on contemporary anti-racist scholar-activism as we conceive of it. We do not intend to suggest that each of the tenets are unique to anti-racist scholar-activism. Indeed, commonalities exist between anti-racist and other forms of scholar-activism, such that we hope some of the ideas contained in this book will resonate with those engaged in resistance movements that centre gender, disability, class, and sexuality. We and our participants have certainly taken lessons from these other movements. Indeed, taking intersectionality seriously requires approaches that are attentive to each of these issues and we hope that the anti-racist scholar-activist praxes we unpack are demonstrative of such attentiveness. Moreover, scholar-activism is also not alone in its counter-hegemonic approach. Critical or applied approaches to scholarship have strong foundations not only in the social sciences and humanities but across a range of disciplines, and yet, in ways both fundamental and subtle, are different to scholar-activism, as should become clearer throughout the book. The same could be said of public intellectualism. As important and overlapping as such approaches are, they are perhaps less insistent on the 'talk-plus-walk'[73] of scholar-activism – that is, its engagement in struggle and embeddedness within communities of resistance.[74] Some might argue that what we have articulated in this section and what we go on to unpack across the book is simply good academic practice. Though we would not disagree, we hold that such good practice rubs against the hegemony of, and hegemonic practice within, the neoliberal-imperial-institutionally-racist university.

The neoliberal-imperial-institutionally-racist university: an overview

Throughout this book, we refer to British universities as neoliberal, imperial, and institutionally racist, or as neoliberal-imperial-institutionally-racist. In this section, we begin to set out why. Despite their outward projection as spaces of enlightenment and bastions of progressiveness, universities are neither democratic nor meritocratic spaces.[75] They are not – and never have been – open, equal, or levelling. Rather, as Osuna – writing in the Black Radical tradition – reminds us, they are a key apparatus in the maintenance of a deeply unequal order.[76] Fundamental to the contemporary maintenance of that order is neoliberalism: that which 'seeks to bring all human action into the domain of the market'.[77] Neoliberalism has had, and at an accelerating pace continues to have, a profound impact upon HE. As the hegemonic discourse, its reach extends beyond the economy into social, cultural, and political domains, disseminating 'market values and metrics to every sphere of life'.[78] Neoliberalism's ubiquity and deep-embeddedness in HE means that it is taken for granted as the norm, making its various manifestations difficult to pinpoint.[79] There are, however, several elements that are worth highlighting for the purposes of this book.

Perhaps most fundamental to the neoliberalisation of universities is the attack on and subsequent demise of the concept of the 'public good' (a concept that we will go on to trouble shortly), such that HE – subjected to the market – has been repositioned as a commodity.[80] The effects of this shift are far-reaching. In particular, the devastating impacts of the introduction of student fees in the UK in 1998, and the subsequent hikes in 2004 and 2012, cannot be overestimated. The message behind the removal of public funding, as Holmwood explains, is that education should be regarded as an investment, the rewards of which will be returned upon graduation into the labour market.[81] Yet in reality, university becomes a financial risk that, for some, is not worth taking. Other young people find themselves saddled with crippling debt, made worse by the abolition of grants for low-income students. They graduate into a saturated labour market. Through fees, and tangled up with the erosion of the notion of 'public good', students have become customers, their education a service that they purchase, and universities and the academics that work within them the service providers.[82]

This consumer–producer dynamic is reified further still by the omnipresence of 'performance indicators linked to customer satisfaction and human capital formation'.[83] In the UK, students are encouraged via the National Student Survey to rate the 'quality' of their teaching, their course, and their university, with the broader neoliberal context of HE making value for money an implicit consideration. The introduction of the Teaching Excellence Framework (TEF), following a 2016 UK government White Paper, promised to promote teaching excellence and empower student decision making around which course to enrol on.[84] Institutions are incentivised to perform well in the TEF through the promise that the best performers can raise tuition fees.[85] As Liz Morrish argues, however, as a neoliberal technology of surveillance and control, TEF 'is only marginally interested in teaching quality'.[86] Rather than improving the experiences of students in HE, these metric-driven processes have been shown to discourage pedagogical practices that facilitate deeper and more democratic learning, depoliticise the classroom, and lead educators to become preoccupied with metrics to the detriment of promoting real learning.[87]

The role of metrics in HE is 'extensive and wide-ranging', even beyond those related to teaching, such that Feldman and Sandoval suggest that 'metric power' is a dominant structuring logic.[88] Much like its predecessor the Research Assessment Exercise (RAE), the UK's Research Excellence Framework (REF) represents another technology of neoliberalism which attempts to make universities and academics accountable via the market. Coordinated by the funding councils of the devolved nations,[89] the REF 'produces a powerful league table by which British universities' fiscal and reputation health is (re)produced'.[90] Despite its dominance, criticisms of the REF abound; not least of these concerns its vast cost in economic terms (£246 million for REF2014), and in terms of academic time and labour.[91] Other critiques focus on its attempt to 'impose a single set of narrowly defined norms' to measure the 'success' of all academic research.[92] As such, those working at the margins of academic disciplines and those producing 'non-traditional' research are disadvantaged,[93] a point that is significant in terms of our focus on anti-racist scholar-activism in this book. As Olssen notes:

> Not only does it place too much emphasis on research productivity and performativity, it militates against 'blue skies' research, encourages dubious research tactics and strategies for maximising publications, citations and team-based research, and from the individual researcher's viewpoint over-encourages conformity to the system of external expectations concerning research.[94]

Unsurprisingly, then, the REF reproduces a culture of high-stakes competition amongst HE institutions and academics, which is understood to stymie scholarship, and negatively affect staff morale and well-being.[95]

The most significant difference between the REF and its predecessor the RAE is its *formally required* assessment of non-academic 'Impact', which refers to the (social, economic, political, cultural) effects or 'benefits' research has beyond academia.[96] As we explore throughout this book, institutionalised notions of the REF Impact and the embedded 'bottom-up' approach to research adopted by scholar-activists may at times – often fleetingly – cross-cut, but we want to be clear here that we do not claim that these things are one and the same. We see Impact as a further attempt to marketise research. There are, for example, significant problems with how Impact is defined and measured, which in turn encourages 'gaming'[97] whereby the successful *performance* of Impact is prioritised over the real benefit to communities and publics. As Horton argues, institutionalised Impact leads to a valuing of 'unabashedly substantial, muscular, large-scale, self-confident' forms of Impact that are 'readily narratable as such'.[98] Given that the REF is often directly tied to career prospects,[99] the Impact agenda also shapes what is researched and dictates 'what researchers must do',[100] encouraging short-termist approaches and 'safe topics'.[101]

Problems with HE did not, however, merely arise from the neoliberal turn. Western universities have historically been, and continue today to be, located within a 'network of state apparatuses of control, discipline, surveillance, carcerality, and violence'.[102] It is in this regard that we, following the educationalist Darren Webb, regard HE to be imperial in nature. To say that the university is imperial is to reject the myth of exceptionalism which sees the university as sitting above the unequal power relations that pervade society. It is to recognise the university as an active reproducer of those power relations, particularly as they manifest along racial and colonial lines. An imperial rendering of the university dispels any illusions that HE exists for the public good. Instead, the university is:

a site for trialling new forms of oppression and exploitation, an institution intimately involved in the reproduction of inequalities ... a corrupt and criminal institution complicit in patriarchal, colonial and racist systems and processes; a criminal institution comparable to the police as a racialized, gendered and class-based force of authority, surveillance, enforcement and enactments of everyday patterns of structural violence.[103]

Whilst an imperial rendering of the university dispels any illusion that the contemporary university exists for the public good, a historically attentive rendering also begins to contest the notion that the university *once* existed for the public good. As Dalia Gebrial urges, if we engage critically with 'how the university has historically produced, sustained and justified violence and domination across the world', we can begin to understand that universities have never been truly public, or at least have only been good for some publics.[104]

Seeing the inequalities that pervade HE as part of a historical process enables us to better recognise the imperial and colonial origins of Western universities. It allows us to see HE institutions as key sites 'through which colonialism – and colonial knowledge in particular – is produced, consecrated, institutionalised and naturalised'.[105] After all, Western universities served both as incubators for and propagators of theories of 'scientific racism' which sought to preserve and improve the genetic quality of the white race, and establish the 'positional superiority'[106] of Europeans. As Bhambra, Gebrial, and Nişancıoğlu argue, Western universities in turn also provided the 'ethical and intellectual grounds' for colonial endeavours that supported the 'dispossession, oppression and domination of colonial subjects'.[107] If we avoid constructing colonialism narrowly as settler-colonialism, we can also see how research and knowledge became a colonial commodity. As Linda Tuhiwai Smith shows, the 'collective memory of imperialism has been perpetuated through the ways in which knowledge about indigenous peoples was collected, classified and then represented in various ways back to the West, and then, through the eyes of the West, back to those who have been colonized'.[108] In this sense, the knowledge of indigenous peoples was transformed into 'new' knowledge – new scientific discoveries – by the West, reaffirming the West's self-construction as the governor of legitimate knowledge.[109]

Though the British Empire has largely fallen, in its formal vestiges at least, the legacies of imperialism and colonialism continue to fundamentally shape the academy (as well as wider society) today, including through its institutional and disciplinary cultures, values, practices, and processes.[110] Indeed, as Bhambra, Gebrial, and Nişancıoğlu contend, 'knowledge remains principally governed by the West for the West' and continues to 'reproduce and justify colonial hierarchies'. We also continue to see the multitude of ways (some of which we outline below) in which the university remains a key site in the enactment of structural inequalities and violence. It is particularly effective in doing so precisely because of its hegemonic construction as a liberal, progressive institution.[111] The academy maintains this construction in spite of – perhaps as a consequence of – its sanitisation and inhabitation of social movements and dissenting voices[112] – an observation particularly pertinent to our focus in this book. Yet we must be clear, the imperial university has long since been a site for struggle.

Whereas we use 'imperial' to look outwards from the university, to locate it within a web of oppressive forces and as an actor in the maintenance of racial capitalism's structural inequalities, we use 'institutionally racist' to describe the conditions within the university.[113] Of course, this separation is rarely so clear in practice – the imperial may capture the power dynamics within the university too. We use 'institutionally racist' *and* 'imperial', however, to maintain an emphasis on both these internal and external elements. Institutional racism is a concept introduced by Kwame Ture and Charles Hamilton in their 1967 seminal work, *Black Power*, and subsequently taken up by activists – in the radical anti-racist tradition – in the British context. It was popularised further still – albeit in an inadequate form[114] – following its inclusion in the findings of the aforementioned Macpherson Report into the police (mis)handling of the murder of Stephen Lawrence. As Ture and Hamilton contend, compared with interpersonal racism, institutional forms are 'less overt, far more subtle, [and] less identifiable in terms of specific individuals committing the acts'.[115] Sivanandan adds that they reside 'covertly or overtly … in the policies, procedures, operations and cultures of institutions … reinforcing individual prejudices and being reinforced by them in turn'.[116]

In the early 2000s, the State pressured HE institutions in the UK to address the disadvantages faced by both 'BME' (Black and Minority Ethnic) staff and students. Yet despite race equality legislation and widening participation initiatives, HE continues to be a deeply unequal space.[117] Indeed, pointing to how processes of racialisation shape hiring and promotion practices, people of colour remain underrepresented amongst academic staff generally and the professoriate specifically. They are more likely to hold temporary contracts, and Black staff face a pay gap of 14% compared to their white colleagues.[118] Students of colour are underrepresented at 'elite' universities, continue to face an awarding gap on their degrees,[119] and are less likely to study at postgraduate level. A report by Leading Routes – a UK-based initiative that aims to strengthen the academic pipeline for Black students – found that of the almost 20,000 UKRI[120] scholarships for PhD students awarded between 2016 and 2018, only 1.2% were awarded to Black or Black mixed-race students.[121] Both staff and students of colour are also subject to racialised securitisation and surveillance, including as part of the hostile environment on university campuses and under the UK government's counter-terrorism duty, Prevent. Creating a climate of fear, the latter functions as a form of censorship of critical discussions around racism, Islamophobia, and counter-terrorism policy.[122] All the while, HE continues to be dominated by white US-Eurocentric scholarship.

Following Sivanandan's understandings of racism, we must view the institutional racism in HE policies, procedures, and cultures outlined above as being reinforced by, and reinforcing, the everyday interpersonal racism that is so widely evidenced as being endemic within the university setting. Yet there is also a need to resist the (narrow) defining of racism in HE as acts of bigotry and the ascription of culpability at the level of the individual, as is commonplace in the neoliberal 'post-racial' epoch.[123] Indeed, if we view racism only in its explicit forms, the structuring conditions of race are readily repudiated and the 'complex entrenched institutionalised'[124] racism within HE becomes easier to ignore. As Harper shows, there is a widespread culture of dismissal of racism within HE, with scholars relying on 'anything but racism' to explain away the racialised disparities that manifest in policies, procedures, and working practices.[125] This is symptomatic of a trend in liberal societies in which 'colour-blind' logic abounds.

The anti-racist scholar-activist praxes we explore in this book are no doubt shaped by the particularities of the institutional context we have outlined in this section. As intimated, our use of hyphenation in describing the 'neoliberal-imperial-institutionally-racist' university represents an attempt to resist a simplistic narrative and to note the simultaneous, overlapping, and interconnecting ways in which these forces operate. Whilst it is essential that we avoid glossing over the particularities that arise from the British context, we expect that the experiences of anti-racist scholar-activists documented in this book will nonetheless resonate with those in other parts of the world. This is particularly the case in countries where the grip of neoliberalism has also tightened on HE, such as those in which frameworks similar to the REF are used to evaluate and govern research,[126] as well as countries where the legacies of colonialism and imperialism continue to shape the contemporary social order.

Our research

The twenty-nine participants in our research worked, or studied as doctoral researchers, in British universities and were involved in anti-racist activism.

Our focus on academics is not intended to privilege them or to reproduce notions of 'legitimate knowledge' – that is, the myth, reproduced by and within the academy, that universities are *the* site of knowledge production.[127] Far from it, we argue in this book that knowledge derives from anti-racist struggle, and is therefore produced, often collectively, within communities of resistance. We focus instead on academics involved in anti-racist organising to, on the one hand, observe the call to action from those who have come before us – from Rodney, Andaiye, Harney and Moten, and many others – and, on the other, to restate and further amplify this call to action. This book should, therefore, be read as an incitement. We also focus on university-based academics because we are interested in the university as an institution, and specifically the ways it enables and constrains anti-racist scholar-activism.

With this in mind, and in the context of a dearth of empirical work on the topic, we conducted semi-structured interviews with participants between the summers of 2018 and 2019, lasting between one and three hours. Reflecting the diversity of perspectives (which we discuss in Chapter 1), those we spoke to either self-identified as scholar-activists (or with scholar-activism as praxes), were identified as scholar-activists by others, or were active in scholar-activist networks. All participants were committed to anti-racism and this inflected their scholar-activism. Whilst the interviews form the basis of the book, our conversations with many of these (and other) anti-racist activists have taken place over a more pro-tracted period. This book is therefore not only based on interview data, but also on our learning from (often far more experienced) scholar-activists. It is based upon long conversations and debates with our co-conspirators and comrades, and our learning through our own anti-racist organising – participant observation or perhaps some form of quasi-ethnography, in social scientific terms. The knowledge we gained during this process, albeit difficult to attribute to its source, has no doubt informed this book in untold ways. The book has also been shaped by ongoing feedback from participants, some of whom read their transcripts and provided annotations and elaborations, and through written comments on chapters of this book from critical friends and comrades as part of an informal process of peer review. In many ways, therefore, the ideas contained in this book, and the contributions it makes, are collective: there are many to whom we are indebted.

The majority of the people we interviewed were people of colour, though we also spoke to several white people. There was considerable variation in career stages, ranging from the very late stages of completing PhDs, to full professors. Throughout the book, we provide ethnicity and career stage information whenever a participant first appears in a new chapter. The ethnicity information provided is non-standardised as we have used the information given to us by participants. This means, for example, that some ethnic identifications are more specific than others (e.g. Bangladeshi versus person of colour), and that some identifications reflect political views and personal preferences manifest in terminological choices (e.g. Black versus African). Some of these choices are also to respect participant concerns about anonymity.

In addition to ethnicity and career stage, there was also diversity in the specific issues that our interviewees worked or organised around, and interviewees were from a range of academic disciplines within the social sciences and humanities, including (but not limited to): sociology, criminology, psychology, education studies, geography, law, social work, business, anthropology, international relations, history, and linguistics. To protect their anonymity, we do not outline the academic discipline of individual participants alongside the accounts that feature, particularly because the whiteness of academia means that many of our participants are among the only people of colour in their departments. Nevertheless, as much as possible, we try to remain attentive to noteworthy disciplinary differences. Whilst disciplinary conventions, frameworks, and traditions no doubt influence our work in (often) unseen and unknown ways, the heterogeneity that characterises anti-racist scholar-activism – a theme we return to time and time again in this book – does not appear to be forged primarily along disciplinary lines. Indeed, in many respects, and as we go on to explore, anti-racist scholar-activist praxes are perhaps informed more by communities of resistance outside of the university than by academic convention within it. This is not to say that academic convention is completely eschewed; after all, our work is structured, to varying extents and in different ways, by the neoliberal-imperial-institutionally-racist university, as much as we might try to resist its structuring forces.

Before we outline the chapters that follow, we want to take a brief moment to reflect on our positionalities, in the spirit of reflexivity – a praxis that we argue throughout this book is hegemonic in scholar-activism. Remi is a Black mixed-race cis-man, a sociologist whose work focuses on race, ethnicity, and (anti-)racism, often in the context of education, as well as in relation to policing. He works at a UK 'Russell Group' institution in a largely research-based role but has previously worked at a teaching-intensive university. Laura is a white cis-woman, working within criminology and sociology. Her work focuses on race, gender, migration, and processes of criminalisation, often in the context of the sex industry. Her academic role combines research and teaching, and having recently become a Programme Leader for three undergraduate degrees, she works increasingly closely with students but also increasingly encounters university administration and bureaucracy. We both come from working-class backgrounds but in many ways, particularly material, are now middle class. Although we understand ourselves as contributing to wider anti-racist movements, we both currently organise within two anti-racist collectives: the *Northern Police Monitoring Project* – a grassroots, abolitionist group based in Greater Manchester, UK that builds (local, national, and international) community resistance against police violence, harassment, and racism; and *Resistance Lab* – a collaboration between anti-racist activists and technology experts to resist State violence and create more equitable communities. Remi also owes a lot of his learnings to his time at the *Racial Justice Network*, a UK-based anti-racist organisation.

The structure of *Anti-racist scholar-activism*

The book is presented in six substantive chapters, followed by a manifesto. Each chapter contributes to our task of understanding anti-racist scholar-activism. In Chapter 1, we argue that although there is some value in 'scholar-activist' as an identification, it is more useful to speak of scholar-activism as something that one *does* – a form of praxis – rather than something that one is. Using the accounts of participants, we build on some of the discussion around terminology touched upon in this introductory chapter. In doing so, we demonstrate both the heterogeneity of participants' views, and the terminologically and conceptually contested nature of scholar-activism. After exploring the perspectives of participants who see utility in adopting scholar-activist identities, we look at accounts that problematise the constitutive elements of the scholar-activist label. We also consider participants' concerns around the currency the label carries, which in turn makes it susceptible to institutional co-optation and to being overclaimed by academics.

Drawing upon Sivanandan's work, Chapter 2 explores the notion of working *in service* to communities of resistance, and to anti-racism.[128] We argue that this represents a counter-hegemony which disrupts the logic of working *for* the neoliberal-imperial-institutionally-racist university, as well as the power dynamics that can elevate academics who organise within communities of resistance. Specifically, considering questions of accountability (are anti-racist scholar-activists accountable, and if so, to whom?), usefulness (is our work useful, and if so, to whom?), and accessibility and reach (is our work accessible and reachable, and if so, to whom?), we contend that the in service orientation provides an important anchoring for the praxes of anti-racist scholar-activism, one that we build upon throughout the book.

In Chapter 3, we introduce the concept of *reparative theft*. We do so by bringing Harney and Moten's seminal work on *The Undercommons*[129] into conversation with a reparations framework.[130] We argue not only that theft is a key component in anti-racist scholar-activist praxis but, particularly given the harms caused and perpetuated by the university, such theft is morally and ethically justifiable: it is a form of repair. This chapter continues to develop the notion of working in service to communities of resistance but focuses specifically on how scholar-activists can redistribute the university's material resources, and use the social and symbolic capital accrued by academics to the benefit of communities of resistance and wider anti-racist movements.

Picking up on a theme that emerges from the preceding chapters, Chapter 4 considers how the values and orientations of anti-racist scholar-activists are different from – if not fundamentally oppositional to – those of the neoliberal-imperial-institutionally-racist academy. Advancing a theoretical framework of *backlash*,[131] we consider the consequences of the ensuing clash. We examine how anti-racist scholar-activism is devalued by colleagues and managers, both within our institutions and our wider academic disciplines, and how the matrix of domination makes backlash particularly acute for some scholar-activists. We show, however, that in the context of this backlash, anti-racist scholar-activists have developed a range of strategies to survive in the academy.

'Struggle where you are', said Stuart Hall.[132] Expanding upon this brief instruction, Chapter 5 explores possibilities for anti-racist scholar-activist praxes within a system of HE that is constitutive of, as well as constituted by, inequality and injustice. To do so, we first focus on the classroom and critical pedagogy. We argue that despite wider pressures and surveillance within the neoliberal-imperial-institutionally-racist university, the classroom offers some space for autonomy, allowing us to drop the seeds of anti-racism. This is particularly so if we are able to construct – what we call – a *classroom-to-activism-pipeline*. Next, we look beyond the classroom to wider acts of resistance in the university such as speaking up and pushing back, and union activism. At several junctures in this chapter, however, we reflect on the risk that our anti-racist scholar-activism is constrained within the academy, leading to it becoming reformist in nature – devoid of its radical potential.

Chapter 6 considers this risk much more by exploring how, by virtue of our academic status and affiliation with power, anti-racist scholar-activists are entangled in the reproduction of interlocking forms of domination within, and beyond, the academy. In this respect, we conceive of the university as engendering dissent, as in Chapter 5, but also complicity. Expanding Gayatri Chakravorty Spivak's notion of *constructive complicity* by applying it in a new setting,[133] we contend that whilst meaningful reflexivity is important in enabling us to recognise, document, and minimise our complicity – and although this politics of declaration might be seen elsewhere in the social sciences and humanities as good practice[134] – anti-racist scholar-activism implores us to put our complicity to work in service to communities of resistance. As *constructive* complicity begets, rather than letting our complicity constrain and inhibit us, we must exploit our affiliation with power both for the benefit of anti-racist movements, and to dismantle the inequitable university and rebuild it in the vision of our freedom dreams.

Our final chapter is a manifesto for anti-racist scholar-activism. Instead of a traditional conclusion, we adopt the form of a manifesto to point to the explicitly political nature of scholar-activist praxes. We do so to signal that we see the conclusion of the book not as the end of a conversation but as a primer for further conversation and collective action. The ten points we include in the manifesto are key themes (some explicit and some more tacit) throughout this book. These themes might be thought of as broad, guiding principles for anti-racist scholar-activism. We hope for this manifesto to be a live document that will be picked up, discussed, challenged, adapted, and expanded. We hope it is filled with the scribblings of 'intelligent graffiti'.[135] The manifesto is our attempt to use the wisdom of the anti-racist scholar-activists that we interviewed to think more concretely about the praxes of anti-racist scholar-activism.

1

Problematising the 'scholar-activist' label: uneasy identifications

As we indicate in the Introduction, although we will delineate some broad principles and orientations of anti-racist scholar-activism, this book is not intended to be a 'how-to' guide. The accounts presented throughout the book show that such an endeavour would not only be incredibly difficult but would belie the nuance, complexity, and multiplicity of what is invoked through the terms 'scholar-activist' and 'scholar-activism'. It is not our intention to present anti-racist scholar-activism as an essentialist entity that can be easily captured and theorised, or to uncritically perpetuate discourses of idealised activism. Nor is it our intention to homogenise our participants, or to ignore the terminologically and conceptually contested nature of 'scholar-activist'. Indeed, in a variety of ways and to different extents, participants were quick to problematise and question the scholar-activist label.

In this chapter, we consider the uneasiness that the label 'scholar-activist' evokes amongst our participants. Their reluctance or hesitance in adopting the scholar-activist identity makes for an interesting starting point given that all of our participants are engaged in the kind of work we might broadly conceive of as anti-racist scholar-activism. In this chapter, we want to show that, ironically, a criticality and wariness of scholar-activist as a label is one of the few consistencies amongst those who might identify and/or be identified by others as an anti-racist scholar-activist. We begin by exploring the perspectives of participants who see utility in adopting a scholar-activist identity, before we problematise the label by examining participants' concerns over its constitutive elements: 'scholar' and 'activist'. Next, we explore another set of concerns around the scholar-activist identity, this time related to the currency the term carries. This currency, we show, makes the term susceptible to institutional co-optation and to being overclaimed by academics. With these problematics in mind, and notwithstanding some value in the identification, we suggest that scholar-activism is more usefully thought of as something that one *does*, rather than something that one *is*.

Claiming a scholar-activist identity

In the introductory chapter, we noted that scholar-activism has utility as a shorthand term to refer to approaches that combine scholarship and activism in pursuit of social justice: it demarcates a distinction from more traditional or hegemonic approaches to academia. It follows, therefore, that 'scholar-activist' refers to somebody who combines scholarship and activism in pursuit of social justice, and invokes a similar set of distinctions. The importance of claiming a scholar-activist identity was something that several of our participants emphasised. This was illustrated by Galiev, an early-career academic of colour:

> In terms of the scholar-activist identification, I think it has pragmatic use now because we have to identify between us and scholars who don't engage in the struggle. There is a resentment against scholars who don't engage within the wider community or that are able to say these hoity toity things from the ivory tower, but they don't engage in it or they don't acknowledge their class privilege which means that the very things that they're criticising, they're largely immune from. I think at this particular moment, it's important that we distinguish ourselves from that.

For Galiev, his identification as a scholar-activist represents not only a connection to others he sees as being like him but is also based upon a disidentification with, or a disavowal of, what he understands the academy to represent. In this respect, the distinction Galiev draws serves to critique the ivory-towerism that positions the academy as detached from wider society.[1] This critique of the current state of universities – which we discussed in the Introduction – is one that motivates the praxes of many of our participants, whether or not they identify as scholar-activists. For Galiev, it is the wider failures of the university (and other academics) that motivates not only his praxis but his claim to a scholar-activist identity too. In contrast to most 'traditional' scholars in higher education (HE), Galiev positions himself and other scholar-activists as being both engaged within wider communities (see Chapter 2), and reflexive about their own (class) privilege. In this sense, the scholar-activist label denotes a particular (counter-hegemonic) orientation – it sets apart the *detached* academic from the *engaged* scholar-activist.

Like Galiev, Zami – an established academic of colour – was particularly forthright in advocating for the claiming and usage of the scholar-activist identity. We should 'make it explicit, name it', she insisted:

> That way it doesn't just name, it forms what it names and [that's] great. Let's have the word activist everywhere but let's [say …] I'm an anti-racist feminist activist-scholar, you know, not just an activist. What are you activist in?

Zami suggests that the scholar-activist identity should be regarded as desirable and something that we are proud to claim. As she indicates, naming scholar-activism is a process of bringing the practice into being: it is, in this sense, performative.[2] Key here is the idea that we can *do* things with words, particularly through repetition. This is what Judith Butler conveys when she argues that 'discourse produces the effects that it names'.[3] Thought of in this way, claiming the scholar-activist identity can be a political act in and of itself – which is not to say that it is sufficient alone – and one that functions to relocate scholar-activism from its marginal position in HE. As Zami implores, 'let's have the word activist *everywhere*': let's establish scholar-activist praxis as a norm within the university. As in Galiev's account, there is a conviction that increasing the visibility of scholar-activism, through naming and repetition, can increase its power.

Zami also makes a case for naming the particular political orientation of our work as a way of further distinguishing the scholar-activist identity. In doing so, she perhaps addresses concerns, which we come to later in this chapter, around the breadth of, or lack of specificity in, what could be considered scholar-activist. As she centres the importance of anti-racist and feminist approaches, situated within a theoretical and practical history of resistance – a tradition we began to chart in the Introduction – she marks out the specificity of her orientation and praxis. She insists that her scholar-activism must be anti-racist feminist scholar-activism.

Writing in the Canadian context, though with an eye on the global picture, Tilley and Taylor offer observations prescient to our consideration here. Reflecting on the questions 'why choose such a label? What is in the name?', they posit:

> A number of people collect together under the umbrella of scholar-activist. There is strength in numbers. When we identify in such a collective way we can find and connect with our allies. We can stand together and work to make visible the limitations of our institutions for promoting social justice and equity goals. We can also support each other as we advance our research and teaching in ways that question the status quo whether in our local contexts or abroad. We can support each other in the face of those who may question the usefulness of our work, particularly when at times it seems more 'activist' than 'scholarly'.[4]

Tilley and Taylor therefore share a similar sentiment to that of Zami and Galiev – that is, the notion that by adopting the scholar-activist identity, we can build a collective or, in Sivanandan's terms, grow our *communities of resistance*.[5] Indeed, developing a collective identity functions to situate people with similar praxes together under the same 'umbrella', which, in turn, enables their collective identity to be consolidated through participation in collective action.[6] On this latter point, Tilley and Taylor point to the more concrete ways in which scholar-activism can be brought into being, including via support networks (the importance of which we discuss in Chapter 4). Key here, then, is the idea that by claiming the scholar-activist identity, we can facilitate scholar-activism as a practice, and that this is a collective process.

Problematising the scholar-activist label

Although Zami and Galiev were not alone in highlighting the utility of identifying as a scholar-activist, the term was problematised by participants in a number of ways. In this next part of the chapter, we explore participants' unease with the constituent parts of the scholar-activist label.

Problematising 'scholar'

When considering the scholar-activist label, several participants spoke of a sense of discomfort that centred on the 'scholar' component specifically. Thomas, a Black early-career academic, exemplified this sense of unease. Having been asked whether he thought of himself as a scholar-activist, he responded:

> Yeah, I'm a lot of things. I guess a scholar-activist [is] one of those things. I don't really like the word scholar. I feel like it's a bit archaic, isn't it?! If you told someone on the street, 'oh yeah, I'm a scholar', people would be like 'what the fuck are you talking about?'

Thomas first makes the point that scholar-activist is not his totality. He occupies a number of identities, perhaps situationally and contextually, and scholar-activist is only one. Whilst he affirms that the term is applicable to him, he shows that, at the same time, it is replete with issues. It is therefore perhaps only useful as a shorthand descriptor, in the absence of more fitting terminology or a more elaborate explanation. Most explicitly, Thomas goes on to trouble the word 'scholar' and questions its utility in everyday interactions. As he suggests that the term is less intelligible outside of the academy, he reveals his own orientation to be shaped by a concern with being intelligible to wider society (or 'on the street'). Whilst Thomas is speaking specifically about scholar-activist as a label, his remarks are microcosmic of a wider set of concerns – evident across all of our participants, including explicitly in the earlier account of Galiev – around the usefulness and accessibility of academic work to those outside of the ivory tower.[7] We return to discuss these concerns more fully in Chapter 2, as well as elsewhere in the book.

When we asked Thomas about how else he might articulate his particular position, he elucidated:

> I'll just say activist. I use the word academic more than I use the word scholar because academic feels a bit less like living in the medieval times, but yeah activist-scholar. I wouldn't tell anyone outside of academia that I was a scholar. They'll probably think I'm being pretentious.

Here, it becomes clearer still that, for Thomas, the term scholar-activist is only useful within the context of academia, where it is more readily understood. Outside of academia, the term is indicative of pretensions which, as we unpack throughout this book, are antithetical to the ambitions that those engaged in anti-racist scholar-activism have for their praxes. Thomas attributes this largely to the outdatedness of the term 'scholar'. Interestingly, Thomas also reframes 'scholar-activist' as 'activist-scholar'. Much like in the work of Reynolds, Block, and Bradley,[8] who draw a distinction between scholar-activists and activist-scholars, this reframing emphasises the prioritisation of activism (or activist communities) ahead of scholarly activities (or the university). As we noted in the Introduction, we use the term scholar-activist in this book in a broad sense to encompass the different stances of our participants, the varying emphasis they place on the constituent parts of scholar-activism, and ultimately to capture the heterogeneous nature of anti-racist scholar-activist praxes.

Whilst earlier Galiev spoke about the utility of the scholar-activist identity, particularly for setting apart engaged scholar-activists from detached 'traditional' academics, he also reflected on how the scholar-activist label can feel ill-fitting:

> I'm sometimes reluctant to call myself a scholar … I'm reluctant to call myself a scholar-activist, but I think that's to do with my own imposter syndrome, which I think actually speaks to a larger structural issue of how particular people feel about their position in academia, particularly as someone who maybe doesn't see people like myself in academia as much.

Although generally positive about scholar-activism as a concept and praxis, Galiev's reluctance to use the label scholar-activist to describe himself rests on the notion that 'scholar' is not a neutral term, but rather is loaded with racialised and classed meanings. As a person of colour from a working-class background – and therefore a 'minoritised' person in academia – Galiev feels that his own positionality jars with what is hegemonically invoked through the term 'scholar'. The imposter syndrome to which he refers has been noted elsewhere to impact academics of colour particularly acutely.[9] Through various mechanisms, and drawing our attention back to the discussion in the Introduction of the university as institutionally racist, academics of colour are often made to feel a sense of non-belonging or outsiderness within HE.[10] Imposter syndrome was also mentioned by Khadija (Bangladeshi, early-career), who remarked: 'I'm still very fresh in academia [and …] my imposter syndrome is pretty severe.' Imposter syndrome is cross-cut and exacerbated by a range of factors in the matrix of domination.[11] Galiev and Khadija's reflections about the ill-fitting nature of the scholar-activist label, therefore, point to structural problems within HE that are no doubt shaped by the colonial project of coupling whiteness and intellect.

In a similar vein to Galiev, Jasmin – a Pakistani PhD researcher – also reflected on how the racialised nature of HE can make the scholar-activist label seem ill-suited:

> as a non-white person in the system, I feel like certain labels are just not really [fitting]. I mean it's kind of invalidated, like I feel that at no point in my time at university doing my PhD have I even been made to feel that I could be considered a scholar.

Because of her racialised identity, Jasmin feels that her identification as a scholar is always already undermined. We see again this sense that 'scholar' is coded as white, and in this respect Jasmin's account points to the active reproduction of white supremacy in HE. It is this that means Jasmin, and many other academics of colour, have never been made to feel like a scholar. Taken together, the accounts of Thomas, Galiev, and Jasmin show that whilst we must avoid uncritically adopting a scholar-activist identity, some of the problems associated with it lie with the deeply racialised, classed, and elitist nature of scholarship in HE, rather than with the scholar-activist label per se.

Haytham – a Pakistani PhD researcher and long-standing activist – also raised concerns around the 'scholar' element of scholar-activist. For Haytham, however, his problematisation related to the significance assigned to the label 'scholar' within Islam:

> It is that word scholar, I guess that it throws you a little bit because, you know, as a Muslim you know there is a certain reverence that is attached to that word … An activist researcher why not? A scholar I am not so sure about yet, even when I am 60 or something it is something I might not say.

Haytham conveys a sense that there is a certain weight attached to the word 'scholar'. Jasmin and Galiev centred race in their problematising of the term, but Haytham shows how religion can also be salient. For Muslims, he argues, there is a 'certain reverence' – due to its usage in reference to Islamic law – that can make one more hesitant in identifying as a scholar-activist. It is for this reason that, whilst supportive of scholar-activism in spirit – that is, as a praxis – Haytham suggests he is more comfortable with 'activist researcher' as a label.

Problematising 'activist'

Participants were generally more comfortable with the 'activist' constituent of scholar-activist than they were with the 'scholar' element. Nonetheless, there were issues raised with the 'activist' component too. Although an abiding theme throughout many participants' accounts was a belief that being a scholar-activist often requires individual and collective risk and sacrifice – an idea this book goes on to unpack later, particularly in Chapter 4 – this appears to pertain primarily to the 'activist' component, at least as far as the 'scholar' and 'activist' of 'scholar-activist' can be disentangled. Put another way, the risk and sacrifice involved in scholar-activist work is not unique to scholar-activism, but rather was felt to be a feature of activism more broadly. In fact, as Barry – an early-career academic of colour – indicated, academics involved in activism can be insulated from many of the risks and sacrifices non-academic activists face. This made Barry reluctant to identify with the scholar-activist label:

> I wouldn't embrace the label scholar-activist myself because I feel like when I meet activists, I'm always impressed by the fact that they're doing shit for free, which takes loads and loads of work and which I don't do.

Barry raises an interesting critique here that points to potential tensions embedded within the scholar-activist label. If activism is conceived as being done, virtuously, 'for free' (i.e. without tangible individual gain),[12] then there is an understandable uneasiness when that activist may also benefit materially as a 'scholar'. Whilst we discuss these tensions in more detail throughout the book, it suffices to say for now that a perceived lack of sacrifice left some participants feeling unworthy of the 'activist' label. Notwithstanding the precarity of many academics[13] – a situation exacerbated by (or exploited by institutions under the guise of) the COVID-19 pandemic[14] and, for some, the UK government's hostile environment (anti-immigration) agenda[15] – these feelings of unworthiness are perhaps tied to the relative economic privilege of HE in comparison to other sectors.

Like many of the participants in this study, Barry is widely regarded by others as a scholar-activist. He is known to be involved in community organising, to support community events, and to be committed to the public dissemination of his work. In fact, whenever we spoke about writing this book, his name was regularly mentioned to us by participants as somebody we *must* speak to. For this reason, it is all the more interesting that Barry is so reluctant to self-identify as a (scholar-)activist.

As well as raising concerns particular to being employed as an academic, Barry's feelings also reflect a wider set of issues regarding idealised activist identities. As Craddock argues, the typical construction of an activist as an 'extraordinary individual … often functions as an unreachable standard that results in individuals feeling unworthy of the title'.[16] With this in mind, it is worth noting that the idealised spectre of the activist is shaped by discourses of race and gender that elevate masculinity and whiteness,[17] and devalue more slow-burning, probing, reflexive, and emotional modes of organising.[18] Barry's contemplation of the term 'activist' is perhaps, therefore, indicative of the ways in which his own approach sits in contrast to the idealised activist, who reasons in 'black and white' and engages in 'direct action' quickly and urgently, often without necessary reflection. In this regard, as we began to suggest when discussing the 'scholar' constituent earlier, reluctance to identify as a scholar-activist cannot be viewed outside of the ways in which logics of whiteness and masculinity – as well as ableism and other factors in the matrix of domination – shape meanings.

Another way in which participants troubled the 'activist' constituent of the scholar-activist label relates primarily to power. This was particularly apparent in the account of Dez – a Black professor – who, like Barry, had been mentioned to us time and time again as an anti-racist scholar-activist with whom we needed to speak. It was again surprising, therefore, that when we asked Dez whether he considered himself to be a scholar-activist, he answered:

> No! I mean I would probably call myself an intellectual worker, to be honest, something like that, I think. Partly because I'm not entirely convinced that academics should have leading roles in activism because there is a certain imbalance of power which is difficult to compensate for, if you push yourself as an activist working in academia.

Dez's critique clearly centres on the 'imbalances of power' that can manifest in activism, especially when academics take up 'leading roles'. Being positioned as an academic means that one's knowledge often comes with a perceived degree of institutional legitimacy that can create unequal hierarchies of knowledge and expertise. It can become the case, therefore, that the privilege and status that scholar-activists have can result in them speaking *for*, rather than *with*, their fellow activists.[19] That said, a number of participants sought to circumvent these power hierarchies by adopting reflexive approaches that were sensitive to (partially) countering the status imbued upon them as academics. Practically, for many, this involved occupying supporting roles in activism, often articulated as doing the 'donkey work'. Nonetheless, as Leon Sealey-Huggins's work on climate change activism attests, hidden hierarchies and power imbalances pervade activist movements.[20] As such, it is important we bear in mind that participation in anti-racist movements is never egalitarian and we must remain attentive to, and committed to addressing, inequities.

Dez's concerns seem to echo those of anti-colonial thinkers such as Amílcar Cabral with regard to the petit bourgeois intellectual,[21] as well as well-documented critiques of W.E.B. Du Bois's writings on the 'talented tenth.' Du Bois argued that the 'negro race' would be 'saved by its exceptional men', who would and should receive 'higher education' in order to lead them.[22] For Andrews, this 'bourgeois sentiment' is the antithesis of Black Radical politics.[23] Whilst more generous interpretations suggest that Du Bois's writings have been distorted, his thesis contains 'the trappings of elitism' at least.[24] Dez's important warning suggests that the unequal power dynamics attached to academics in activist movements are so deeply entrenched that they 'are difficult to compensate for'. Indeed, regardless of the extent to which they adopt a scholar-activist identity, power imbalances were a significant concern amongst participants (an issue we discuss more throughout the book).

Much like those in the previous section about the 'scholar' element of scholar-activist, the concerns raised here around the 'activist' identity could also be understood as pointing to problems with the academy. For Barry and Dez, academics occupy a position of privilege, both in terms of their relative lack of sacrifice and in terms of their relative power. Of course, these positions of privilege are always mediated by the interlocking structures of power that constitute the matrix of domination, such that some academics are subject to less risk and occupy more power than others.[25] It is important, therefore, that those taking up the scholar-activist identity are attentive to Barry and Dez's concerns, as well as how processes of privilege and disadvantage shape our scholarship and activism, regardless of the labels we do or do not adopt.

The currency in scholar-activist identities

Critiques around the scholar-activist label not only pertain to its constitutive elements. Rather, some of the most resounding concerns raised by participants were tied to a recognition that, in some circles, the scholar-activist identity carries a certain amount of currency: 'it does feel very much like a new buzzword … it has market value in the capitalist system', noted

Amara, a mid-career academic of South Asian heritage. As the renowned activist and educator Aziz Choudry similarly writes:

> There is a currency in this terminology – with many universities promoting themselves as community engaged, with academics who perform and construct an 'edgy' or 'radical' identity and image, without necessarily engaging in radical politics or taking political risks.[26]

As Choudry shows, currency manifests in an interlinked set of concerns. Firstly, we have the institutional co-optation of scholar-activism and secondly, academics' overclaiming of the identity and therefore its dilution. Here, we look at each in turn.

Institutional co-optation

Barry was one of several participants who raised concerns around the institutional co-optation and marketisation of scholar-activism. As he put it:

> these terms get picked up and co-opted by the institution to show that it's right on in some way … If they were to say that they are a place where there are a lot of scholar-activists – if the university is still run like a business, if the student body is still really middle class, and if the fees are still extortionate and there's not that much engagement with people in the local area – then I don't want to see it marketed basically. So, the scholar-activist thing, I don't think it's one of them but it could be. It could become a thing that I guess is co-opted basically.

We see through Barry's account that there is some currency in the scholar-activist identity in that it allows the university to portray a favourable external image. Much like Choudry,[27] the problem for Barry lies in how the university's deployment of a scholar-activist identity is superficial. It is not indicative of structural change. As Barry indicates, whilst the university might brand itself as being an advocate for and vehicle of social justice, it is simultaneously perpetuating inequalities through its fees, class demographics, and poor engagement with local communities. But as Barry also argues, the institutional co-optation of the scholar-activist identity would also be market-driven. In this regard, anti-racist scholar-activism could be repurposed by the university to yield profit and extend inequality, aims that are antithetical to anti-racist scholar-activism. Although Barry suggests that this co-optation moment has not yet arrived, he implies that it could be on the horizon.

The neoliberal market-driven paradigm that has overtaken academia means that Barry is right to urge vigilance, particularly given that universities often prefer to create the illusion that they are doing anti-racist work, rather than actually *doing* the disruptive work of anti-racism.[28] There are clear (albeit, not absolute)[29] parallels here with the co-optation of 'decolonisation'. As Dar, Dy, and Rodriguez write, '[d]ecolonising has entered consumers' imaginations'.[30] In their powerful analysis, they ask important questions that, as Barry's account attests, we might well apply to a consideration of scholar-activism:

> is decolonising becoming familiar to power structures in ways that its consumption, circulation and reproduction in the academy is diluting its radical politics? We question whether the rapid uptake of decolonising as the new buzzword of critique has become a new form of academic production that adds value to one's reputation as a critical scholar while also opening a pathway to profit through making the histories, bodies, and experiences of Black people and people of colour consumable and marketable, transforming them into a viable subject for the entrepreneurial academic agenda. We identify a new form of appropriation, where it seems that decolonising is becoming factionalised along a political spectrum so that only parts of it are easily absorbed by Universities (and the people who govern them). This in turn supports the legitimation of HEIs as inclusive spaces without demanding that they engage in the painful process of self-accountability.[31]

In this critique, Dar, Dy, and Rodriguez show how the (market-driven) overuse and misuse of the term 'decolonisation' threatens to undermine its transformative potential. This is particularly apparent given that the more radical elements are hollowed out to enable easier entry into the politics and processes of (what we established in the Introduction to be) the neoliberal-imperial-institutionally-racist university.

The argument set out by Dar, Dy, and Rodriguez aligns closely with Barry's pre-emptive concerns around scholar-activism. Ultimately, they do not call for radical scholars to eschew the term 'decolonisation', but rather for greater attentiveness to the radical framework that the term invokes. Such attentiveness must be resistant to – even oppositional to – the co-optive forces of the neoliberal-imperial-institutionally-racist university, and the same might be said about scholar-activism. In their warning, Dar, Dy, and Rodriguez are not only concerned about institutional co-optation but also the sudden, widespread, and superficial uptake of 'decolonisation' by academics (who use the term but do not adhere to any radical framework).[32] We now go on to explore similar concerns with the overclaiming of the scholar-activist identity.

Overclaiming

There was a palpable sense amongst our participants that the scholar-activist identity was overclaimed by academics who, quite often, were not doing the 'real' work. As Amara argued:

> You have people talking and writing about scholar-activists and it just makes you wonder why is it so valuable, why is this being so widely circulated … People are writing about it because they are gaining market value from it. If I was wrong, then we would be having a revolution in the country, wouldn't we?

For Amara and others, then, the currency in the label means that the number of people identifying as anti-racist scholar-activists far exceeds the number of people doing anti-racist scholar-activism. As such, the identification can become what Sara Ahmed refers to as 'a substitute for action'.[33] The 'entrepreneurial spirit is overriding the structural critique that we need', as Amara put it. In so doing, she draws attention to how the radical framework of anti-racist scholar-activism can be cast aside by academics as, spurred on by research performance metrics such as the UK Research Excellence Framework (REF), they jostle to market themselves in an increasingly competitive academia.

Much like Amara, Dillon – a British Asian early-career academic who is involved with several anti-racist community groups – also reflected on whether scholar-activist is a desirable identity (for some):[34]

> It's fine to use the term, anyone can call themselves a scholar-activist, but are you doing the work of the scholar-activist? It's fine to write on your Twitter handle scholar-activist, interested in de de de, but are you actually engaging with the groups on the ground?

Underpinning Dillon's provocations is the idea that scholar-activism can come to be superficial, merely 'acting out the motions of activism to gain social capital rather than engaging in real action'.[35] In this superficial sense, it is a form of branding ('on your Twitter handle') that can lack substance. Dillon is clear that the performance is 'fine' but it must be supported by action to avoid what Ahmed calls the non-performativity of anti-racism.[36] For Dillon, this action should involve 'engaging with groups on the ground', a notion that is reminiscent of Walter Rodney's conceptualisation of 'groundings' – that is, the praxis of embeddedness that we identified in the Introduction as a tenet of anti-racist scholar-activism.[37] The importance of engaging with community groups was a key and recurrent theme in participants' accounts and we return to it in the next chapter.

This sense that people were more likely to adopt the label than do the work was also apparent in the account of Neville (white, mid-career). As he explained:

> You can definitely carve out a little career niche for yourself, as the activist-academic I think, if that's what you want to do. I don't really label myself like that in public, I think partly because I feel a bit uneasy about it, and I feel like there's probably a lot of quacks around who are claiming that identity, and so I feel a bit nervous about being one of those people.

Whilst noting that it is 'niche', Neville is clear that there is some currency to be extracted from the 'activist-academic' identity and that this leads 'quacks' to overclaim it. In this regard, much like Dar, Dy, and Rodriguez's observations in relation to 'decolonising',[38] the scholar-activist identity can add 'value to one's reputation as a critical scholar', at least in certain academic circles. Showing how perceived currency enters such considerations, it is clear that both Neville and Dillon share concerns about – and are keen to distance themselves from – the 'quack' who takes the capital without doing the work. It is the spectre of the quack that, by hollowing out the term, leads Neville to disassociate (publicly at least) with the term; although, importantly, not with its essence.

Seeming to share much of the sentiment expressed above, Sajid – a mid-career British Pakistani man – calls for a closer consideration of the scholar-activist label:

> I would describe myself as that but then I guess that you're always a little hesitant in prescribing labels to yourself, you know, that I'm a scholar-activist … people might equate you to other scholar-activists who, you know, who aren't that scholar-activist *really* if you look at their profiles. And I think we need to really drill down into what this term means and who benefits from it. Because, if I'm a scholar-activist, it's not because I want to benefit from that label, it's because I'm seeking to shift debates and policies and discourse in progressive directions with my very limited capacity. I think the reasons why people do it are complicated. Of course, some of them, many of them perhaps, are genuine, but I think also there's many people who may be misleading not only others but themselves.

Although Sajid begins by saying that he identifies as a scholar-activist, as he ponders, he reflects the nuances and complexities manifest in the term, complexities that make him somewhat 'hesitant' to adopt the label. As Sajid indicates, there is a slipperiness to the term scholar-activist, perhaps resulting from overinflation, that leads to a need to 'drill down' to consider its meaning more closely. Amara similarly suggested that 'it is important to think about what [scholar-activism] is and what it isn't. What politics does it fall under and what methodologies does it refuse?' These are prescient questions that we, and our participants, consider throughout the book.

In Sajid's account we see, again, a suggestion that there are more people who claim the anti-racist scholar-activist identity than do the work, and it is from those who are 'misleading' – the 'quacks', as Neville put it – that Sajid seeks to distinguish himself. Whilst these 'quacks' are there only to benefit from the label by offering a particular presentation of Self, Sajid is clear that his motives are more productive and less individualistic. He is seeking to use his capacity to contribute towards progressive social change. By 'drilling down', therefore, Sajid is seeking to excavate the *practice* behind the label, and in doing so he reveals a distinction between himself and the 'quack'. Put another way, the 'quack' is concerned only with the scholar-activist identity; the genuine scholar-activist is concerned (primarily) with praxis.

In a similar vein, Galiev touched explicitly on the need to refine the scholar-activist concept and be specific with regard to what we are invoking through its use:

> I think if you don't engage in the struggle, man, in concrete, practical, grassroots, on the frontline action, I think it's bollocks … there has to be some kind of intersubjective definition of what we consider a scholar-activist [to be,] over which there is consensus. Part of that has to be that you engage in the struggle. You can't be someone who talks a big game but doesn't walk the walk.

Like Neville and Sajid, undergirding Galiev's suggestion that we must develop a shared understanding of what constitutes a scholar-activist is the spectre of the 'quack'. With this in mind, for Galiev, consensus over the term ought to centre around what one *does*. As he puts it, there is a need to tangibly and concretely 'engage in the struggle'. This seems to reiterate Dillon's claim earlier that one must be 'engaging with groups on the ground'. Galiev's emphasis on 'frontline' action might threaten to erase those less typically masculine and less confrontational forms of (scholar-) activist work,[39] but his call for a need to 'walk the walk' is reflective of several of our participants' accounts. It is also reflective of Ruth Wilson Gilmore's emphasis on 'talk-plus-walk',[40] which we noted in the Introduction to be a defining feature of scholar-activism, and of Kevin Hylton's discussion of walking the walk as an important component of the 'lived activism' of Critical Race Theory.[41] By raising concerns around the overclaiming of scholar-activist identities, Galiev, Sajid, and Dillon do something important: they centre in on the *doing* (Galiev), *practising* (Sajid), and *engaging* (Dillon) elements of scholar-activist praxes. This sentiment was reiterated by Oliver, a Black senior academic involved in community groups, who insisted:

> If you're going to be a fellow scholar-activist, alongside me, you need to bring it to the table. If you don't have proper community roots, and if you're not really embedded in your communities, then you're just *chatting*. You're not going to be part of anything I'm *doing*.

Whilst we pick up on this theme of embeddedness more in the next chapter, for now Oliver's emphasis on *doing*, rather than *chatting*, is our key concern.

In the next section, we think a little more about this idea of doing – of walking the walk – but before we do, it is important to note that we tread a fine line here between definitions of scholar-activism that are too narrow and those that are too broad. Those that are too broad threaten to overinflate the concept of scholar-activism to such an extent that it becomes claimable by all. At this point, the term comes to be devoid of specificity: it becomes vacuous, an empty or floating signifier. As Bobel writes, '[w]hen anything is activism, and, by extension, anyone is an activist, then the definitional power of the word is compromised'.[42] This is why Galiev calls for some 'consensus', Sajid urges us to 'drill down', and Amara seeks clarity on 'what it is and what it isn't'. Definitions that are too narrow, however, might fall into the trap of drawing upon an idealised version of (scholar-)activism. As we have argued, this idealised image is shaped by (white) ableist masculinity and operates to privilege certain forms of (frontline) activism, forms that can often be problematic, knee-jerk, and short-lived.[43] As Taylor argues, 'there is more to do to embed inclusive notions of activism within scholar-activism […] if it is to avoid the problems of exclusion and disempowerment associated with "capital A" notions of activism.'[44] In part, it is this balancing act that makes scholar-activism such a slippery concept. This slipperiness is evident when we recognise that, on the one hand, there are people who claim the scholar-activist identity who are not doing (what could generally be agreed upon as) scholar-activist work, but on the other, there are people who are doing (what could generally be agreed upon as) scholar-activist work who (actively or inactively) do not claim the identity.

Walking the walk: doing scholar-activism

Building on the arguments above, here we want to further problematise the scholar-activist identity. Indeed, a significant number of our participants noted (either explicitly or implicitly) that they are more comfortable with the idea of scholar-activism as something that one *does*, rather than scholar-activist as something that one *is*. Similar notions are evident in wider literature on activism and social movements,[45] and this is encapsulated by Khadija, who said: 'I participate in activism, I do what I can within academia and outside, but no, I wouldn't use the term to describe myself.' Expanding on this sentiment, Rosa, a mid-career white woman who migrated to Britain, explained:

I'm generally uncomfortable with labels and identities, and I'm aware that there has been an increasing interest in – for the most part, of radical academic research – into this topic. So, my fear is always that if we start defining ourselves in this way then we almost reproduce a new form of identity which could be comfortable or too comfortable, and then it becomes more about who we are, rather than what we do.

Like participants in the preceding section, Rosa is concerned about the currency embedded in the scholar-activist label, which has manifested in an increasing interest in the topic. To identify as a scholar-activist risks the reproduction of an identity that, at the point when we become 'too comfortable', lacks substance. It is, as Rosa puts it, more about 'who we are, rather than what we do'. Rosa's emphasis on 'what we do' is important here. She went on to explicate this point a little further: 'there is something [problematic] about naming itself, defining oneself as an activist. I believe in political practice; I believe in *practice*' (emphasis her own). As she calls for practice over naming, Rosa paves a way for responding to concerns raised earlier around the currency that is associated with the (superficial) performance of scholar-activist identities. In doing so, she bolsters Galiev's assertion that scholar-activism is not about talking the talk but about walking the walk.

Oliver seemed to concur with Rosa, suggesting that 'the terms aren't hugely important. It's about the work you're doing.' There seems to be an impetus in these accounts, therefore, for a shift from *noun* to *verb*: from *being* to *doing*. We find this to be a useful framing, not least because the shift from being a scholar-acti*vist* to doing scholar-acti*vism* situates scholar-activism as a process. It is something towards which we must continually strive, rather than a fixed and reachable entity. This idea of continual reflexive praxis is perhaps encapsulated by the becoming 'too comfortable' that Rosa warned against.

The idea of scholar-activism as something one does, rather than something one is, is made clearer still by Barry. Earlier in this chapter, he expressed his reluctance to identify as a (scholar-)activist because of the positions of privilege we occupy as academics relative to most non-academics engaged in activism. For Barry:

> Part of me feels a bit like when I have met activists doing the [frontline] stuff. They're the ones who don't have a wage. They're the ones who are more likely to end up with criminal records and more likely to be surveilled, and I get invited to give talks and I'm applying for jobs with like thirty-five grand starting salary. So, that's why I wouldn't be too keen on saying I'm a scholar-activist, but I would be keen to say that scholars should be doing some kind of activist work.

As Barry makes clear, his salary, activities (invited talks), and relative lack of surveillance and criminalisation[46] all mean that he does not embody the risk and sacrifice that he sees as constitutive of being an activist. Though Barry's recognition of power and privilege is demonstrative of an important degree of reflexivity, it is also possible that his initial reflections here are caught up in discourses of *capital A activism*[47] – discourses that restrict understandings of activism to its more masculine, rapid, and/or idealised forms. In research with menstrual activists, Bobel found that her respondents – many of whom felt unable to claim an activist identity – often defined activism through 'romanticized, abstract allusions to tireless commitment, selfless sacrifice, [and] unparalleled devotion'.[48] This is, however, as one of Bobel's focus-group attendees put it, 'a paralyzing way to look at it'.[49] As Barry continues, he appears to find a way out of this paralysis by shifting his focus from being an activist to 'doing some kind of activist work'. For Barry, *doing* (some kind of) activist work is an imperative as an academic, and his use of 'some kind' creates space for more expansive understandings of what constitutes that work. In this sense, Barry echoes Ali – an Arab early-career man – who warned against 'essentialising scholar-activism as one monolithic entity'. As such, Barry's framing enables him to acknowledge his particular orientation (and commitment to acting for social change), whilst also recognising the relative privileges he holds.

Barry's view that scholars should be engaged in activism was commonly held amongst participants, with some seeing activism as part of their duty as an academic. As Ali put it, 'I have a responsibility towards myself. I have a responsibility towards my family and towards my community.' Throughout our interviews there was an abiding sense that doing (what some might call) scholar-activist work is merely what ought to be considered good academic practice. Daiyu Suzuki speaks fittingly to this point:

> In an ideal academia, this would not even be an issue because scholarship and activism would be one and the same, together composing a cyclical process of learning and social interventions for the betterment of the world. In an ideal world, we would not even have the word 'activist,' because living attentively to social injustices and seeking ways to address them would be considered a natural part of living as human beings.[50]

As Suzuki suggests, when redressing social injustices becomes the norm both within and beyond the university, there will be less need for terminological and conceptual discussions over the utility of scholar-activist as an identity or scholar-activism as praxes. With this in mind, moving anti-racist scholar-activism from the margins to the centre within HE should be a goal; although, in the process, there will be a need to be attentive to the danger that scholar-activist praxes lose their radical edge or transformative, anti-racist, anti-capitalist potential.

In this section, we have called for the need to give primacy to the praxes of scholar-activism – to recognise that it is something that we *do* – ahead of the identity or label. Notwithstanding this point, we still maintain, as participants suggested in earlier sections, that there may also be some value in identifying as scholar-activists. Our point here then is that although the *doing* should be our focus, identifying as a scholar-activist does not necessarily foreclose the possibility of seeing the work as always ongoing – that is, the verb and the noun need not be seen as at odds. Indeed, our identities and our very existence are always in process.[51] Recognising this, we can see our scholar-activist identities as always in a process of becoming. When we understand identity and existence in such a way, we can adopt the identity, whilst recognising the need to continue to do the work. The anti-racist scholar-activist identity, then, is forged through praxes.

Conclusion

In this chapter, we have unpacked the contested nature of the scholar-activist label. We have shown that even amongst those that are regarded by others as such, there is a tentativeness in identifying as an anti-racist scholar-activist. Terminological criticality is perhaps one of few consistencies in how our heterogeneous group of participants self-identify. Although there are some that claim scholar-activist identities as a way to demarcate themselves from the academy writ large, there was a general consensus that we must be attentive to the problematics of the scholar-activist label. Some participants raised concerns about the 'scholar' constituent, including the datedness and pretensions of the term, and its racialised codings. Others drew attention to the problems associated with the 'activist' component, specifically in relation to the privilege of academic-activists relative to non-academic activists, and the power dynamics arising from academic involvement in activist movements. These concerns were raised in discussions around the scholar-activist label; however, they point to a broader set of structural problems within the academy. Indeed, concerns around the ill-fitting nature of the 'scholar' element point to the deeply racialised, classed, and elitist nature of scholarship in HE, whilst, in a similar vein, concerns over academic privilege and power within activism point to how the academy is invested in reproducing inequality and hierarchies of knowledge.

Concerns also centred around the misuses of the scholar-activist label and the dilution of its meaning. Participants warned about the dangers of the (neoliberal-imperial-institutionally-racist) academy's co-optation of the term, and how this may not only blunt the radical potential of scholar-activism but may result in it being marketised to drive profit and ultimately to extend inequity. Concerns were also raised around the currency the term carries for academics (in certain circles) and how the 'quack' takes up an anti-racist scholar-activist identity without engaging in the 'real' work. To resist the dilution of scholar-activism, participants urged us to 'drill down' and develop an 'intersubjective' understanding of what is invoked through the term. In this regard, we argue that a balance needs to be struck between narrow definitions that promote *capital A activism* and definitions that are so broad that they become bereft of their discursive power. Importantly, and as per the tenets we set out in the introductory chapter, our intersubjective understanding should focus on anti-racist scholar-activism as *praxes*. Indeed, whilst we have explored the problematics of scholar-activist *identities*, our participants are much more comfortable with the notion of scholar-activism as something we *do*. Although we do not intend to discount the identity or label entirely, this praxis-oriented framing – one we adopt in the rest of the book – allows us to situate scholar-activism as a constant process, as something we must continually strive towards rather than a fixed and reachable entity.

2

Working in service: accountability, usefulness, and accessibility

Through the concerns of participants, the previous chapter began to show that anti-racist scholar-activism describes a form of praxis that is characteristically distinct from traditional approaches to working in academia. Building on these foundations, this chapter looks more closely at what governs, and therefore distinguishes, anti-racist scholar-activism. By drawing upon Sivanandan's notion of *working in service*,[1] we show how the orientation of those engaged in anti-racist scholar-activism is fundamentally shaped by a commitment to *communities of resistance*.[2] The in service orientation is a counter-hegemonic one, often bristling against the neoliberal technologies of the contemporary university – technologies that see academics come under pressure to orientate their work to performance metrics like the UK Research Excellence Framework (REF). As we intimated in the Introduction, whilst at first glance non-academic Impact under the REF could be seen to overlap with and even encourage or enable scholar-activism, we show the cross-over of institutionalised Impact with anti-racist scholar-activism to be both superficial and fleeting. Rather, working in service to anti-racism requires a long-standing, genuine embeddedness that only comes from a deep grounding within communities of resistance.

We begin this chapter by offering a theorisation of *working in service*. This is important not only because it is little developed as a concept in relation to scholar-activism but because it lays the foundations both for the rest of this chapter and for the rest of the book. Building upon these foundations, we consider three elements to working in service: questions of accountability (are anti-racist scholar-activists accountable, and if so, to whom?); usefulness (is our work useful, and if so, to whom?); and accessibility and reach (is our work accessible and reachable, and if so, to whom?) In each of these sections, we conceptualise the notion of working in service as a counter-hegemonic principle. In doing so, we argue that the notion of *working in service* should be conceptualised as a fundamental orientation of anti-racist scholar-activism.

Theorising in service

The notion of servicing appears in the work of Ambalavaner Sivanandan who, as we suggested in the book's Introduction, is a key figure in the history of anti-racism in Britain (and beyond). Having been part of a takeover that promised to ensure the organisation played an active role in anti-racist resistance, Sivanandan directed the radical think tank, the Institute of Race Relations (IRR), for forty years.[3] Under his directorship (1973–2013), the IRR adopted more radical and structurally focused understandings of race and racism that were always contextualised by imperialism and colonialism.[4] As he described in reflections on his vision for the IRR:

> there was a plethora of grassroots, community movements at the time (unlike now, alas) that *we could serve*. If we could not be at the barricades in the fight for racial justice, we could, at least, be *servitors* in that cause. We could do research that spoke to the issues and problems confronting Black communities. We could be a *servicing station*. We could put gas in

the tanks of Black and Third World peoples on their way to liberation. That, in any case, was our pious hope.[5]

Although he was referring specifically to the orientation of the IRR, and was never a university-based academic himself,[6] what Sivanandan offers is a radical orientation that we show throughout this book to be central to anti-racist scholar-activism. Indeed, he foregrounds the 'bottom-up' nature of anti-racist scholar-activism – that is, the proximity to and embeddedness in struggle that we identified in the Introduction as a key tenet. He also points to how this orientation enables research that can be *put to use* within anti-racist movements and thus shuns the relegation of communities of colour to the category of victim – a category that can be deeply depoliticising – in favour of recognising that a dialectic exists between domination and resistance.[7] It is to capture the agentic nature of marginalised communities that Sivanandan uses the term communities of resistance, a term we deploy throughout this book.[8] In this sense, the in service orientation offers a hopeful outlook that casts scholarship as performing an important (supporting) role both in the communities and groups we organise within, and in wider liberation struggles.

Whilst the notion of working in service is most often associated with Sivanandan, the sentiment is present too in the work of others we might think of as influencing the anti-racist scholar-activist tradition. It is, for example, implicit in the thought of the Martiniquais anti-colonial revolutionary Frantz Fanon, who declared that 'we are nothing on earth if we are not in the first place the slaves of a cause, the cause of the people, the cause of justice and liberty'.[9] Much like Sivanandan, Fanon encourages us to take up a productive orientation, one that is dedicated not simply to understanding but to changing the social world as we know it. We are, Fanon urges, to work in service to an anti-racist cause. The Guyanese anti-colonialist Walter Rodney spoke more explicitly of working in service. He contended:

> If we [the petit bourgeois intellectuals] have a role, it has to do with the shift of the initiative into the hands of workers and peasants and then for a change we begin to serve those classes. Because mostly we have been serving other classes anyhow. Mostly we have been serving the capitalist class. So for a change, we may begin to service the working people, service the working class.[10]

For Rodney, working in service to 'the working class' is counter-hegemonic. It signals an orientation that breaks with the norm under racial capitalism. To adopt this orientation, the petit bourgeois intellectual must relinquish the social and material rewards they acquire through their servicing of the capitalist class, and instead allow the needs of working-class communities to set the agenda.[11] It is in a similar vein that the Black feminist Patricia Hill Collins describes intellectual activism as 'the myriad ways in which people place the power of their ideas in service to social justice'.[12] Thus, key to working in service is the notion that academics should use their power against, rather than in support of, the ideologies, institutions, structures, and systems that maintain the status quo. In this rendering, in service sits at the very core of anti-racist scholar-activism, serving as an important anchor point for our praxes.

The counter-hegemony of the in service orientation of anti-racist scholar-activism becomes more apparent still when viewed in the context of, or in contrast to, the neoliberal university. As we discussed in the book's Introduction, the neoliberalisation of higher education (HE) has engendered conditions in which academics work under increasing pressure to fulfil the demands of a high-stakes metric and audit culture. Most notably in the UK context, academics are required to meet publication quotas and engage in quantifiable, self-confident forms of non-academic Impact as part of the REF,[13] or else face repercussions in terms of job security and/or progression. These metrics operate as State-funded technologies of neoliberalism,[14] and are afforded a tremendous amount of power to dictate labour in HE and thus secure neoliberal hegemony.[15] It is against this backdrop that, by allying with communities of resistance and operating in service to anti-racism (which, as far as possible, involves an eschewing of neoliberal imperatives), anti-racist scholar-activist praxes can be considered counter-hegemonic. As we discuss in Chapter 4 and elsewhere, it is also against this backdrop that anti-racist scholar-activists frequently rub against those adopting traditional approaches to scholarship in the contemporary university, such that they form mutually antagonistic relationships.

There is another way in which the notion of working in service to anti-racism is counter-hegemonic too, and it lies at the nexus between scholar-activists and the wider activist communities within which they organise. Whilst problems can arise from unequal power relationships when academics (and the 'petit bourgeoisie' more broadly) involve themselves in activism,[16] working in service implies an attempted break with hierarchies that elevate academics within social movements. It marks an approach that is critical of, as Liz Fekete puts it, the 'academic voice that tends to lead and not serve'.[17] As Huerta elucidates, scholar-activism 'means being a bridge between these asymmetric spaces: institutions of higher education and racialized/working-class communities. It means for the former, with its privileged members, to *serve* the latter – not vice versa, as is the norm.'[18] Reflecting a similar sentiment to Rodney above, Steven Osuna argues – in his instructive development of Amílcar Cabral's concept of class suicide – that to become transformative agents, those of us working in the academy must 'break free from the chains of the neoliberal university and struggle with the people'.[19] This might involve relinquishing our class positions, our power and privilege, as Cabral conceived, or it might involve using that power and privilege to exploit the contradictions of the university and 'struggle with and for aggrieved, oppressed and exploited communities'.[20] In this light, the notion of service ensures that our work is orientated to and for anti-racism, rather than for our individual publishing or career interests.[21]

The praxes of working in service

The idea of working in service to anti-racism as a counter-hegemonic orientation ran through the accounts of many of our participants, some of whom were directly influenced by Sivanandan. Alison (white, mid-career), for example, attributed the inspiration for her own praxis – 'working in service to social movements' – to Sivanandan's aforementioned framing of the IRR. There were echoes too in the account of Amele, who explained: 'I'm committed to a certain kind of politics, and I do what I can within my means to service those politics.' Oliver – an established Black academic who we met in the last chapter – also made clear that he saw his orientation as being in service to the community. As he explained:

> I'm an academic and scholar but actually, I'm a public intellectual, which means I'm owned by the community and there to service the community. I'm a public intellectual who happens to have access to a range of resources through the academy.

Here, Oliver situates himself firmly as being 'in but not of' the university, as Harney and Moten would put it.[22] As we began to suggest in the Introduction, we borrow this phrase from them to invoke a praxis that – underpinned by a fierce critique of the university – is subversive, oppositional, and counter-hegemonic. It gets at the idea that scholar-activists may be employed by the university and may reap some of the benefits that follow from such employment but their priorities lie elsewhere, in the communities of resistance that they organise within. In this regard, there is clear convergence between Harney and Moten's notion of 'in but not of',[23] Osuna's aforementioned formulation of Cabral's class suicide,[24] and the orientation of working in service. Put another way, to work in service as a scholar-activist requires that we adopt the position of being 'in but not of' the university, which in turn enables us to put our class privileges to work for the benefit of communities of resistance.

It is telling that when Oliver reflects on the service he offers to the community, he speaks of the resources he is able to access, rather than the knowledge he might bring as an academic. Indeed, working in service should not be understood to imply that there is an intellectual deficit in activist movements that needs to be filled by the institutionalised knowledge of the academy. As Oliver intimates, and as we show – particularly in the next chapter – the role of anti-racist scholar-activists is often less about knowledge production (though this can sometimes be important), and more about exploiting the contradictions of the academy and/or leveraging (often material) resources and institutionalised power to bolster resistance movements.

Before moving on with the rest of this chapter, there is one vital point that we want to make with regard to the idea of working in service. Whilst we hold that working in service is generally a useful orientation – one that participants invoked explicitly and implicitly, and a guiding principle in our own work – it must come with a degree of criticality and reflexivity. There needs to be careful consideration of who or what we are working in service to. As Alison reasoned, we have to question the 'assumption that your politics and your ideas align so neatly with that social movement that therefore you would work unquestionably in service'. In reality, she explained, consideration needs to be given to the role and practices of those groups because 'you're working out whether you're sharing those [values]'.

Talking about an instance where he felt a community campaigner's approach worked *against* anti-racism, Elroy – an established Black academic – offered reflections that echo Alison's:

> I guess that taught me to just be a little more hesitant about who you get into bed with, who you fight with. That's being in service to. Here is my

role. This is what I can do. This is what I can contribute. This is my research. But, for me, it's being careful about how deep we go in there.

Both Alison and Elroy show that the notion of working in service cannot operate without parameters. If a group with whom one is working starts to engage in a politics that is regressive and moves against one's anti-racist aims, we ought to be critical enough not to work in service to those ideas. Although this might seem an obvious point, it is nevertheless an important one. It is a point that is necessary to make because reflexivity over the relative power we have as academics can, in some cases, lead us to become overly deferential to non-academic movements and the activists within them, and this can blunt our criticality. As Laura Pulido explains, 'among progressives there is a deeply entrenched narrative that confers a nebulous moral authority upon nonelites'.[25] When working with community groups or movements, our political positions may temporarily align on specific issues but it cannot be assumed that that alignment is limitless. That alignment may not extend to other (related) issues, just as it may not last over a period of time. Movements are dynamic, heterogeneous entities that can often obscure internal differences. They are, as Zygmunt Bauman puts it, *cloakroom communities* that are 'put together, temporarily, around a shared focus'.[26] In this regard, it is important to continually revisit the question of whether or not we should remain in service to a particular group or movement.

In our own work as members of the *Northern Police Monitoring Project*, we have at times worked in collaboration with other anti-racist groups and activists. Whilst we have shared a commitment to tackling institutionally racist policing, at critical moments schisms in our respective politics have emerged. We believe that policing is fundamentally and structurally problematic and that, by embracing the spirit of *freedom dreaming*,[27] we should strive for the abolition of the police.[28] During one particular collaboration, it became clear that our collaborators were in fact only interested in equity to the extent that white young people are arrested, punished, and imprisoned to the same extent as Black young people. In instances like this, the notion of uncritically working in service to community groups shows itself to be deeply flawed. Recognising that 'subordinated communities can also be sites of unethical conduct and/or political disagreement',[29] it becomes necessary in such instances for us to challenge regressive logic or disband the cloakroom community. It is therefore perhaps more useful for us to orient ourselves towards working in service to anti-racism more broadly, rather than to specific community groups. In practice, our broader service to anti-racism will see us working (critically) in service to community groups as a means to achieve our broader goals, but nevertheless our anchor will ultimately be to the broader project of anti-racism. We turn now to consider how working in service to community groups and anti-racism more broadly impacts upon, and is guided by, concerns around accountability.

Accountability

Central to working in service to anti-racism, we want to suggest, should be the notion of *being accountable*. Establishing accountability has been a long-standing concern in UK HE, particularly since the neoliberal turn. Indeed, accountability is a key driver behind metrics such as the REF and the Teaching Excellence Framework, both designed to ensure that universities remain accountable to the State for public investment and to the student consumer.[30] As we suggested in our introductory chapter, these technologies of neoliberalism are incredibly limiting, including in the forms of accountability they encourage. Rather than facilitating meaningful accountability to the public, they encourage academics to jump through hoops that are dictated by market logics, leading in turn to a culture of competitiveness, stress, and anxiety.[31] Whilst the UK's REF Impact agenda might at first glance be seen to encourage an accountability to various publics or to social change more broadly, normative conceptualisation of Impact in HE can, as noted in the Introduction, 'often lead us to value only those modes of social impact which are unabashedly substantial, muscular, large-scale, self-confident, and readily narratable as such'.[32] Institutionalised forms of Impact – those that are causal and readily measurable – might therefore cross-cut fleetingly with the genuine, long-term (albeit, unquantifiable) forms that arise from scholar-activists' embeddedness in communities of resistance, but the nature and extent of accountability in each are incomparable.

Anti-racist scholar-activist notions of accountability stand in stark contrast to those that pervade HE. Pointing to the relationship between embeddedness within, and accountability to, communities of resistance, Laura Pulido notes:

> Accountability refers to the fact that scholar activists are not lone mavericks. Indeed, the idea of a scholar activist operating alone is something of an oxymoron. The whole point of being a scholar activist is that you're embedded in a web of relationships, some of which demand high levels of accountability to a community or other groups of individuals.[33]

In a similar vein, and tying the notion of working in service to accountability, Patricia Hill Collins explains:

> there is an important distinction between scholarship *in support of* social justice and scholarship *in service to* social justice. Scholarship *in support of* social justice implies a lack of accountability on the part of the scholar – others are engaged in social justice projects and the thinker in question aims to make a contribution but is not held accountable for how his or her contribution works out.[34]

Understood in this way, accountability should be at the heart of what it means to work in service to anti-racism and thus, in turn, central to anti-racist scholar-activism.

Our participants were keen to subvert the pressures of hegemonic forms of (neoliberal) accountability within contemporary HE, and to suggest that they were primarily accountable to the immediate groups that they worked with, wider communities of resistance, and ultimately anti-racism. For some, particularly academics of colour, this accountability came from working within the communities they had grown up in. For others, this sense of being accountable was something that had to be managed more consciously and proactively. This is apparent in the case of Maria (white, mid-career), who worked at an institution and in a city to which she was relatively new:

> that takes time in a community, and it takes relationships and the relation-
> ships, I think, are the most fundamental part. And for me to do it ethically,
> it involves me having personal relationships with people that are regular
> relationships, where there's accountability. Especially being a white person
> within the discipline and working around issues of race. So that's going to
> take time, but it's a thing that I am committed to doing if I stay in a place
> and it's always my central goal.

Maria talks of the importance of building relationships with local communities and, as Gramsci puts it, being 'an active participant in practical life'.[35] She emphasises that these relationships should be both personal and regular, and thus – like Clarke, Chadwick, and Williams – appreciates the importance of 'being present, being consistent, being approachable, being engaged and being a support'.[36] As Maria indicates, relationship-building takes time and effort, but 'for many activist researchers in movements, the significance of relationships will be one of the first things people emphasise'.[37] Relationships are particularly pertinent for Maria – and other scholar-activists like her – both because she is working within a community with which she is unfamiliar and because she is racialised as white working primarily with Black communities.

There is a clear counter-hegemonic tendency in Maria's account. Time has been commodified in our capitalist society, the effects of which are very much felt within the academy. Indeed, the pressure to use time 'wisely' – that is, to be 'productive' – is ubiquitous in (as well as beyond) the contemporary HE sector both nationally and globally.[38] It is in this context that Aziz Choudry observes that 'maintaining relationships with movements, organisations, and activist groups involves considerable work, which often goes unrewarded and unrecognised in terms of pressures to win research funding and the ways in which academics are evaluated'.[39] One of our participants, Jay (Asian-British, mid-career), noted something similar, suggesting that 'one of the biggest barriers to doing that sort of stuff [scholar-activism] is just sheer workload, time pressures, and the bureaucracy that comes with all of that'. Therefore, to build meaningful, regular, trusting relationships with local communities – as opposed to the short-term, hollow, extractive relationships that so often characterise academic interactions with wider communities[40] – is to swim against the neoliberal tide. The counter-hegemonic nature of this practice is particularly apparent when we consider that it can be 'easier to build a CV' or meet the demands of performance metrics 'with nominal engagements and positions in "the community"' than it is to invest the time and energy in cultivating embeddedness.[41] Of course, the former becomes tempting in a context whereby the neoliberal logics of competition, precarity, and overwork characterise HE.

The embeddedness that Maria strives for creates opportunities for direct and tangible forms of accountability, and this is part of her motivation for building such relationships: it is what informs and guides her orientation as an anti-racist scholar-activist. Dillon – a British Asian early-career academic – similarly reflected on the more direct forms of accountability that arise from embeddedness:

> you get called out as well. I've had many conversations with Linton [anonymised] where he said to me, 'no, you're focusing on the wrong thing here'. Or where he said, 'that's not the issue, it's this. You need to look more at this.' Because he's involved with the people on the ground, he has a strong idea of what academia should be focusing on and writing about. So, then I go back to my work, thinking actually I need to refocus it if it's going to

be of any use to people. So that's pivotal. Sometimes when you hear community groups saying 'oh the work doesn't speak to us' that's part of the reason why – because some academics are so detached from the groups that are mobilising and resisting, and hence they're not writing about the things that people on the ground care about. It's only by mingling with, being with them, being part of them, and actually *being* them that you understand what matters and what doesn't.

Whilst being called out by non-academic activists can often produce defensiveness and a sense of vulnerability, Dillon shows that such instances can be important, even formative. In activist circles, this is particularly the case when one occupies a position of relative privilege, such as that of an academic. For Dillon, the process of being challenged leads him to refine and refocus his praxis to ensure it is of 'use to people'. In this sense, the accountability that comes from 'staying connected to and informed by struggle'[42] enables scholar-activists to better service communities of resistance and anti-racism more broadly.

Much like Dillon's argument that one needs to be embedded within a community in order to understand what matters to it, Sara (British Muslim, early-career) suggested that working within communities of resistance is important because:

It centres you and it grounds you and it connects you back to those experiences … it moves your scholarship from being behind the paywall of a journal, to being grounded in the community you are working with.

There are clear parallels here between the views of Sara, Dillon, and Maria since each of them speaks to what we noted in the Introduction to be a key tenet of anti-racist scholar-activism: a deep commitment to the collaborative production of knowledge through grounding as *part of* – rather than as a detached observer to – communities of resistance.[43] This embeddedness enables one's scholarship to be informed by 'the sounds and visions'[44] that emerge from struggle. As Choudry contends, this is 'real work' which 'cannot be easily converted into "outputs", "partnerships" or "future collaborations"'.[45] In this sense, embeddedness is productive of an anti-racist scholar-activist rendering of account-ability that is radically distinct from the neoliberal accountability of HE metrics.[46]

Thus far, we have focused on the importance of embeddedness and direct accountability. Here, however, we want to argue that anti-racist scholar-activism also necessitates less tangible – perhaps even imagined – forms of accountability. There are at least two reasons why imagined accountability can be important. Firstly, it is not practicable or ethical for communities outside of the university to constantly manage and check on the work of university-based scholar-activists – that is, although we should be accountable to communities of resistance, anti-racist scholar-activists should not need to be supervised by (often unsalaried) community members and/or activists. Secondly, the sheer size and scale of marginalised and dispossessed communities means that we must adopt a larger concep-tion of accountability that extends beyond those with whom we have direct contact. In this sense, and to borrow from both Benedict Anderson and Sivanandan,[47] we might think of ourselves as being accountable to *imagined communities of resistance*.

Notwithstanding the need to and possibility of building more direct international networks, the 'expanded notion of community'[48] in *imagined communities of resistance* can enable us to look beyond the borders of 'methodological nationalism'[49] to adopt a more internationalist approach to our anti-racist scholar-activism. This internationalist approach encour-ages us to see 'our struggle as closely related to' or a part of 'liberation struggles around the world'.[50] In this sense, it recaptures those elements of the radical anti-racist tradition (discussed in the Introduction) that seek to understand struggles in their global context, tied to imperial and colonial histories.[51] Our argument here is not intended to suggest that imagined forms of accountability should overshadow or preclude direct and tangible forms of accountability, or should discourage us from building international networks. Our intention is simply to acknowledge that, for the reasons set out above, imagined forms of accountability can be both necessary and generative. As our last point on the matter, we want to take this one step further. Earlier in this chapter, we suggested that whilst we work in service to communities of resistance, our ultimate service is to the broader project of anti-racism. We might say the same here in terms of accountability: our ultimate accountability is to anti-racism. Thus, our accountability is governed by our ability to live up to the principles and orientations of radical anti-racist traditions – that is, those that centre on racism in its institutional and structural incarnations. Such a rendering will regularly leave us at odds with the neoliberal-imperial-institutionally-racist university.

Usefulness

A concern with the usefulness of academic work ran through many of the accounts of our participants. In essence, such a concern is somewhat unremarkable. Not only is it shared by many (if not all) academics, but it is also institutionalised through the REF Impact agenda – albeit, in a somewhat reductive and economically calculated form. As we will show throughout this book, however, scholar-activism invokes a particular way of thinking about usefulness which breaks with the market-driven understandings advanced through HE's technologies of neoliberalism. More specifically, the notion of working in service anchors to whom (or what) we strive to make our work useful.[52] In an anti-racist scholar-activist tradition, work is useful if it helps to empower communities of resistance and if it fuels anti-racism.[53] The usefulness we are describing here is something akin to that which Richard Johnson and others, charting traditions of radical education, have referred to as *really useful knowledge* – that is, usefulness that does not merely operate 'as a tool of social reproduction and a guardian of the status quo' but which 'demands changes by unveiling the causes of exploitation and tracing its origins within the ruling ideology'.[54] We use 'usefulness', therefore, to describe that which serves 'practical ends' that are shaped by the 'social standpoint and political purpose' of communities of resistance, in pursuit of liberation.[55]

Focusing specifically on research, Sajid (British Pakistani, mid-career) provided insight into how we might think productively about this notion of usefulness:

> Your research agenda is often derived from your involvement in community or grassroots organisations and campaigns and movements ... to me that's where good research comes from. It doesn't come from a research gap or a gap in the literature. And I think often that can be the worst excuse to do a project: because I've seen a gap in the literature. I don't think that should be a motivation to do a project. For me it's about how socially useful is your research?

By starting with the 'research agenda', Sajid situates usefulness as being fundamental to the entire research process, with communities of resistance playing a key role within it. In this regard, his understanding of usefulness ties into earlier accounts from Dillon, Maria, and Sara in relation to accountability, in that all suggest that community embeddedness produces 'good research' and good praxis. Part of the value in embeddedness, we argue, derives from its facilitation of attempts to combine theory and practice, which we noted in the Introduction to be a key tenet of anti-racist scholar-activism. As Walter Rodney conveys, embeddedness enables linkages between one's theoretical ideas and 'the practical realities of the experiences of the masses'.[56] In turn, as Mathiesen remarks, we can take as 'our point of departure the interests of those out of power rather than those in power'.[57] This is the crux of anti-racist scholar-activist notions of usefulness. It is in recognising that research should be socially useful that Sajid juxtaposes his own work against that of an academic whose research is motivated by a perceived 'gap in the literature'. Talk of the proverbial gap in the literature is commonplace in academia and is

encouraged through the operationalisation of 'originality' within the REF,
but for anti-racist scholar-activists like Sajid, the importance attributed
to knowledge gaps is apt to sound self-indulgent. In a context where
marginalised communities often have pressing needs, scholar-activists
cannot afford to practise detached forms of scholarship (this point is
complicated a little in a moment).[58]

The importance of allowing communities to drive the research agenda
was unpacked further by Sajid, who went on to say:

> it's about trying to figure out what communities want and I think in the
> times that we live in which are highly polarised politically, which are danger-
> ous with the rise of the far-Right and with the rise of the more respectable,
> or *so called* respectable, alt-Right, we live in dangerous times and I think
> it's about trying to respond to the needs of communities as opposed to
> preaching to communities.

Here, Sajid reiterates his commitment to taking direction from marginalised
communities but, importantly, he also points to the wider socio-political
context that surrounds his praxis. To be sure, 'we live in dangerous times'
that, as the prominent American philosopher George Yancy writes,
underline the 'urgency of addressing and attempting to eradicate our
collective dehumanised existential condition, of overthrowing hegemonic
structures that render our Black and Brown bodies dispensable.'[59] Responding with urgency can be counter-hegemonic because 'the academy is not
geared towards immediacy or urgency',[60] at least not in service to social
justice. We will return to exploring how urgent scholar-activist agendas
jar against slow university bureaucracy when we consider the backlash
against scholar-activism in Chapter 4.

It is perhaps this sense of urgency that leads many, like Sajid, to be
absolutely clear in their commitment to communities of colour. There is
no time or space for ambiguity; we must, as Routledge and Derickson
put it, engage with an 'insurrectionary imagination'.[61] Barry (early-career
academic of colour) picked up on this thread when he noted:

If you're not trying your best with your position, whatever wage you get, and [a] permanent job, to feed into some kind of struggles, [then] I do struggle with that. I also think sometimes you want to do an intellectual project and that's okay as well, but I do struggle to see how you can justify making your funding bid about a bowling alley in the shadows of Grenfell or whatever. Or, how you can get involved in certain kinds of representational stuff around gender when women's centres are being closed down and such. There's always that balance to be struck between saying you always have to do the most insurgent, radical, on the ground feeding into the movement work, because it is important to, [but] also do[ing] some theoretical work even if it's really abstract.

For Barry, the urgency of the moment dictates the need for work that feeds into anti-racist struggles and prioritises a focus on the material conditions of dispossessed communities above purely representational politics.[62] When grappling with this urgency, we want to suggest that there is work to be done to connect the immediate and the symptomatic (e.g. Grenfell) to the underpinning structural conditions (e.g. capitalism, racism, nationalism, and borders) – that is, there is a need to respond to the urgency of the moment, whilst also feeding into struggle against wider structural forces. In this sense, there is a tension that some scholar-activists might work to reconcile between urgent and responsive research on the one hand, and more long-term theoretical explorations of the structural conditions (that give rise to the events that require urgent attention) on the other. As Barry indicates, there is 'always a balance to be struck'.

Notably, Barry's comments do not constitute a disavowal of theory. Indeed, in contrast to stereotypes that often construct scholar-activism as anti-intellectual,[63] there is clear acknowledgement from Barry that there is a place for theoretical and/or traditionally intellectual work. As we suggested in the tenets we set out in the Introduction, the utility of theory, in this balance, would be informed by and situated alongside the (urgency of the) needs of communities of resistance. In this sense, as the Black Power activist Kwame Ture and others have maintained, theory is used to propel anti-racist social change.[64] Though this is a feature of activism generally, it underscores the *scholar* in scholar-activism particularly. This serves as a reminder, as Patricia Hill Collins so aptly puts it, that 'the overarching goal of scholarship in service to social justice is not to explain social inequality or social injustice, but to foster social justice, to bring about some sort of change'.[65] In this sense, Sivanandan's notion of 'not just thinking for thinking's sake, but thinking in order to do'[66] – as we noted in the Introduction – is far from an anti-intellectual position. Instead, it is better understood as pointing to the importance of making theory useful in resistance struggles.[67]

Situating his thoughts in a longer genealogy of anti-racist scholarship and activism, Barry traced his concerns around usefulness to what he described as a disagreement between the 'two powerhouses' of Stuart Hall and Ambalavaner Sivanandan. Barry recalled that Sivanandan had charged Hall with a 'betrayal of the struggle against racism' for his turn to 'culture and identity' in the 1980s and away from more radical, socialist, anti-racist politics.[68] For Barry, this represented a 'really healthy debate' that illustrates how the contemporary moment 'has become watered down to a whole new level'. Put more plainly, we might ask: if Sivanandan could make that critique of Hall, despite Hall's socialist politics and his work as a leading public intellectual in Britain, what might he think of contemporary scholarship? As Barry put it, contemporarily:

> you have policy-oriented migration studies which are shit, carceral everything everywhere, criminology being full of people who are basically police officers, [and you] can't talk about race and identity without being 'Leftist'. We talk about migration without talking about race!

Barry reminds us here that scholar-activism must be fundamentally based upon a radical and critical anti-racist analysis, if it is to be most useful (or work in service) to communities of resistance and anti-racism. In keeping with the Black Power-influenced strand of anti-racism we outlined in the book's Introduction, such an analysis situates racism within broader social, political, and economic process, and ties it to histories of colonialism and imperialism.

There is one final point we want to make with regard to questions of usefulness and this was captured most forcefully by Dez, a Black professor:

> If you are a critical scholar or a critical theorist, or someone who does that kind of stuff, it's not that you're not useful but that a lot of what you write about is, by and large, known by people who are at the front of the thing. You do critiques of power. You might be able to write it a little bit more eloquently, but basically you're not going to wow anybody, like 'fuck, I never knew power was like that!' Do you see what I mean? Often what people want is a particular kind of expertise, and a particular kind of expertise which actually a lot of critical theorists don't have! Do you see what I mean? For example, I know a few of the people around the Grenfell Tower stuff, and one of the things that they were really wanting was in-depth investigations into local council stuff, and legal issues and all that kind of stuff, not globalisation and the city and justice.

In speaking back to assumptions that elevate the knowledge of academics, Dez's analysis here is vital. As he puts it, the knowledge that 'critical theorists' possess is usually already known by activists on the frontline or by individuals living through inequality and injustice.[69] Often, movements may not need the research of scholar-activists at all, but rather more practical skills. It might even be that buying pizza for a community meeting, stacking chairs after a meeting, or being a shoulder to cry on is far more useful than one's academic work.[70] In this respect, as Gargi Bhattacharyya advises, we must avoid rushing 'to commentary before [we] are able to do everyday work': the 'donkey work'.[71] To engage in work within communities of resistance, scholar-activists might therefore find themselves having to upskill and move beyond their comfort zone: to learn the craft of activist organising. As Castle and McDonald warn, however, 'given that excelling in the academy often requires submission to the same power structures that activists are organising against',[72] academics can be less willing or able to engage in necessary confrontations with power. We might add here that, particularly for those in precarious positions (and with marginalised positionalities), it might not only be a case of excelling in academia but of merely surviving or remaining in it. The analysis of Dez therefore is sobering and offers food for thought for those of us committed to anti-racist scholar-activism.

Accessibility and reach

Participants were also concerned with ensuring that their work is accessible to, and reaches, the groups and communities for which it is intended. A fundamental concern in this regard pertains to the US-Eurocentricity of knowledge production and discipline formation,[73] and the interrelated dominance of the English language, both of which speak to the university's ties to colonialism. This has implications for which voices, and which forms of knowledge, are valued. It creates disadvantages for those academics for whom English is not a first language and feeds into unequal (academic) power relations.[74] It also means that such knowledge is only shared to English-speaking audiences. For anti-racist scholar-activists, this places significant limits upon our abilities to work in service to communities of resistance, particularly as – in the spirit of internationalism – we look to move beyond borders. It is for this reason that participants like Malaika – who had migrated to Britain from South America – spoke of translating academic writing in different languages as part of their scholar-activist praxis. Notwithstanding the irony of this book being written in English, we want to suggest that it is necessary that we push for the decentring of the English language and – wherever possible – call for the production of materials in multiple languages.

Concerns about language also bring forth strong critiques of the opacity of academic jargon, and the subsequent exclusion of people outside of the academy,[75] including those we claim to be working alongside. As Haytham (Pakistani, PhD researcher) explained, academic norms can lead you 'to stop writing like a human being'. It was in a similar vein that Galiev (person of colour, early-career) said:

> There's always this problem of the knowledge that we produce being incredibly impenetrable. I know so many people that say, 'You talk a big game of being radical and this, that and the other, but first of all we don't have access to your scholarship. Second, when we do it's completely impenetrable, man.' I think this is something we can no longer think is okay: to acknowledge this as a problem and then that's enough. I think it's the biggest problem within critical scholarship.

For Galiev, it seems that critical academics are largely unable or unwilling to move beyond (the hollow performance of) critiquing the exclusionary nature of academic jargon, and towards a change in their own praxis. For those of us engaged in anti-racist scholar-activism, questions over the accessibility of language should raise important questions. Namely, who are we writing for? Or, put another way, to whom are we working in service? As Patricia Hill Collins acknowledges, working in service to social justice 'raises a distinctive set of concerns' that includes questions over style, 'intended audiences', and accessibility.[76] If we are to work in service to communities of resistance, should our work not speak the language of those communities? This should not be taken to mean that scholar-activist work should be 'dumbed down' to patronising, monosyllabic writing. It is certainly a fallacy to assume that those outside of the academy cannot understand precise, complex language; this is a point we return to soon.

Alongside questions about the accessibility of language sit questions over where and how work is published. 'Paywall journal articles are shit and always have been shit, really', Barry insisted:

> and yet they're the things we are valued on in terms of getting a wage, getting a permanent job, getting a promotion. So, I think it's more important

than ever to try and write some shorter stuff, and also that's where the
political intervention is.

Bringing a critique of academic publishing to the forefront of our considerations of accessibility, Barry draws attention to the issue of journal paywalls
(although much the same can be said of extortionately expensive academic
books). Journal paywalls create conditions of exclusivity, meaning (in
theory at least) that articles are only accessible to those who are willing
and able to pay, or who have an institutional affiliation that grants them
access. Thus, journal paywalls not only accelerate the commodification
of knowledge, but they (attempt to) ensure that certain forms of knowledge
remain the preserve of the privileged.[77] Noting that publishing in journals
is what we are valued on (and what keeps us employed), Barry points to
how, through the pressure it creates to publish in particular journals, the
REF constitutes a barrier to accessibility. In this sense, the REF bolsters
the locking of knowledge into the academy and away from communities
outside of it.

In addition to paywalls, the form of academic journal articles is itself
limiting. Alex – a mixed-race, established academic – conveyed sentiments
similar to Barry's:

> I think it [blog writing] is very important because people read blogs, people
> outside of academia read blogs and they have a much wider circulation.
> They're free, they're outside the heinous academic publishing system. And
> yes, I think that obviously they're shorter, they're not as rigorous, but then
> you can also be more creative and more free and I think that, politically,
> it's important to write blogs.

Extolling the virtue of writing short form pieces, Alex, much like Barry,
suggests that accessible writing is politically important. Thus, the motivation
for writing is to advance the political interests of the communities and
causes to which we are in service. Alongside her substantive point about
the need for knowledge to be free, Alex places emphasis on the importance

of engaging a wide readership, including publics beyond academia: there is convergence, here, between the interests of scholar-activists and the interests of public intellectuals. Alex conveys a desire to 'speak the truth to the people',[78] an impulse that we traced in the tenets of anti-racist scholar-activism set out in the Introduction. This tendency underscores a tension between the orientation of scholar-activists (who are concerned with political change and engaging wider audiences) and the norms of HE (which are more conservative, and often exclusionary). In 'speaking to the people', Patricia Hill Collins argues that scholar-activists can undermine the 'belief that elites are the only social actors who count'.[79] As Alex puts it, in contrast to academic journal articles, blogs are something that people (beyond academia) actually read.

Having spoken of the virtues of blogs, Alex also notes that they are sometimes less rigorous than academic scholarship. Whilst she importantly ties this to the opening up of opportunities for more creative interventions that are perhaps better suited to working in service to communities of resistance, we might also read her comments as an intimation that blogs alone are not enough. Rather, blogs play an important role alongside longer, more in-depth and more typically 'academic', peer-reviewed work. We agree with Gargi Bhattacharyya that 'sometimes understanding important things can be laborious, and the labour is an important component of developing understanding'.[80] Indeed, defending complexity, Sivamohan Valluvan asserts that 'to always eschew complex language in the interests of clarity and simplicity is not necessarily a virtue and not necessarily consistent with the aspiration to provide sufficiently searching argumentation'.[81] It would be a misapprehension to presume therefore – as critics of scholar-activists often do (see Chapter 4) – that anti-racist scholar-activists disavow or devalue academic rigour and precision. As we began to establish in the Introduction, there is a strong tradition within anti-racist scholar-activism (and relatedly, public intellectualism) of producing rigorous scholarship that is tested and refined through resistance.[82] It is worth reiterating here, as Sivanandan's work – as a non-university-based intellectual – attests, this rigour is not only confined to academia.

Concern over the dissemination of one's work to wide-ranging audiences was a recurrent theme amongst our participants. Whilst public dissemination is a concern for many academics and is an imperative within the REF Impact agenda, the concerns of participants were inflected by a specific concern for reaching communities of resistance in pursuit of anti-racism. Ali – an early-career Arab man – reflected on his sense of responsibility in this regard:

> I feel a lot on my shoulders which is that, because I am privileged to read and think about these things, I do have to give back and try to rephrase and transform things in ways that are digestible for people who don't have that space and time to think about these things, and legitimately so, who are concerned with other things in their lives.

What Ali describes here is a responsibility to demystify some of the exclusionary tendencies of the academy as a way of opening up knowledge. Echoing much of this sentiment, Ereene, a British Muslim early-career academic, asserted:

> People are not inclined to read [academic] books. They're not inclined to read papers. Who's going to read papers? Blog articles and things get shared on social media, shared on WhatsApp, shared in so many different forms and people are reading them. They're quick, they're snappy, and it's important because that's how you spread the news, that's how you build a movement and that's how you get people involved.

Ereene speaks damningly here of the capacity to engage with wider publics through academic books and articles. It is for this reason that she sees blogs and shorter digital forms of writing as being important for engaging the groups and communities that she works within. Her motivation is to 'build a movement' and draw others into it. For this reason, she is clear who her audience is and how to engage with them. Making explicit reference to mobile messaging services, Ereene reflects where she believes her communities are most likely to be reached.

Whilst we agree to some extent with the point being made here, we also want to push back a little. We want to suggest that many communities of resistance do want to, and are able to, engage with books and papers to inform their praxis. Indeed, our activist friends and comrades based outside of the academy often contact us to help them to access paywalled journal articles, books, and other academic materials. Moreover, many of our participants listed non-academics as amongst their fiercest and most generative critics. It is important, therefore, to resist a binary that presents those in the academy as being engaged with rich knowledge and theory, and those outside of the academy as only wanting to engage with 'snappy' blog posts. Ereene is right to call for shorter forms of engagement in order to draw people into movements, but this should not be extended to imply that non-academics in movements are not engaged with theory, or that meaningful engagement with complex theory is not a worthwhile task.

Ereene is not alone in emphasising the importance of social media. The possibilities that are opened up by our entry into the digital era are widely recognised in academic literature, including how digital technologies open up the university to public pedagogy.[83] In this latter respect, Michael Eric Dyson observes that 'the advent of technology has enabled [a] new black digital intelligentsia to share their ideas more widely and publicly'.[84] In the spirit of *freedom dreaming*,[85] we might even think of how digital technologies enable us to engage in community education as an alternative to the university and/or as a way of undermining the university. Yet, the ability of these technologies to accelerate anti-racist movements cannot be taken for granted. Not only have anti-racist scholars long since found ways to reach wider publics, but we should also question whether our ability to rapidly communicate our thoughts in pithy formats 'moves us closer to the truths that will sustain us'.[86] Natalie Fenton has warned about how the rapid communication of the digital world may '[run] roughshod over the slower process of political organization' that is needed to sustain movements.[87] Similarly, Bhattacharyya and colleagues warn of 'the power of social media to undo the historically informed, internationally contextualised and carefully thought-out analyses of racism so desperately needed in these times of multiple crises'.[88] Thus, whilst offering opportunity for anti-racist activism, it cannot be assumed that new technologies will lead to social justice.[89] This rings particularly true when we are cognisant of the existing (imperial) power structures in our societies, and how they shape access and engagement online. Given that internet connection and media literacy is not available to all,[90] digital technologies – much like journal paywalls – can lock out already marginalised members of society.

There are other considerations in relation to digital technologies, too. After echoing much of the sentiment of Ereene, Sara (British Muslim, early-career) went on to unpack some of her thinking around the utility of social media for anti-racist resistance:

> I mean I am in two minds. I absolutely do believe it's so important. You can literally connect to millions, right, and I think that is what is really important … However, I am now also aware of how Twitter is used to literally tear you down. Especially as someone who is part of a marginalised community, I am extremely aware that that is the downside of it. I am very cautious with what I tweet now, especially in relation to the research that I am doing because I know that it is used by those who are advocates of the policies against me. I think that I have to be really mindful of that.

As Sara makes clear, the role of social media in social movement building is a complex one. On the one hand, social media has the potential to propel movements and to reach huge audiences instantaneously. The rise of Black Lives Matter from a hashtag to a movement is a case in point,[91] as was the Arab Spring,[92] the Egyptian Revolution,[93] and the global #MeToo campaign,[94] among others. Pew Center research has shown that communities of colour are more likely to find political utility in Twitter than their white counterparts.[95] As Sara acknowledges, there are, however, issues around the relative impunity with which people can enact racist abuse online. There are also significant issues around surveillance and demonisation, and evidence that social media can be weaponised to undermine social justice efforts.[96] In these and other regards, critical work on social media and online spaces offers notes of caution. The respective works of scholars such as Cathy O'Neil, Safiya Noble, Yarden Katz, and Ruha Benjamin all point to how – in contrast to their assumed objectivity – digital technologies in fact reinforce structural inequalities, with racism often hardwired into and reinforced by online spaces and the digital. Online platforms are saturated by whiteness, often reflecting biases and assumptions present in design, development, and usage.[97] Moreover, Michael Kwet's work details how US 'domination of digital technology' reinscribes or 'reinvents' imperial and colonial relations (through 'economic domination', 'imperial control', and 'imperial state surveillance').[98] Social media – as per the digital more broadly – is, therefore, an incredibly difficult terrain for scholar-activists to navigate. This underlines the need for reflexivity to lie at the heart of scholar-activist praxis and for that reflexivity to be exercised in the context of online engagement, if we want to work effectively in service to anti-racism.

In addition to blogs and social media, many of our participants shared a general commitment to using a range of other platforms to engage with non-academic publics. Ali captured this sentiment when he noted that 'there are definitely different ways … I say we hit them all. We do what we can with what we have.' Thomas (Black, early-career) similarly reflected on his efforts to utilise a range of dissemination methods:

> I do a lot more kind of audio-visual academic work than most academics, which I think is a lot more accessible than writing in a journal and in incomprehensible language. I go to schools and community centres and teach on the same topic as I wrote my highbrow thesis on and deliver workshops on the same topic.

Thomas's praxis here is based upon a critique that relates to two themes discussed earlier in this section: the inaccessibility of academic language and the exclusivity of journal paywalls. In response, Thomas draws upon other methods of engagement – often appearing on the news, the radio, and on podcasts – to better communicate ideas related to his research and issues that pertain to anti-racism more broadly. His reasoning for doing so reflects a desire to reach more people, and move beyond academic echo chambers, in order to strengthen anti-racist resistance. As Thomas also reflects on his use of workshops in schools and community centres, he returns us to the question of who our work is for. In doing so, he highlights the need to speak to different audiences which, in turn, requires the adoption of different registers – an idea we introduced in the Introduction. The individuals, groups, and communities with which we work are not homogeneous; we should be prepared to use different methods and registers to reach them.

Taking us back to the notion of working in service explicitly, and expanding on the point raised by Thomas, Elroy explained:

> Researchers, if they're talking 'in service of', then those findings should be 'to the benefit of'. Sometimes, that means, therefore, presentations locally. Feeding back to those individuals for whom that research is intended, who that knowledge may be of use to. To those individuals, for want of a better term, who commission that research. Accessible, transparent. But it has to go back through those groups. That's the impact, isn't it?

Here, Elroy reaffirms the idea that researchers must feed their research back to the groups they claim to work in service to. Not only this, but that feedback must be 'accessible' and 'transparent'. In this regard, there are lessons that university-based scholar-activists can learn from wider activist and organising communities about effective and useful dissemination of knowledge. In contrast to popular understandings that centre the university, Elroy situates communities of resistance as the *commissioners* of the research. He also suggests that the measure of the research lies in the extent to which it is 'to the benefit of' those communities. By making reference to impact, he pushes us towards a reclamation of a term that has been co-opted and institutionalised. In this sense, impact is not to be measured by institutional metrics but by our engagement with communities of resistance.

Conclusion

In this chapter, we have introduced the notion of working in service as a foundational principle – an orientation – that guides anti-racist scholar-activism. We have suggested that by working in service to communities of resistance and to anti-racism more broadly, anti-racist scholar-activism is counter-hegemonic. This is so, not only because it disrupts the power dynamics that often elevate academics who work within communities of resistance, but because it disrupts the idea that academics work *for* the university and therefore should be governed by the neoliberal technologies that pervade contemporary HE. We have shown that the working in service orientation guides anti-racist scholar-activism in a number of ways. Firstly, it induces a sense of accountability. In the most immediate sense, this accountability is to those communities with whom one directly works. Given that some of us work in service to communities beyond those we have direct contact with, however, we have argued that accountability (necessarily) exists on a much broader (perhaps imagined) level too. We are accountable to *imagined communities of resistance*. Secondly, we have also shown that the in service orientation can guide anti-racist scholar-activist concerns about how useful (or otherwise) one's work is, and to whom/what it is useful. In this respect, we maintained that usefulness to the broad project of anti-racism should be the primary goal of our work, and this should often be mediated by (or overlap with) questions around the usefulness of one's work to the groups with whom one works more directly.

Lastly, we reflected on questions of accessibility. Here, we suggested that language is an important consideration, both in terms of the dominance of the English language and the exclusionary logics of academic jargon. Language can, therefore, serve as a barrier or enabler of our ability to 'speak the truth to the people',[99] and thus to work in service to communities of resistance. We also reflected on the exclusion and exploitation that manifests in academic publishing, and the ways participants circumvent such obstacles. From these criticisms arose calls for a commitment to wider engagement with publics beyond academia and, in this regard, public intellectualism can be a vital component of scholar-activist work, particularly in the quest for the mobilisation of a larger anti-racist public. Whilst we are (trying to become) mindful of the problematics of social media, and have emphasised the need for reflexivity when utilising digital technologies, we have suggested that they offer opportunities to reach wider audiences and move beyond our academic echo chambers. We cannot be complacent about these opportunities, however. It is not inevitable that they will work in service to anti-racism. In the next chapter, we continue to draw upon the idea of working in service, as we think about 'stealing' from the university as a key component of anti-racist scholar-activist praxis.

3

Reparative theft: stealing from the university

In the previous chapter, we set out an orientation for anti-racist scholar-activism that is governed by the notion of working in service to communities of resistance,[1] and to the broader project of anti-racism. For the purposes of this chapter, we want to set the praxes of servicing against the backdrop of two coordinates. On the one hand, we have the relative lack of wealth and resources in communities of resistance, whilst on the other, we have the significant wealth and resources of the contemporary university,[2] of which we, as academics, are affiliates. Given the importance of such resources in determining the successes or failures of social movements,[3] opportunities for anti-racist scholar-activism lie in this stark contrast. Our access to resources within our institutions and the wider academy, and our orientation towards communities of resistance and anti-racism, make it incumbent upon us to redirect resources out of the university and into communities. As we argue, it is our duty to 'steal' from the university.

In the first part of this chapter, we explore Harney and Moten's work on the subversive praxis of 'stealing' from the university.[4] We bring these ideas into conversation with a discourse of reparative justice, in order to introduce the concept of *reparative theft* – a concept that then underpins the rest of the chapter. Building on these foundations, we introduce the accounts of participants to make the case that reparative theft is morally and ethically justifiable. Thereafter, we look at reparative theft in practice and do so in two sections. The first focuses particularly on the reparative theft of more material resources – for example: money, time, labour, and space. The second considers how social and symbolic capital constitutes a resource that can, and should, be stolen from our institutions. Ultimately, we argue that reparative theft is a key form of praxis – a fundamental component – of anti-racist scholar-activism, one that enables scholar-activists to exploit the contradictions of the university in service to communities of resistance and anti-racism more broadly.

Towards a theory of reparative theft

The notion of stealing from the university emerges out of *Black Studies*, and specifically the seminal work of Stefano Harney and Fred Moten. In *The Undercommons*, Harney and Moten declare that the 'only possible relationship to the university today is a criminal one'.[5] As they explain, given the university's underpinnings:

> one can only sneak into the university and steal what one can … abuse its hospitality … spite its mission … join its refugee colony, its gypsy encampment … be *in but not of* – this is the path of the subversive intellectual in the modern university (our emphasis).[6]

We touched briefly on the idea of being 'in but not of' in the Introduction and in the preceding chapter: it strikes at the heart of what it means to work in service to anti-racism. As we suggested, the notion of being 'in but not of' the university, as we take it from Harney and Moten, reflects a radical orientation that is fundamentally committed to anti-racism, and is also fiercely and necessarily critical of – and often operating in opposition to – the neoliberal-imperial-institutionally-racist university. To be 'in but not of', as we see it, is to be employed by the university but to work at its margins. It is to work 'inside' a university, whilst holding allegiances that are grounded 'outside' of it.[7] Scholar-activists – or subversive intellectuals, in Harney and Moten's terms – are in the university to *service* the undercommons of resistance: they 'came under false pretences, with bad documents, out of love'.[8] As Lennox and Yildiz rightly suggest, the question becomes, therefore, 'how can we mobilize the resources and privileges of our position within academia to service radical movements?'[9] How can we exploit the pockets of possibility the university presents to us?

Reminding us of the counter-hegemonic orientation of scholar-activists, Harney and Moten describe how, after taking what can be taken from the university, the subversive intellectual:

> disappears into the underground, the downlow lowdown maroon community of the university, into the undercommons of enlightenment, where the work gets done, where the work gets subverted, where the revolution is still black, still strong.[10]

As we argued in the previous chapter, once again we see in this conception that communities of resistance are prioritised by scholar-activists over and above the university. Underpinning Harney and Moten's notion of stealing is an understanding that the university is an unjust and extractive space: it 'cannot be accepted' as a 'place of enlightenment'. Its current form is 'built upon the theft, the conquest, the negligence of the outcast mass intellectuality of the Undercommons', they argue.[11] With this in mind, recognising the (racial) inequities of the university – as we seek to capture through our use of 'neoliberal-imperial-institutionally-racist' – is vital to our understanding and gives a particular inflection to the theft committed by subversive intellectuals. Not only do many universities have direct and indirect *material* and *financial ties* to African enslavement, colonialism, and contemporary racial capitalism,[12] but – through knowledge production – universities played (and continue to play) a key role in the development and perpetuation of the white supremacist ideologies that underpinned slavery, colonialism, and contemporary coloniality.[13] Moreover, historically and contemporarily, universities reproduce and reinforce structures of race, class, and other systems of oppression that make up the 'overarching structure of domination': the matrix of domination.[14]

It is in taking account of this long extractive history, a history with an afterlife, as Sharpe puts it,[15] that Harney and Moten remark that 'to be a critical academic in the university is to be against the university'.[16] A critical understanding of the university not only renders 'stealing' ethically and morally justifiable but – for anti-racist scholar-activists at least – positions it as a duty. In this sense, to steal from the university in service to social justice might be thought of as an act of *reparative justice*. Struggles for reparative justice have a 'long and varied history', beginning in 'chattel enslavement', 'interwoven into the histories of African-led resistance to enslavement', and contemporarily hinging upon 'the legal concept of a crime against humanity'.[17] Although this complex history makes succinct definition difficult, at its essence reparative justice, or reparations, invokes a framework of repair.[18] To speak of *repair* is to recognise that harms have been caused and that it is only right and proper that actions are taken to redress those harms. As such, the concept of reparative justice enables us to think about the university's complicity in (re)producing harm (see Chapter 6) and to seek reparations accordingly. Notwithstanding initiatives at institutions like the University of Glasgow – which in fact 'does more to bolster the university's liberal image than serve restorative justice'[19] – the relative unwillingness of higher education (HE) institutions to (meaningfully) reckon with their pasts and free up their resources for the dispossessed makes it incumbent upon anti-racist scholar-activists to *serve*, duplicitously, as a conduit of redistribution. In using this concept, our intention is not to be so naive as to imply that the work of individual scholar-activists can do the monumental work needed to realise reparative justice. Rather, we seek to locate 'stealing' from the university in a historical and sociopolitical context, and to recognise the small role that academics can play in lieu of (or as we agitate for) a deeper institutional commitment.

Despite Harney and Moten's searing critique of the university, they leave space in their analysis to acknowledge that, in spite of its extractive and oppressive tendencies, the university presents opportunities for subversive intellectuals. This is a key point for us. As la paperson implores us to see, despite all of its ills, the university is a site of contradictory forces and competing visions – that is to say, it is better viewed as an assemblage than a monolith.[20] The heterogeneity and complexity of the academy creates pockets of possibility through which anti-racist scholar-activists can exploit the contradictions of, and tensions present within, their institutions. Importantly, universities present opportunities for us to 'steal'. With this in mind, it is necessary to resist the temptation to overdetermine the university as a homogenous site of oppression and extraction in order to recognise these possibilities, as few and fleeting as they may be.

The reparations movement has gone to great pains to move beyond 'reductive interpretations of reparations as demands for individual payments, or simply as a "pay cheque"'.[21] We agree with Kehinde Andrews, however, that it is important for anti-racist movements to not shy away *entirely* from a focus on economic justice.[22] In the rest of this chapter, therefore, we conceive of 'stealing' as a form of reparations that both includes, and reaches beyond, the immediately economic. We want to turn now to our participants, as we develop the concept of reparative theft a little further and, in particular, think about reparative theft as a praxis that is entirely justifiable.

There is justice in reparative theft

Much like Harney and Moten and others,[23] participants acknowledged that the university has vast resources and that these resources should be redirected towards, or 'stolen' for, communities of resistance. This was encapsulated by Aaliyah, a Black early-career academic:

> I like the idea of just exploiting the university and its resources, *everything*, because it's exploiting my students and my colleagues. So, I don't owe it anything. That's really how I feel.

Bearing witness to the ways her institution exploits its constituents, Aaliyah makes clear that she does not feel indebted to the university. Instead, she affirms, it is the university that has a debt and, as a consequence, it ought to be (justifiably) exploited for its resources. In emphasising that it should be exploited for 'everything', we might read Aaliyah's comment as pointing to resources beyond the economic. Galiev (person of colour, early-career) picked up this thread:

> It's a form of redistribution. I think that what we've got to remember is that the university has a massive accumulation of not just economic capital but social capital. That social and economic capital is not entirely self-generated. That comes off being able to exploit the social and economic capital of people that work within, but also outside of the university and people within the university that may not necessarily be academics … They don't get their prestige, they don't get their wealth, purely because it's self-generated. It's because of the community that they kind of come into. I think, because of that, the people outside of the university are fully entitled to use the resources that the university often excludes them from. It's a form of, I guess, redistributive justice in that we've got to recognise that we wouldn't have the kind of prestige and resources that we have, were it not for being in the particular space that we were in and the exploitation that the university engages in.

As Galiev makes clear, the university exploits both its constituents and wider society. The position of the university – its social and economic capital, prestige, and wealth – is inextricably tied to the subordination of others, particularly the communities surrounding our institutions: communities which are often excluded physically and symbolically from the university.[24] What Galiev argues, therefore, is that dispossessed communities are entitled to forms of 'redistributive justice'. Like the concept of reparative justice, Galiev's notion of redistributive justice engenders a framing that is cognisant of an injustice that must be equalised or repaired. It is a framing which recognises that the university is built on ill-gotten gains and that anti-racist scholar-activists should redistribute those gains.

Sharing the sentiments of Galiev and Aaliyah, Maria was directly influenced by Harney and Moten's work: 'I think there's a justice in stealing from the university', she explained. We asked Maria – a white, established academic – about the framing of theft and whether a reparations discourse might be more appropriate:

> I think it should be reparations. It's an unjust institution that owes something to communities. So, for me there's a justice in the stealing, it would be like, enslaved people, theft does not mean the same thing. The morality of theft is subjective when the structure of opportunities and equalities are skewed towards some over others. So, yes, for me it's not theft, but the word 'theft' is nice, because it situates me as being subversive against what it's doing. It makes me clear about my position, which is that I'm a part of it but I'm on the edge of it. I'm critical of it the whole time, and I think some of that is not even just for the benefit of saying to other people I'm not a part of this; it's for myself, so that I don't trick myself into thinking that what they're offering here is what I want or what they've got for me here is worth it. That's not what I'm about here. I'm about taking the resources, stealing the resources, and trying to keep focused on the reasons I came in here to do this work.

Maria's starting point, like Galiev's and Aaliyah's, is that the university is an 'unjust institution'. The university is exploitative and extractive, and, contrary to the myth of meritocracy, is not a levelling space. As Maria puts it, 'equalities are skewed'. It is from this critical base that we must understand notions of 'theft' and the praxes of 'stealing' – that is to say, given the inequitable distribution of power, it is morally justifiable – morally imperative, in fact – to steal from the university. As Harney and Moten urge,[25] we *must* steal. It is part of the 'criminal relationship' we should have with the university.

Rather than dispensing of theft to simply talk about reparative justice, however, Maria contends that there is virtue in the notion of theft because it reflects her subversive 'in but not of' relationship to the university. Reflecting her positionality and orientation, it serves as a reminder that Maria's priorities lie not with the university (whose allure under capitalism can, of course, be seductive)[26] but with communities of resistance or, in Harney and Moten's terms, with the Undercommons. Maria's emphasis on the need to 'keep focused' also reminds us, as we argued in Chapter 1, that scholar-activism is best thought of as something that one *does*: a form of ongoing praxis that is shaped by *action and reflection*,[27] rather than a fixed or static identity that can simply be attained. As well as serving as a reminder with regard to her own orientation, Maria's retention of the notion of theft also urges us to recognise that, despite presenting pockets of possibility that we can exploit, HE institutions are generally resistant to radical anti-racist scholar-activism. As Gargi Bhattacharyya observes, 'state-funded institutions are unwilling to support and fund the work of revolutionary movements or to promote ideas that promote their own demise'.[28] This unwillingness to fund anti-racist scholar-activist work – which should not be mistaken for impossibility – therefore necessitates theft. Resources (material or otherwise) will not be given to anti-racist scholar-activists readily; we must *take* them.

When Maria continues to elaborate on her point, she shows us the importance of the notion of *reparative theft*:

> the goal is not to make the institution love you, that's not the goal. In fact, my struggle shouldn't centrally be around just the university. If I'm in here to steal the resources of the university to empower communities and to be involved in more radical organising, then my esteem in this institution should not be the central focus. My time in this university and the support they give me is not the central focus even though I'm concerned about those things. So, I think maybe I picked the university for those reasons ... It gives me a space that has a lot of resources that I can leverage for other people, that I wouldn't have had otherwise if I was working in a different type of job.

Maria's perspective brings our attention back to the notion of working in service, an orientation we discussed in the preceding chapter. As she notes, her goals and her sense of esteem come from 'more radical organising' within wider communities of resistance, rather than from her relationship with the university. Like many of our participants, Maria entered the university because of the opportunities it presents to plunder its resources for the benefit of anti-racist movements. Thus, as Maria reminds us, our fervent critique of the neoliberal-imperial-institutionally-racist university should not preclude us from recognising the pockets of possibility the university presents for anti-racist scholar-activism. Whilst these pockets of possibility or spaces within the university might be, as Darren Webb puts it, 'fleeting, transitory [and] small-scale',[29] they can nonetheless be leveraged in service to our communities of resistance, and anti-racism more broadly.

Reparative theft in practice

Having shown that notions of *reparative theft* inform anti-racist scholar-activist epistemologies and orientations, we want to turn now to consider what forms this reparative theft takes and what it might look like in practice. Writing on what they refer to as a *politics of resourcefulness*, Derickson and Routledge describe how:

> scholar-activists can commit to channeling the resources and privileges afforded academics (e.g., time; access to research, technology, and space; grant writing experience; expertise legible to new organizations) to advancing the work of non-academic collaborators (community groups, activist networks, local insurgencies, etc).[30]

Many social movements and community groups lack resources, power, and privilege. This is important to acknowledge given that the successes or failures of social movements are inextricably (although not solely) tied to their ability to access those things.[31] In contrast, universities have a wealth of resources. It is because of this contrast that Derickson and Routledge's remarks about the practice of redistribution become all the more salient. In the remainder of this chapter, we first explore how those engaged in anti-racist scholar-activism undertake the reparative theft of material resources, before we consider social and symbolic capital as a resource that can be stolen from the university.

Stealing material resources

There is a broad array of resources available within the university that can be repurposed for communities of resistance, and anti-racism more broadly. As Rosa – a white, mid-career academic who migrated to Britain – explained:

> It can be financial resources; it can be money, it can be human time, labour. It can be knowledge sharing, critical information sharing. So, maybe also help communities that are hit by austerity [gain] access to some resources through those resources that are available for research, as such. I'm certainly not the only one trying to do this. Then also, if you think about PhD studies … you can actually use your own self as a PhD student to help out groups that have limited access to resources. So, in a way, you are also allowing a transfer of resources through your own activism.

As Rosa's account indicates, when asked about the transfer of resources from universities to communities the most common response from participants was economic redistribution – that is, the filtering of university money, or money accessed via a university affiliation, into community groups. Although often requiring some careful (re)framing – what we refer to later in this chapter as *strategic duplicity* – academics can secure funds for communities of resistance in a variety of ways, including: through the inclusion of payments on (internal and external) research funding applications; by framing activism as/through Research Excellence Framework (REF) Impact activities;[32] and through university community engagement or social responsibility funding streams. The possibility to actualise (relatively small-scale) economic redistribution reminds us again that the university is not a homogenous entity, but rather a site of contradictory forces and competing visions that create pockets of possibility for anti-racist scholar-activism.

Securing university funding for activist groups is important and something that we seek to do in our own scholar-activist work. In our experience, and as our participants attest, amounts of funding that are considered to be small in the university's own terms can be incredibly impactful in grassroots community settings (such is the unequal distribution of resources). This is not, of course, to underestimate the ways in which funding can get wrapped up in university bureaucracy and is tied up with State surveillance. By way of example, Laura has encountered some of these problems when requesting the university pay sex worker activists for their labour on one of her research projects. The rigid managerial systems of the university offer no space to be responsive to sensitivities around sex workers not wanting to disclose real names and addresses to the university for fear of being 'outed'.[33] Many times, when anxiously (and embarrassedly) waiting for our respective universities to pay our community partners, or when our partners have been made to jump through the hoops of hostile environment policy,[34] we have wondered whether it would simply be easier to find funding outside of the university machine.

Notwithstanding the importance of funding, there are also, as Rosa explains, university resources beyond the immediately financial. Time can be stolen and so too can labour. Indeed, without people and time (amongst other factors), funding is not enough to sustain an effective activist movement.[35] Many of our participants spoke of how, academic workloads permitting, they use some of their salaried time to engage in activist work – that is to say, with scholar-activists acting as a conduit, the university comes to unwittingly resource activist time. This is the *reparative theft* of time that not only bolsters communities of resistance in the more immediate sense but which also rubs against – or seeks to undermine and redress – a neoliberal capitalist system that steals all of our time. Rosa uses an example of PhD study, but this can perhaps be extended to research studies and our work more generally. If studies are designed in such a way as to overlap with or be fundamentally informed by the interests and needs of activist groups, as they should (see previous chapter), then it is possible for one's research to be contributing to wider activism. Put another way, if one can (perhaps duplicitously) frame their activism in such a way as to see it recognised as part of their academic work, then time can be redirected from the academy to communities of resistance.[36]

On this point, Dez (Black, senior academic) spoke about the possibilities for finding space to do subversive work in the context of the contemporary university:

> On the one hand, if a new variable of university success is public engagement and Impact, then so long as you can narrate your work as public engagement or as Impact, then in actual fact its content is emptied out. It doesn't mean anything. All that it means is that you can make a claim to say that you'll do public engagement or Impact. In other words, part of it, at least over the last few years, is that no one cares what you're doing, but you're valorised if you can *say* that you're doing it. Again, there are problems with that, but at the same time, if it allows me to be able to do that stuff, then I don't really have that much of a problem with it.

As we have discussed, there are myriad issues with neoliberal mechanisms like the REF and its concern with Impact. Amongst a litany of other problems – some of which we touched upon in the book's Introduction – we are particularly concerned here about its promotion of short-termist and superficial engagement with communities.[37] As Dez explains, the hollowness of the REF Impact agenda means that it can be much easier to *perform* the work of community engagement than it can be to actually do the work, and indeed it is only the performance that is needed: 'its content is emptied out'. Put another way, it is the performance that is 'valorised', whilst (as we explore in the next chapter) the work of anti-racist scholar-activists – who invest significant amounts of time and energy in building genuine relationships within communities and community groups – is often undervalued within the academy. Having said that, Dez also points to how the hollowness of institutionalised notions of Impact and public engagement means that anti-racist scholar-activists can find space to do more counter-hegemonic work in service to anti-racism, as long as it can be articulated through the discourses of the REF. Our point here is not a defence of the REF because, as we noted in the Introduction and the previous chapter, its negative impacts are profound. Following Dez, we simply seek to point out how contradictions in the system can be manipulated for the benefit of communities of resistance,[38] or how we might find breathing space within academia.[39] We must bear in mind, however, that these benefits might be short-term in nature and may come at the cost of legitimising university processes that bring about damaging longer-term consequences.

Several of our participants noted that academic jobs can often provide the time and space to produce particular forms of knowledge that support wider resistance struggles. Such sentiment is evident in Chomsky's writing on the *Responsibility of Intellectuals*:

> Intellectuals are in a position to expose the lies of governments, to analyze actions according to their causes and motives and often hidden intentions. In the Western world, at least, they have the power that comes from political liberty, from access to information and freedom of expression. For a privileged minority, Western democracy provides the leisure, the facilities, and the training to seek the truth lying hidden behind the veil of distortion and misrepresentation, ideology and class interest, through which the events of current history are presented to us.[40]

In Chomsky's analysis, there is clear recognition of the relative privileges experienced by academics. From this privilege, he argues, comes a sense of responsibility or duty. This was keenly felt by many of our participants. Ali (Arab, early-career), for example, spoke of feeling 'very, very blessed, very grateful' for the 'space to be able to read and write and think'. With this, he noted, comes a 'responsibility that weighs down very heavily'.

The sense of responsibility that both Chomsky and Ali capture was echoed by Thomas, a Black early-career academic, who perhaps pushed towards a more overtly activist framing:

> Sivanandan described it as providing the intellectual fuel for the motors of resistance, which I quite like. So, it's the fact that all of these communities are engaging in troubles against the police or against the education system or against our borders, but academics have the resources, space, and time to do the, kind of, the knowledge producing that aids those struggles. To better understand the border system. To make connections between different forms of policing in parts of the country or part of the world or different parts of a specific empire. I think being able to have the space to make those kinds of connections, both historical or geographical or theoretical is what makes us scholar-activists.

For Thomas – who draws directly on Sivanandan and expresses sentiment not unlike Chomsky's – scholar-activists can work in service to (or provide 'the intellectual fuel for') wider resistance movements (see Chapter 2). We can do so through the production of knowledge that 'aids those struggles', for example, by drawing connections between sources and systems of oppression, connections between struggles, and developing understandings of the bigger picture. There are two points we want to make here. Firstly, Thomas is not suggesting that academics have a unique intellectual capacity to do this work, but rather it is the 'resources, space, and time' offered by a position in the academy that makes such work possible. This is an important point if we are to challenge dominant (colonial) constructions of legitimate knowledge – that is, those that position the university as *the* site of knowledge production. Secondly, as Thomas insists, the knowledge production we engage in must be to service anti-racism ('aid those struggles'). It is worth adding here that the form that this takes will likely differ across academic disciplines and – for a range of reasons – may be less direct in some instances than others (this relates to the point we made in the previous chapter about how we may be accountable *directly* to the communities of resistance we work within and/or more *indirectly* to broader anti-racist movements).

It is this second point, we argue, that returns us back to the notion of theft. If the university does allow time and space for anti-racist scholar-activism, why is it useful to think of our practice as *theft*? Whilst the university may offer some space for scholar-activism (which in fact was a key reason why many of our participants work in the academy), there are limits to the work that can be done *legitimately* within the academy.[41] Moreover, as suggested in the introductory chapter, the neoliberalisation of HE means that time is increasingly being squeezed and compromised. The task of scholar-activists, therefore, is to exploit the contradictions of the university,[42] and to push (back) these limits: 'abuse its hospitality … spite its mission' and 'subvert the work', in Harney and Moten's terms.[43] We must '*steal*' more than is on offer or, as Elroy puts it, constantly 'operate in the margins', from our 'in but not of' position. Choudry is right then that 'despite changing times, and notwithstanding all of the pressures on new academics to publish and perform in a certain way, there remain possibilities to use resources and locations in universities in the service of struggles and movements'.[44] This work often requires a degree of *strategic duplicity* with regard to what is being presented to the university, compared to the work that is actually being done.

In practice, some of the contributions that academics can make to social movements appear relatively insignificant (in that they place almost no burden on the academic) but can actually be incredibly impactful in terms of the benefit that they produce for communities of resistance. Thomas provided an example of this low-effort/high-reward work:

> it's very, very difficult to get a central London location where people from the north and south, east, west can access quickly for free and all that kind of stuff. So, I was like, bang. It's fine. I'll just book you a room at the university.

It's a very small act but it meant that that convening could go ahead, and a lot of academics don't think about that I don't think, because I'm constantly booking rooms all the time.

As Thomas acknowledges, booking university space for community groups and/or activists is 'a very small act' that many academics simply 'don't think about', but it is one that many of our participants recognised as being important and undervalued. It is one that is enabled by our affiliation with the university. When we consider the ways in which universities lock out so many, and the growing real estate and gentrification practices of HE institutions,[45] to reopen those spaces to wider communities can be an important political act: it can be a reparative act. It is an act that many of us, scholar-activist or not, can and should engage in. This is all the more apparent when we consider the ways that so many community groups struggle for access to space, for example, as a consequence of prohibitive city centre rents.

The value in university space has been apparent to us on several occasions in recent years. In 2019, for example, we were working on a project with *Resistance Lab*[46] that required physical space for us to get together. We needed the space to have a strong internet connection, accessibility, space for a sizable group, relative privacy (not to mention heating and relative comfort), to be geographically central to us all, and of no (or low) expense. University buildings transpired to be one of the only appropriate spaces that allowed us to do our work.

On another occasion, as part of the *Northern Police Monitoring Project*,[47] we hosted the former Black Panther Kathleen Cleaver at a public event in 2018. Given the number of people wanting to attend, and the project's lack of resources, finding a suitable venue was a challenge. Despite it meeting our criteria in terms of size, location, and equipment, we ruled out university space early on. We did so because of the detachment of Manchester's universities from the communities we organise with, and because university spaces can be exclusionary and alienating. We eventually found a community venue and the event was largely regarded as a success, but as we followed up with fellow organisers and attendees after the event, one point of feedback really stuck with us. It was possible that, because we held the event in one specific geographical area of Manchester, potential attendees from other areas of Manchester might have felt unable, or too uncomfortable, to attend. We had, potentially, prioritised one community over others. Although there was likely no perfect solution and the afore-mentioned problems related to university space still hold true, the uni-versity's central location and 'neutrality' might have offered us a way to circumvent the issue that was raised. Indeed, reflecting on a community project of his own, Ornette Clennon notes the underconsidered and underutilised value in university meeting rooms as 'neutral space'[48] to bring together various constituents of groups.[49] Using the university may also have allowed us to open it up to communities of resistance, to reclaim that space and to, temporarily at least, chip away at the exclusionary politics of the university in order to alter campus dynamics.

There are two other small acts that are worth mentioning here, and both might be considered forms of reparative theft that are somewhat unglamorous. The first is printing. Whilst community campaigns and groups can spend considerable amounts of money on printing, academics are usually able to print at work, at no cost to themselves (although their usage is sometimes monitored by their institutions). Particularly where anti-racist resistance is antithetical to the dominant logic of the university, repurposing university printers to produce materials for community groups can be a subversive act. As Elroy (Black, established academic) explains, it is about using the resources that we have and asking 'What do you need? A hundred flyers? Yes, I can get those printed off.' The second act relates to accessing academic resources, particularly paywall-protected journal articles but also academic books. The institutional protection of these resources acts to lock knowledge into the academy, even when that knowledge can be useful to wider communities. By opening up these resources (for example, by sharing journal articles), scholar-activists can engage in small acts of subversion that, on the one hand, undermine the exclusive logics of HE, academic publishing and the commodification of knowledge, and, on the other, bolster and resource communities of resistance.[50] Particularly with these smaller acts, we are not suggesting that only scholar-activists do this work, or that printing for a community group (on its own) makes a scholar-activist. We are merely suggesting that these are some very easy examples of ways in which academics can better support communities outside of the university. Given the in service orientation of scholar-activists, such acts can form a (very small) part of a broader arsenal of scholar-activist praxes.

Stealing social and symbolic capital

Our participants were keenly aware of the relative status accrued from their position within the academy. For some, the prospect of using this status in service to communities of resistance was the main reason behind their entry into the academy. Elroy encapsulated such motivation:

> I remember reading an article by Chuck D in the '80s. He was talking about notions of power, and where power is concentrated. I remember him saying, 'Where are all the black researchers?' Because we know knowledge is power; we know that data is power. And yet, we don't have black researchers doing this work for us. I just thought, 'Fuck, that's what I want to do. Right, Chuck, I'm going to do it.' It was one of those moments, just as a kid growing up, 18–19, thinking, 'That's what I'm about.'

Central in Elroy's reflections is his desire to increase the power of Black communities. In his framing, the university is positioned as a site of power and it was, therefore, the prospect of harnessing this power that motivated Elroy to become an academic. He is motivated to engage in acts of reparative theft, as he seeks to repurpose the university's power – perhaps read here as social and symbolic capital – to the benefit of

Black communities. In this sense, as well as the more tangible material resources outlined in the previous section, Elroy's account nods to wider notions of resource. We want to think here, then, about how anti-racist scholar-activists can utilise the symbolic and social capital of the university, through forms of reparative theft, in service to anti-racism.

One of the most common ways that participants felt that they were able to support wider struggles was through the use of their status and, specifically, their symbolic capital.[51] This is evident in the following account from Dez. Having asserted in the previous chapter that academics often lack the specific skills that movements need, here he claims that what he does offer relates to status and symbolic capital:

> it's the fact that I bring a title and an institutional affiliation which valorises the work, just because of that. I'm not afraid of it, I don't care ... use that, I don't mind. I don't mind that at all.

Dez recognises that there is capital embodied within academic titles and associated with institutional affiliations. Notwithstanding the dangers of situating the academy as *the* site of knowledge production and of reproducing hierarchies of knowledge, the symbolic capital of academics can strengthen movements and campaigns.[52] As Dez puts it, it 'valorises the work'. He is therefore happy for movements to 'use' his capital. A similar point was conveyed by Elroy:

> To be a doctor affords you a privilege and perspective which opens those doors ... It's exploiting or working in the margins of, I would say, the privilege that is afforded from being in a university.

As discussed in the last section, we are reminded here of the relative privilege afforded to academics and the responsibility that comes with it.[53] For Elroy, who echoes both the language and sentiment of anti-colonial thinkers within the Black Radical tradition,[54] this privilege can be exploited in the interests of communities of resistance. To facilitate this exploitation, one must work in the margins or be 'in but not of' the university.[55] In this sense, although he is referring to the privileges that derive from symbolic and social capital, Elroy's framing is similar to those who discussed more material resources above.

Elroy elaborated on the notion of exploitation. He explained: 'that sense of being in service almost means sometimes opening yourself up to be exploited, for want of a better term, and that exploitation is important'. The idea of exploitation is a valuable one here. It is present in Elroy's accounts, is an underlying theme in Dez's, and can be seen too, both implicitly and explicitly, in other accounts across this and the previous chapter. Our participants often work with, and write about, communities that are subject to the exploitations that manifest as a result of the matrix of domination.[56] In siding with communities of resistance, and resisting those forms of structural exploitation, scholar-activists can engage in subversive work. By looking to exploit the university (an institution that is usually exploit*ing* rather than exploit*ed*), the counter-hegemony of scholar-activism becomes all the more apparent. In this respect, anti-racist scholar-activists can serve as *conduits* for reparative theft, in that they can enable communities of resistance to move from a position in which they are the subjects of exploitation to one in which they are effectuators of 'exploitation' – the latter position being one that, as we established earlier in this chapter, is morally and ethically justifiable.

This idea of exploitation also came up in our interview with Alison (white, mid-career), in which she spoke about her work with a local community campaign:

> I think they see the university and the university connection as a resource, like as a legitimating resource … I had a text from [someone] this morning saying 'Oh, I've got an opportunity to go on the radio to discuss [my] case and … will you come with me? You can do your university bit' … there's all sorts of stuff there. [There is being] an individual, on an interpersonal level, supporting that person through that experience, but there's also something about my being there, my relationship to the university can

legitimate things that she's saying … I think there's quite a bit of that. Good, let's use [it] … Because that's power, isn't it? That relationship to power can maybe be positively exploited.

Alison reiterates the earlier point that a 'university connection' constitutes a form of symbolic capital and that this capital can be harnessed for anti-racist movements. This argument was made time and time again by participants. Whilst many were reflexive and critical about the processes that construct the university as a legitimating institution, there was nevertheless a degree of pragmatism that led Alison and others to explore how the university's power could be 'positively exploited' or, put another way, 'stolen' in service to communities of resistance. In offering this example, however, Alison also points to how her role within the community group is about more than the symbolic capital she brings. As we discussed in the last chapter, it is also about the interpersonal: the 'being there'[57] and the 'bearing witness'.[58] It is about the work that is often unseen and uncelebrated. It can be about 'trying to feed into a conversation or be supportive or respond to the emails of people, direct people to lawyers' (Barry), or something as simple as 'getting on the phone' (Elroy). Engaging in this feminist-inflected relational work of giving and caring sees us countering the neoliberal, masculinist, extractive, white politics of the university and it, again, involves us stealing back time.

Thus far, the accounts in this section have largely focused on how anti-racist scholar-activists can harness their social capital to support wider movements. Alex (mixed-race, mid-career) continues in this vein:

There are people who I really respect, who are activist-scholars, who successfully are in both worlds, and part of what they do, I think, is to amplify the insights and voices of activists, groups or individuals within activist circles, who otherwise wouldn't be heard beyond their immediate political circle.

For Alex, key to being a scholar-activist (or activist-scholar in her terms) is a commitment to raising the collective voices of, or individual voices within, communities of resistance. This should be contextualised against a backdrop in which universities often operate as gatekeepers in terms of whose voices are elevated. Alex's use of 'amplify' is significant and instructive here, and it is this point that we want to linger on. To *amplify* is to raise the volume in order to allow a message to be heard. Importantly, amplification leaves that original message intact. In this sense, to amplify is characteristically distinct from the *speaking for* communities that so often characterises academic practice. Unlike amplification, the act of speaking *for* risks distorting and silencing rather than elevating. As the American philosopher and activist Cornel West explains, 'the vocation of the intellectual is to let suffering speak, let victims be visible, and let social misery be put on the agenda of those in power'.[59] It is not to speak *for* that suffering. The praxis of amplifying therefore requires a degree of reflexivity. Firstly, it is necessary to recognise one's own social capital and relative power. Secondly, one needs to harness that power in service to communities of resistance. And thirdly, and vitally, in doing so, one must guard against the reinscribing of unequal power dynamics. Underpinned by the orientation and sense of accountability we discussed in the previous chapter, reflexivity becomes most important in navigating the inherent tension between step two and step three: to utilise power, whilst resisting the perpetuation of unequal power relations. We want to turn now to consider this apparent tension a bit further.

For our participants, it seems that the aforementioned tension was largely understood and reconciled in terms of a need to be strategic when working in service to communities of resistance. This was articulated clearly by Abiola, an African man and long-standing activist in the final stages of his PhD:

> As a scholar-activist, I'm not about performance. Not unless I'm doing performance stuff. That's not my game. It's to communicate the idea in the most effective way possible. The most practical way possible. And that means that if I have to talk in a certain register – if I had to wear a suit

and tie … You've never seen me in a suit and tie. But if I *had* to wear a suit and tie, then that's what I'd do as an activist, I'd make those compromises, those decisions. But it also works the other way around. If I can be communicating my ideas without that performance, without falling into those tropes, then I'd equally do so. Because it breaks down and chips away at that veneer, these respectability politics that state this is how an academic must sound, must look. This is how an activist behaves.

Here, Abiola discusses the strategic ways in which he draws upon and manipulates his status for the benefit of the communities he works within, as well as wider anti-racist movements. He is concerned with practicality. Therefore, when he draws upon his status, he does so based upon a strategic assessment that the manipulation of such status can be of some benefit. It is in these instances that he will engage in performance: he will 'wear a suit and tie', he will 'talk in a certain register', if that is what it takes to be most effective. Drawing upon the work of Keith, Bhattacharyya notes that:

the role of the scholar is, at best, changeable, ranging from playing the expert to trimming knowledge to fit the demands and attention span of the audience, to speaking in whatever dubious tongue will achieve the desired end … the value added by scholars is the ability to move between different presentations of knowledge with some understanding of which register will yield influence and with whom.[60]

Whilst Abiola and others clearly embody some of this spirit, what is important for Abiola is that he remains cognisant and critical of the processes that make it advantageous for him to engage in impression management and different presentations of knowledge. If he can avoid the superficial performances then he does so because he knows that such performances perpetuate hierarchies of knowledge and harmful stereotypes about who possesses that knowledge. In this sense, anti-racist scholar-activism is dually concerned with utilising symbolic capital for communities of resistance, but also deconstructing knowledge hierarchies.

To pursue the dual concerns of utilising and deconstructing status requires reflexivity. This point was reiterated by Alison, who draws us explicitly to a notion that, aside from a couple of brief mentions, has lay just beneath the surface of this chapter – that is, the notion of *strategic duplicity*:

> I think it's important to, in this space at least, recognise the duplicity, you know, in that space I won't have these [campaign wrist bands] on. I'll have a suit and I'll wear my hair differently. I might even tap into a different accent. There is a level of performativity in those spaces whereby the scholar-activist dynamic to your work is turned down in order that you know, so you're managing yourself in those different spaces, for your message to be received.

Alison's primary concern here is with the message being received. To this end, she, like Abiola, is happy to engage in performance management if the situation demands it. What is important in these accounts is the acknowledgement of the superficiality of these performances. Both Abiola and Alison are critical enough to know that these performances lack substance but reflexive and strategic enough to know that they can bring benefits to the struggles that they are engaged in. We might understand this praxis as duplicity, therefore, since it involves a doubleness of thought, speech, or action. Drawing our minds back to the work of Harney and Moten,[61] to be duplicitous is to engage in deceit and deception, or *subterfuge* in their words, in the interests of communities of resistance. It is therefore always a *strategic* duplicity.

For several participants, this strategic duplicity manifests in a manipulation of the myths of objectivity and rationality that surround academia. Neville (white, mid-career) made this point:

> It's quite useful if you want to get access to elites, if you don't necessarily always wear your politics on your sleeve. So again, kind of assuming the role of the disinterested, impartial observer, can be quite useful if you want

to get access to people and places, where waving a red flag might be a bit more difficult.

Much like other participants, and recalling the tenets we set out in the Introduction, Neville is influenced by traditions that show objectivity and rationality to be a fallacy that protects power and the status quo.[62] Nevertheless, there is recognition that those mythologies can be harnessed in the interests of communities of resistance. In these cases, academics may be able play the role of 'the disinterested impartial observer' in order to give an air of legitimacy to the interests and demands of the groups and communities that they work within. As Alison explained: 'At certain times, you want to look more like the sort of neutral evidence producer, yeah? Rather than the kind of person politically motivated by social change.' Some anti-racist scholar-activists, like Alison, can therefore harness the notions of impartiality that are attached to the academy to the benefit of anti-racist movements. There are two additional points to make here though. Firstly, this praxis of strategic duplicity should perhaps (and often does) sit alongside longer-term work that looks to dismantle the hegemonic privileging of 'objectivity' in research – that is, the very logics that make such duplicity possible. Secondly, it is necessary to acknowledge that not all academics or scholar-activists are able to play the role of the impartial academic. We are thinking here, for instance, of those who have a documented and known histories in social movements, or those who are racialised in ways that see them viewed as always already biased. We return to this theme of racialised experiences of scholar-activism in the next chapter.

Conclusion

In this chapter, we have drawn upon Harney and Moten's work on stealing from the university,[63] and the discourse of reparative justice, in order to introduce the concept of *reparative theft*. Reparative theft invokes a form of theft that – in the context of coloniality, white supremacy, and the matrix of domination – is both morally and ethically justifiable. In fact, for many of our participants, such theft is understood as a duty. This rendering is premised on a recognition of the university as an extractive and exploitative institution that is built on ill-gotten gains. It is through this lens, therefore, that we come to think of this theft as a form of reparation, small-scale and incomplete though it may be. We cling onto the notion of theft in this chapter, however, to acknowledge the subterfuge that scholar-activists must engage in, in order to exploit the contradictions of the university and take its resources for the groups and communities we work within. The idea of theft acts as a reminder of whose side anti-racist scholar-activists are on or, put another way, that we are 'in but not' of the university. Our orientation is in service to communities of resistance, and wider anti-racist movements.

We have shown that the university holds a range of resources that scholar-activists can and do leverage for communities of resistance. As well as directly economic resources, there are also other invaluable resources such as labour, time, and space. In terms of space, we might think of this both as physical space – which can be booked for community events – and as space to think and produce knowledge for social movements. There are also those resources that might be less glamorous but are still significant, for example, access to printing. Albeit very small acts, all of these practices of resource redistribution are acts of reparative theft, with anti-racist scholar-activists – and hopefully academics more widely (particularly given the relative ease of these acts) – serving as a conduit.

We also focused on those forms of resource that are less material, in the immediate sense. Specifically, we situated the social and symbolic capital of the university, which can come to be embodied in university-based academics, as something that can be stolen. Here, we explored how scholar-activists navigate an apparent tension between using this knowledge for communities of resistance and perpetuating harmful hierarchies of knowledge and power. Mediated by accountability and embeddedness (see previous chapter), we argue that reflexivity is key in this regard and to anti-racist scholar-activist praxes more broadly. Ultimately, this chapter has built on Chapter 2's notion of *working in service*, in order to show that *reparative theft* is a key component of anti-racist scholar-activism.

4

Backlash: opposition to anti-racist scholar-activism within the academy

As we have shown in previous chapters, the values and orientations of those engaged in anti-racist scholar-activism are starkly different to – if not fundamentally oppositional to – those of the neoliberal-imperial-institutionally-racist university. After all, scholar-activism involves recognising that 'what is best for your department is not necessarily best for humankind'.[1] The explicitly political, radical scholarship and praxes of anti-racist scholar-activism can situate us in mutually antagonistic relationships with much of the academy. As Harney and Moten contend in their discussion of the subversive intellectual, 'the university needs what she bears but cannot bear what she brings'.[2] This tension results in attempts to curtail, dismiss, ridicule, or silence anti-racist scholar-activist work, casting it as not theoretical or objective enough, and too political and threatening. As scholar-activists clash with their institutions, they are habitually 'pushed to the margins, forced to take risks, situated in politically and emotionally vulnerable positions, [and] rendered illegitimate by the structure'.[3] Those engaged in anti-racist scholar-activism are therefore confronted daily with backlash – and the ubiquitous threat of backlash – from within (as well as outside)[4] of the academy.

   In this chapter, we consider how anti-racist scholar-activism evokes backlash within the academy. We begin by foregrounding theoretical understandings of *backlash*,[5] before we draw upon participants' accounts to explore how anti-racist scholar-activism is devalued by colleagues and managers within both our institutions and our wider academic disciplines. Next, we focus on how backlash is particularly acute for scholar-activists of colour and others who are marginalised by the interlocking systems of oppression that constitute the matrix of domination.[6] Finally, in the context of (the threat of) backlash, we explore a range of mechanisms that our participants employ to navigate life within academia – their strategies of survival.

Theorising backlash

Backlash, Aoki conveys, might be understood as the "'getting back to", "returning back to", or "restoring" [of] a real or imaginary status quo ... before those that prompted one to "lash back" were on the scene'.[7] We might conceive of backlash, therefore, as negative reactions or responses to social change, whether that be actual change or the potential for, or threat of, change. The more counter-hegemonic that change threatens to be, the more backlash we can expect to see. In the context of the university, the real or imaginary status quo to which Aoki refers is one that is underpinned by whiteness.[8] Indeed, Nirmal Puwar urges us to see how, in the context of intersecting structures and systems of power, spaces are constructed and imagined over time: 'social spaces are not blank', she asserts.[9] With this in mind, we can understand the university as an exclusionary space, historically dominated by white men and Eurocentric (and racist) knowledge production.

Increasingly diverse student demographics are, however, threatening to change the landscape of higher education (HE), in the representational sense at least.[10] Karis Campion notes that there was a 60% increase in the number of Black, Asian, and 'minority ethnic' students entering UK HE between 2003 and 2020.[11] Such change can be disruptive and, as Puwar reminds us, disruption 'is not without consequence'.[12] Whilst some of these consequences may manifest in institutional transformation or the illusion of institutional transformation, they also manifest as backlash against change and those seen to be its harbingers. In this sense, backlash offers a lens through which we can think about the particular forms of institutional and interpersonal racisms that people of colour, constructed as *space invaders*,[13] face within universities. Put another way, we can consider how racism manifests as a lashing back against the entry of significant numbers of people of colour into HE.

We can also conceive of backlash in other ways too, particularly as a response to the social gains made by anti-racists, feminists, the LGBTQ+ movement, and other liberation movements in recent decades.[14] In this regard, we might talk not only about backlash against the presence of Black and Brown bodies, but backlash as a response to liberatory ideas and praxes that threaten the status quo. By way of an example, we might think here of the backlash against student decolonise movements, and specifically the *Rhodes Must Fall* campaign at the University of Oxford. Though no doubt shaped and accentuated by the racialisation of the students involved, the backlash primarily manifested as a response to the counter-hegemonic ideas of the students, which made visible the colonial underpinnings of the University of Oxford. Understood in this way, backlash is the desire to obstruct and prevent the forward movement of social progress. Thus, central to our theorisation of backlash in this chapter is what Nayak and Bonnett call *anti-anti-racism*: the backlash that comes in response to anti-racist ideas, scholarship, praxes, and movements.[15]

Writing in the US context, the philosopher George Yancy examines the backlash to his viral *Dear White America* letter published in the New York Times in 2015, in which he implored white Americans to recognise the role that they play 'in a system that continues to value Black lives on the cheap'.[16] Reflecting on the responses he received to his letter, many of which were vitriolic in nature – replete with violent racist language – Yancy lays bare the explicit racism that continues to pervade contemporary Western societies.[17] As with the Rhodes Must Fall campaign, the backlash that Yancy faced was in response to the disruptive arguments he offered. It was, however, no doubt also inflected and exacerbated by his racialisation as a Black man. The point we want to make here, therefore, is that backlash is mediated by one's location within the *matrix of domination*.

Yancy's focus is not only on explicit racism, however. He also draws attention to the systemic nature of, and culture of indifference and inaction that sustains, anti-Black racism. In so doing, he encourages us to think about the less explicit forms that racism takes.[18] This intervention extends the utility of the concept of *anti-anti-racist backlash* in a way that is helpful for our purposes in this chapter – that is, we can employ it not only to help us understand explicitly racist lashing back, but also the more subtle, subterranean, and seemingly non-racial racism that characterises the contemporary epoch, and particularly the contemporary neoliberal-imperial-institutionally-racist university.[19] Conceived in this way, we can understand backlash as serving the simultaneous functions of penalising those that do speak out and deterring those that might.

There is one final way that we want to think about backlash, before we move on to look at participant's accounts – that is, backlash against the praxes of scholar-activism. As we have shown in previous chapters, scholar-activism can signal a break with traditional and hegemonic approaches within academia. It often departs from the established conventions within our academic disciplines. In a range of ways, it constitutes a disruption and it is perhaps unsurprising, therefore, that it evokes backlash. When we look at the experiences of anti-racist scholar-activists, the distinctions we are making here between types of backlash does prove to be somewhat superficial. Indeed, the backlash one faces in reality is often a consequence of a complex combination of one's position within the matrix of domination, one's anti-racism, and one's scholar-activist praxes, and these factors are not easily disentangled. In what follows, we take these various forms of backlash as our concern, whilst holding on to their fundamentally entangled nature.

Devaluing anti-racist scholar-activism

Backlash against anti-racist scholar-activism comes in many guises. An observation common among participants was that their work is devalued by colleagues within their departments and institutions, and within their wider academic disciplines. Malaika, a Black early-career academic who migrated to Britain, for example, noted:

> I think I'm seen sometimes as a troublemaker, sometimes as someone who is doing a subcategory of sociology, not real sociology.

Through the label of 'troublemaker', Malaika conveys a sense that she is seen by others to routinely cause problems and disrupt the status quo (which for her interlocutors is a negative thing). To borrow from Sara Ahmed, unequal power dynamics mean that it is often the person who shines light on racism that comes to be regarded as the problem, rather than racism itself.[20] Although no doubt wrapped up with her being a Black woman in a white-imagined discipline with a history of marginalising Black feminist thought,[21] Malaika being regarded as somebody who does not do 'real sociology' may in part derive from her scholar-activist approach to research. Indeed, many participants suggested that scholar-activists are constructed by others in the academy as less intellectually competent than those engaged in more traditional (often pseudo-objective) forms of theoretical or empirical research. This construction may, however, be felt particularly acutely by those pursuing an anti-racist agenda given that anti-racism is routinely marginalised within disciplines such as sociology, and positioned as a 'subset' – a niche element – of the discipline.[22] It is apparent, therefore, that backlash can be mediated not only by the institution but by an academic discipline that is disciplining of its margins.

Malaika was not the only one who felt that they were viewed by colleagues as a 'troublemaker'. Reflecting on their relationship with colleagues, Aaliyah, another Black woman and early-career academic, noted:

> They're like, quite conservative a lot of them. There's quite a lot of feminist academics actually around me, but I feel they're quite liberal. So, that's why I introduce myself a lot as a troublemaker because I know that's how they see me. I think I'm kind of a bit at peace with taking that role, because also they know that I'm needed … So, they welcome it, but they're also critical of it as well. But I do feel precarious even though I'm on a permanent contract, precarious in being a scholar-activist.

As Aaliyah makes clear, she has reappropriated the troublemaker identity for herself, by taking a label with negative connotations consistently conferred upon her and using it to introduce herself to others. Given the many ills of the neoliberal-imperial-institutionally-racist university (some of which we outlined in the Introduction), why would we not want to cause trouble? As Judith Butler contends, 'perhaps trouble need not carry such a negative valence'.[23] In this sense, we can understand trouble to be what Ahmed calls a feminist political ontology: 'something we can claim *to be*, as feminists, which is to say, something *we do*, without assuming ourselves as behind that deed'.[24] The trouble attributed to the feminist troublemaker is, of course, exacerbated when one's praxes and positionality within the matrix of domination cause trouble too. In Aaliyah and Malaika's cases, their 'troublemaker' status may be a consequence of both their activist approach and the specific anti-racist orientation of that activism, as well as how race and gender are constructed in the academy (and in wider society). Given that 'intersectional experience is greater than the sum of racism and sexism',[25] the effects of the construction of race and gender as 'troublesome' are particularly pronounced for women of colour.

Although Aaliyah recognises the precarity involved in occupying the troublemaker role, she is proud of the disruptive work that she does within the academy and believes that her white feminist colleagues – whilst unwilling to occupy the role themselves, even though their racialisation offers them greater protection – also recognise that someone needs to take up the position of troublemaker. There are some deeply concerning dynamics here that we do not want to gloss over. These dynamics reflect longstanding issues regarding the whiteness of feminist politics,[26] and similar critiques regarding the gendered dynamics of anti-racist movements.[27] Aaliyah's account serves to remind us that it is too often women of colour and/or those with other marginalised positionalities that are laboured with the task of taking up adversarial positions within academia (and elsewhere) and, in so doing, expose themselves to backlash.[28] Those with the privilege and power to better insulate themselves from the negative repercussion of backlash too often stand idly by: an act that is nothing short of 'white complicity'.[29]

Reminiscent of Malaika's sense that her work is not perceived as 'real sociology', Okoye reflected on how her anti-racist scholar-activism is constructed by others in the academy as not intellectual enough. In duCille's terms, not intellectual enough should be read as not 'legible as white or male'.[30] As a Black Muslim early-career academic, Okoye noted:

> It almost delegitimises your space as an academic by saying, because you're doing activist work, that the community aspect of it is where your specialisation lies and not with the academic. They don't see the balance together … you're presented as the expert of your own experience but not an intellectual in that area. So, I research around race and I research around intersectionality, but I'm not approached about my research around race and intersectionality. I'm approached about my *experience* of it … So, it's almost as if there are certain aspects of my identity that are valued by the academy, and that's the physical experience and physical body, but not the actual work and the theory that would actually help change practice.

Black feminist thought has resisted the binary between academic knowledge and lived experience, instead showing how lived experience shapes knowledge and how the standpoint of Black women can enrich scholarship.[31]

Nevertheless, Okoye's account reveals that this (false) separation endures to shape her experiences, as well as those of other Black women in the academy. Her *representation*, as a Black hijabi woman, is valued more by her institution than the contributions she makes to the development of anti-racist theory and praxes. In this regard, anti-anti-racist backlash within the university context may be subtle, but it is, nevertheless, deeply pernicious. In Okoye's case, it involves colleagues within her institution redefining her utility in their own terms – that is to say, her anti-racist scholar-activism has little value to her institution, whilst her bodily presence as a Black Muslim woman has superficial value within a sector seemingly more interested in *appearing* non-racist than *being* anti-racist. Okoye's body might be seen, for example, to enable institutional performances of 'diversity' or act as a buffer against accusations of racism, even though the intellectual contributions generated through her scholar-activist praxis remain both uninvited and unvalued. In this sense, we see the tokenistic elevation of Black and Brown anti-racist scholar-activists, and the simultaneous delegitimising and silencing of their scholarship.

Reflecting on being labelled as 'not intellectual enough', one established Black academic, Dez, highlighted how he confronts this form of backlash – which he suggested is often experienced as 'ridicule' from his colleagues – by engaging more deeply with theory than his traditional academic (non-scholar-activist) counterparts:

> I know my Marx and I've read all his fucking letters. I know my Hegel. I've read the books which other people haven't read. I've read *Logic*. They've just read one or two chapters from *Philosophy of Right*. I've read all these fuckers, and they're very good. It's an education. Now, because of that, it means that some of the people I'm talking about can't quite say that I'm not a proper intellectual.

Dez implies something commonly felt by participants – that is, that they must work harder than their 'traditional' academic colleagues to be viewed as 'proper intellectuals'. An obligation to work twice as hard in order to gain the respect of colleagues was felt particularly strongly by participants who were earlier in their academic careers, on precarious contracts, and/or working at particular (elite) universities (which reproduce traditional approaches to research). As Reynolds, Block and Bradley note, because community-based or activist research is often regarded as less theoretical – and of less 'value' – it can be perilous for academics 'whose continuation in the academy hinges on publishing peer-reviewed, theoretical work'.[32] Backlash against anti-racist scholar-activism, therefore, has real consequences in terms of job security and career progression, and all of this is exacerbated by race (and other stratifiers), a point we develop in the next section.

Another perception common amongst participants was that their work is viewed by colleagues within their departments and wider institutions as biased, lacking the objectivity of 'proper' scholarship. Aaliyah epitomised this viewpoint:

> I think they definitely think that I'm biased towards feminist and Black liberation work. I think they think they're neutral and I'm the one bringing in all of the politics.

The framing of scholar-activism as too political – and its juxtaposition against so-called 'neutral' research – is a key feature of the backlash against anti-racist scholar-activism within the academy. It is predicated on the construction of the university as white space and the normalisation of hegemonic approaches to scholarship, which render anti-racist scholar-activism disruptive and therefore problematic. As Patricia Hill Collins warns, 'calling anything "activist politics" is the kiss of death in academia, because it is often assumed that one cannot be "academic", in other words, appropriately objective, and "activist", which many academics see as synonymous with irrationality'.[33] Yet, the 'objective academic' versus 'irrational activist' binary is one that scholar-activists are fundamentally critical of; although, as we suggested in Chapter 3, it can sometimes be useful to strategically exploit the fallacy of objectivity in order to carve out pockets of possibility for scholar-activism. Generally, as set out in the Introduction, we do not engage in the pretence that research or teaching (see Chapter 5) should be – or can ever be[34] – value-neutral. Rather, anti-racist scholar-activism is intended to agitate for social change both within and outside of the university, whilst upholding high standards of rigour and criticality. This position stands in conflict with the neoliberal academy which, through its instrumentalisation and commodification of knowledge, strips pedagogy and research of moral and political practice.[35] In this context, backlash is not only about devaluing the explicitly political work of anti-racist scholar-activism, it is also about establishing the superiority of 'neutral' traditional (non-scholar-activist) work and maintaining the neoliberal-imperial-institutionally-racist status quo of HE.

Amele – a mid-career academic of Indian heritage – expanded on the false construction of traditional academic work as objective. She argued:

> Everybody is a subject. Everybody has a positionality. You can do your quants and your statistics as much as you like, you know, and try and claim some kind of distance from them as if they're separate, but the way in which you organise that data, the way in which you classify that data, the way in which you manipulate and make sense of that data is all subject to your own views or ideas about the world. There is no distance. This is utter bollocks. So, yes, I think it becomes a way of critiquing intellectuals and academics who are political.

Although many (perhaps most) academics within the social sciences and humanities acknowledge that research cannot be completely value-free, Amele points to how the scientific validity of explicitly political work is still routinely questioned on the grounds that it is not detached enough, that the researcher is too emotionally involved. In this sense, the subjective nature of traditional research is deliberately downplayed and (explicit) subjectivity is instead framed as undesirable: 'a way of critiquing', or lashing back against, 'academics who are political'. Yet, as Hale writes, whilst (the fallacy of) neutrality is privileged within the academy, for scholar-activists 'claims of objectivity are more apt to sound like self-serving manoeuvres to preserve hierarchy and privilege'.[36] Indeed, recognising the urgency of what is at stake, scholar-activism involves the deliberate politicisation of academic work, often, though not always, through the rejection of the myth of objectivity, in the name of social justice.[37]

Reflecting on a presentation that he gave to colleagues within his department, Dillon (British Asian, early-career) highlighted how anti-racist scholar-activism is framed as lacking in nuance. We might understand this, therefore, as another manifestation of backlash:

> I gave it to academics in my department and not a lot of the people are involved in activism and I had one person, a white male scholar, who said that my discussion of the gangs matrix sounded like I was a conspiracy theorist ... Where I've talked about institutional racism in policing or police militarisation, academics have said to me 'well you need to be a bit more nuanced'. Well, I understand nuance and I think it's important, but there's nothing nuanced about the statistics. If you have statistics that are saying in London a Black person's ten, twelve, fifteen times more likely to be stopped by police than a white person ... there's nothing nuanced about those statistics. You can clearly see that the police are a racialised institution.

Here, Dillon draws attention to how some academics, particularly those invested in the maintenance of the status quo, seek to undermine the radical work of anti-racist scholar-activists by questioning the 'nuance' of their analysis as a way of implying that their work is simplistic or 'one-sided'. Once again, scholar-activists who highlight injustice – in this case in relation to widely evidenced institutionally racist policing[38] – are recast as the real problem. Dillon's experience also shows the way in which scholar-activists are not only constructed as fundamentally lacking (in their capacity for nuanced analysis) but also, as a threat. As Flood, Martin, and Dreher contend, scholar-activists 'may be criticised as politically biased, dangerously subversive, or tarnishing the name of their institution'.[39] The framing of Dillon as a 'conspiracy theorist' – which in turn constitutes a denial of racism – might therefore be understood as a particularly explicit form of lashing back: a clear attempt to cast Dillon as something other than a 'real' academic. This delegitimisation of oppositional voices not only threatens to marginalise anti-racist scholar-activists, but also undermines our work and the challenges we raise. In response to this, and as explored in Chapter 3, we might find it useful to engage in *strategic duplicity*, adopting particular performances to achieve our anti-racist aims.

When the reputation of the university and/or its standing with partner organisations is threatened – particularly amongst those with which it wishes to 'do business' – HE institutions may lash back against anti-racist scholar-activists by seeking to silence us. Alison (white, mid-career) has some experience of this:

> We operate within a department whereby at certain times, our research has been actively silenced because the institution is developing relationships with control agencies locally, and then other times the same research is celebrated and awarded an Impact award from the institution because of its contribution to such and such a change and challenging injustices in the community.

Rather than take heed of Alison's work, which highlights how control agencies create and perpetuate inequalities through the criminal justice system, her institution instead chose to strategically silence her work in the interest of developing partnerships with these very same criminal justice agencies. As Alison explains, however, her research has at other times been celebrated by the university for its social impact outside of the academy. Jay (Asian British, mid-career) had a similar experience:

> I remember when I was doing the pro bono stuff, at graduation and on the webpage they'd always shout out about it, saying what a wonderful thing it is. When it came to getting promoted, it was very much that it doesn't count for anything.

As we suggested in Chapter 1, it is clear that the value of anti-racist scholar-activism may be recognised by our institutions if it enables them to (superficially) perform social justice – that is, if it bolsters their public image or falls within, what Jay refers to as, the 'very, very narrow definition' of Impact included in the Research Excellence Framework. Of course, the value that is recognised by our institutions is a much hollowed out version. It is 'value' only in the institution's (metric-driven, capitalistic) terms. Nonetheless, we are reminded here that the university is not a monolith. Instead, it is an assemblage of contradictory forces within which we can operate.[40] Backlash within our institutions or the wider academy may therefore not be constant, but rather repressed at times or superseded by competing logics, to suit the university's agenda.[41]

Scholar-activism within the matrix of domination

In the previous section, we explored backlash as it emerges in response to praxes of scholar-activism and anti-racism, and the mutually reinforcing relationship between the two. In doing so, we began to unpack the notion that anti-racist scholar-activists' experiences of backlash are not undifferentiated. Rather, it was clear in a number of accounts that race and gender (though not exclusively) shape experiences of backlash within the academy. As Sudbury and Okazawa-Rey explain, 'the distribution of the costs of doing this work [are] differentiated by race, gender, sexual orientation, gender identity, and national origin'.[42] In this section, therefore, we consider more directly how experiences of anti-racist scholar-activism, including the backlash against it, are shaped by the location of scholar-activists within the matrix of domination.

The following account from Thomas (Black, early-career) is a useful place to start for thinking about how race structures experiences:

> I guess also when you're Black, you've got to do that intellectual work to prove that you are as intellectually competent as your white peers, and if

you're not doing that intellectual work, if you're not seen to be doing that intellectual work, it will reaffirm the existing assumptions that Black people are less intellectually competent than their white colleagues. So yes, I guess you have a double obligation as a Black activist-scholar.

Here, Thomas reinforces a point made earlier in this chapter by Dez, that scholar-activists – or activist-scholars in Thomas' terms – are viewed to be lacking in intellectual competence. As he also explains, however, the competencies of *Black* scholar-activists are particularly subject to questioning. It is Black academics (and other academics of colour) who are forced to 'prove that [they] are as intellectually competent' as their white counterparts. It is not enough for Black scholar-activists to be doing intellectual work – they must be '*seen* to be doing the intellectual work'. Put another way, whilst white academics might always already be assumed to be 'intellectual', the racism underpinning academia means that Black academics have to prove their intellectuality because, in Puwar's terms, *space invaders* 'don't have an undisputed right to occupy this space'.[43] In this sense, constructed as bodies out of place within the academy, Black academics are subject to hyper-surveillance,[44] all of which is exacerbated when those Black academics are also scholar-activists.

Similar to how Thomas talks of a 'double obligation', Zami – an established academic of colour – reflected on how the challenges of practising scholar-activism within the academy are compounded by intersecting structures of power:

If you're trying to do that (scholar-activism) anyway, that's one hurdle, but then slap on your colour and gender and your sexuality and everything else, it just, it'll make the hurdles higher. Yeah. But I mean on the other hand you learn to be, well, we have to be don't we, very rigorous in what we do? And learn to be articulate.

The influence of Black feminist theory on Zami's praxis is evident. She is all too aware of how systems of oppression intersect, reminding us that racism, sexism, and heteronormativity (amongst other structures of domination) make the work of some scholar-activists more difficult – the 'hurdles higher' as she puts it – whilst imbuing others with power and privilege. Yet as Zami continues, she also refers to the *resistance* that is so central to Black feminist praxis.[45] Cognisant of the double standards to which she will be held, Zami, like many of our participants, has developed strategies to overcome the 'hurdles' she encounters within the academy. She has learned to be 'very rigorous' and 'articulate'. In this regard, and notwithstanding the problematics herein, Zami recognises that within the academy, as well as outside of it, respect is more readily conferred upon those that adopt the 'legitimate' language and those who are seen as the legitimate speaker. Later in this chapter, we return to consider the strategies that anti-racist scholar-activists employ to navigate life in institutions that are, in many respects, hostile towards them.

Like Zami, Galiev reflected on the racism he has faced as a person of colour within the academy:

> there were definitely impediments that I faced as a person of colour in my previous institution where I think I was seen as radical, not in the Angela Davis sense of grabbing at the root, but more as someone who was ideological, fanatic.

Galiev suggests that his interpellation through processes of racialisation as 'ideological' and 'fanatic' means that his work is not seen by colleagues as radical in the way he intends it, but rather is reframed through racist stereotype. We heard from participants that, all too often, their anti-racist scholar-activism was perceived as too excessive: too political, too radical, too 'ideological'. It reminds us of Quaye, Shaw and Hill's reflections about their own scholar-activism: how the Black – or 'non-white' – body, already hyper-visible within the white space of the university, is made all the 'more visible, threatening and dangerous' when it engages in activism.[46]

The imagined threat posed by minoritised bodies was also highlighted by three of our Muslim women participants, all of whom were early-career academics. Ereene believed that she was the 'wrong kind of Muslim. Too vocal and too passionate about activism and too passionate about social justice, racism, and Islamophobia. Too outspoken.'[47] Jasmin, on the other hand, felt that she was perceived by her colleagues as less threatening than other Muslim academics (which is not to say that she was perceived as entirely non-threatening): 'I don't wear a headscarf. I'm not like an overtly looking Muslim woman … I guess I kind of hit that diversity quota without being *too* Muslim.' Both speak to the way in which more visible forms of Muslim-ness are rendered unwelcome in the academy and are thus subject to the threat of backlash. This point was made explicitly by Khadija: 'It's obviously worse when you're a visible Muslim.' All three accounts speak to the limitations of the university 'diversity' agenda. Diversity might create, what Sara Ahmed calls, a 'happy impression', enabling the university to create the illusion that it is 'welcoming to those that appear different by drawing upon those that appear different'.[48] But the lived experience of being a symbol of diversity is starkly different to the illusion, particularly for Muslims who are subject to surveillance under the UK government's counter-terrorism duty, Prevent.[49] For Ereene, being 'too passionate' and 'too outspoken' means that whilst she serves a purpose to the university as a symbol of diversity, she is not considered to be doing diversity in the 'right' way.

Albeit cognisant of her racialised privilege as a white academic, Rosa reflected on the challenges she has faced within her institution as an academic who has migrated to the UK:

> I had encountered some obstacles, as compared to other British, white, relatively privileged, if radical, academics in my career. I haven't been helped when I applied for my promotion by some people; only by some others. Until the very end there was a moment when I was about to give up, but then because I'm a fighter I continued. I think I always tend to look more on my privilege than my disadvantage.

For Rosa, her non-British status presents 'obstacles' that other colleagues – even radical ones – have not been forced to encounter. Indeed, there is little doubt that xenophobia within UK HE compounds the challenges that scholar-activists face in obtaining promotion.[50] Despite comprising 20% of all UK university staff,[51] international academics are also excluded from applying for some academic jobs and routinely experience challenges in obtaining work visas, hyper-surveillance under Prevent and/or the hostile environment agenda, and the threat of deportation.[52] Rosa's reflections about leaving academia were common amongst our participants and are reflective of how hostile the academy can be towards anti-racist scholar-activists, especially those who are marginalised within the matrix of domination. But, like Zami earlier, Rosa speaks of resistance, of being 'a fighter'. What she also points to here is the importance of recognising that privilege and disadvantage can co-exist.

Others spoke about how privilege can be used strategically to enact change within the academy. Aaliyah, for example, noted that one of her supportive colleagues – a white woman – is sometimes better placed to do the 'radical work' than her, a Black woman:

> Also, it's easier for a white man or a white woman to say a lot of these things. One of my colleagues who I'm really close to, she does pretty radical work. I feel like she can carry some of the more difficult things for me. So, she's the one who keeps pushing and I'm the one who pushes too – but also, I'm walking a line. I also have to be really nice to people. I have to ingratiate myself.

As Aaliyah intimates, 'radical work' is often made more palatable when it is undertaken by white academics and, as a result, is subject to less backlash. Their whiteness (partially) privileges them from the accusations explored earlier in this chapter of being too invested, not objective enough, or lacking nuance, as well as from accusations of having the proverbial 'chip' on their shoulder.[53] In a context where academics of colour are often made to feel like outsiders in the academy, Aaliyah indicates that, owing to her positionality, she feels obliged to ingratiate herself. She is all too aware that she is subjected to a level of surveillance that her white colleagues are not. The very fact that Aaliyah names just one colleague who carries 'some of the more difficult things' for her, however, suggests that such colleagues – those prepared to use their whiteness to support colleagues of colour and as an act of resistance – are few and far between. It seems (racialised) privilege is still too rarely used in pursuit of an anti-racist agenda both within and outside of the academy; rather, it manifests most often to stifle an anti-racist agenda – that is, to bolster anti-anti-racist backlash.

Haytham – a Pakistani PhD researcher and long-standing activist – also reflected on the role of white people in anti-racist resistance, though he was critical of the strategic deployment of white people to 'front' anti-racist work:

> I mean how many times have we seen [with] Black scholarship the need for white liberals to front the work that we know that Black scholars have been doing for a very, very, very long time, right? And how unfortunately sometimes our own communities are complicit in putting those voices forward because, for some reason, there is a sense that it will have more credibility if that happens.

Here, Haytham recognises that whiteness is perceived by some to add 'credibility' to anti-racist arguments. Whilst clearly conscious of the structural conditions that encourage a perception among communities of colour that 'white liberals' should 'front the work', he is nonetheless disappointed that this practice continues. We see that disappointment clearly in his use of the term 'complicit', which implies that the practice of encouraging white people to front Black scholarship feeds into the maintenance of white supremacy. Thus, the strategic deployment of white voices may be considered useful in the short-term – because the authority and legitimacy that is routinely conferred upon whiteness adds 'credibility' – but for Haytham, the anti-racist project is hindered in the longer term. Centring white voices reproduces the power and legitimacy of whiteness, further silencing and delegitimising the voices of people of colour in the process. Of course, there is a tangible difference – albeit, a very fine line – between what Aaliyah and Haytham are talking about. Aaliyah appreciates the help of her white colleague to push for change within the academy, while Haytham is talking about white colleagues *fronting* Black scholarship. His use of the term 'fronting' perhaps implies that he is referring to white colleagues who take credit for Black scholarship, rather than those that use their privilege to support colleagues and communities of colour.

Surviving backlash in academia: building networks and playing the system

As the previous sections have shown, the backlash against anti-racist scholar-activism comes in many guises and is particularly acute for those who are confronted by racism, sexism, and other structures of domination in the academy. Participants have, however, developed a range of strategies of resistance, and in this next section we explore just some of the tools that anti-racist scholar-activists employ to survive backlash within academia. Central to these reflections is the cultivation of networks of support. For many, including Zami, these networks exist outside of the academy:

> I've always had a network outside the university, always. And I always will … so, I'll always be part of about four other organisations very actively which take as much time as being inside the university. And I know there are times I feel I have been able to walk in those other spaces where everyone will say hello and I feel a belonging, where I might not feel a belonging in the place that pays my mortgage.

Zami juxtaposes the sense of belonging she feels within her activist networks outside of the university, against the lack of belonging she feels within the university setting. This is characterised by her framing of the university as 'the place that pays my mortgage', which implies emotional distance and suggests that a motivation for working in the university might simply be the need to earn a wage – that is, to survive under capitalism (we discuss this further in Chapter 6). It comes as little surprise that some participants felt a lack of belonging within their workplaces, given that their values are not only different to, but in many respects antithetical to, the dominant values of the neoliberal-imperial-institutionally-racist academy. This unbelonging is demonstrated and exacerbated by routine experiences of backlash and by the racism that permeates HE. In this context, it is also not surprising that strong networks of support are built via our activism and that strong emotional connections develop via our shared experiences of anti-racist struggle.

In addition to the networks we build outside of the university (which we discussed more fully in Chapter 2), there is also the development of supportive networks within our institutions. These networks allow us to develop organic pockets of belonging, perhaps in what Harney and Moten refer to as the Undercommons.[54] Alison, for example, spoke about the importance of being part of an institutional research collective that is committed to an anti-racist agenda:

> I'm not in a common position. I work in partnership with two colleagues that I implicitly trust and I can have these conversations and work through some of this stuff with, and as a collective we are quite powerful within our department and institution, and that enables something that I don't think I could have on my own.

For Alison, the research collective that she is a part of not only provides her with a reciprocal support network of colleagues that she 'implicitly trusts', but also enables her to wield more influence within her department, institution, and the wider academy than would be possible as an individual. In this sense, the power cultivated through collectives of scholar-activists both *protects* us against backlash within the academy and enables scholar-activists to *exert* our own influence. Thus, collectives can facilitate scholar-activists to exploit the pockets of possibility within the university for our own ends – that is, in service to anti-racism. As explored in Chapter 3, by engaging in reparative theft, scholar-activists can, for example, redirect the resources of the university to the communities that they work within. Although this practice may be a challenge for individual scholar-activists, particularly those new to or unfamiliar with university systems and processes, it may be easier for a collective to strategise together,[55] and teach one another new and better ways to engage in reparative theft.

As Alison acknowledges, opportunities to work in research collectives within our institutions with colleagues that we trust are not all that common. Yet, as Barry (an early-career academic of colour) notes, it is possible to develop relationships with scholar-activists *across* institutions:

> So, I think that it is kind of on us to create that community of people across unis who are doing critical work and see what can come of that. Maybe that's writing books together or making sure you're being mates and helping each other out and stuff because I don't think it's possible for all of us to get jobs where we do radical work.

Whilst those engaged in scholar-activism may draw much of their nourishment from the activist communities that they belong to beyond the academy, we should not underestimate the importance of protection and support from colleagues also employed by a university. These cross-university networks of support can help to sustain us as anti-racist scholar-activists. They can, as Aaliyah elucidates, redress the 'toll on your body and your mind and your spirit … that's why the networks that we develop are really important'.

Of course, our institutions and the wider academy may not welcome these networks. Lip service is often paid by universities to the importance of cross-university collaboration, but institutions rarely free up our time or bestow us with the resources to actively support network building. This experience is not unique to anti-racist scholar-activists, but may be felt more acutely by us. After all, it is oppositional to the interests of much of the academy – which, as we have shown in this chapter, is committed to an anti-anti-racist backlash – to support a highly coordinated anti-racist resistance. As such, this reinforces Frances Fox Piven's observations that:

We should work to fashion the environment that will nourish our activist commitments. At first glance that injunction may sound illogical, or at least impractical. After all, our environment, in this case our colleagues and reference groups, the scholarly associations and journals they sustain, are outside of us. But we also to varying degrees choose our colleagues and reference groups, and select our associations and journals. There is a lot to be said for thinking carefully about where we place ourselves in a complex and variegated academic world … If nothing else, we can cultivate the scholar comrades who share our activist commitments and can come to our defense if the occasion arises.[56]

Creating anti-racist scholar-activist networks and wider coalitions built upon solidarity should, therefore, form part of our praxis, particularly as we strive to insulate ourselves from institutional backlash.

In a similar way to Barry, Oliver (Black, established academic) also spoke of the importance of helping other anti-racist scholar-activists succeed within the academy, in a context where they may otherwise be marginalised:

I've been very conscious in being the mentor for my colleagues, to share the knowledge that I have, to make sure that we all progress up the ladder because what I don't want is for me to reach becoming professor and I'm the only one. I'm marginalised. I've only got one voice. My position is precarious. Why do I want to do that? I'm already in that position, so why do I want to do it when the stakes are that bit higher?

Whilst early-career scholar-activists are particularly precarious within the academy, Oliver reminds us that precarity does not disappear entirely for all academics as they climb the academic hierarchy. Indeed, although there is an underrepresentation of staff of colour within HE generally, this underrepresentation becomes even more pronounced at the level of the professoriate.[57] In a 2016 report on the experiences of Black and 'ethnic minority' staff in further and higher education in the UK, the University and College Union found that 90% of survey respondents faced barriers to promotion.[58] Thus, for Oliver, supporting staff of colour and/or anti-racist scholar-activist colleagues is essential in order to ensure simultaneous progression within our respective institutions, so that there is a groundswell of anti-racist scholar-activists (particularly, of colour) occupying positions of power and influence in years to come.

Although we were conscious of the time burden we placed on participants in this research project, many remarked on the importance of the nurturing that comes from conversations with other anti-racist scholar-activists. Zami, for example, said:

> These kinds of discussions are absolutely crucial because for those who do feel isolated or for those who don't feel that there is a place ... there's always a strength in numbers, isn't there? So, the more that are speaking, the louder the voice, isn't it? You're a big rock in the ocean rather than little droplets in an ocean, and that's important. Absolutely important.

In some ways then, and not to overstate this point, there is a silver lining that arises from experiencing the emotional toll of backlash within the academy: our shared experiences and a shared threat can foster collectivism and solidarity. From these positions of collectivism, we are more effective in pushing back against the neoliberal-imperial-institutionally-racist university, and we wield more power as we move from marginal to more central positions within the academy. In this way, as bell hooks urges, we can think about how to use conflict constructively 'as a guide directing and shaping the parameters of our political solidarity'.[59] Whilst some of us might be isolated in our respective institutions, contributing to conversations around anti-racist scholar-activism can empower us, amplify our voices, and create collective social change within and outside of the academy.

Another key mechanism that anti-racist scholar activists may employ for surviving in academia is to *play* the system. Oliver, for example, fundamentally disagrees with the neoliberal values of the academy, but he recognises the importance of understanding how 'the business' works in order to be able to navigate it as an anti-racist scholar-activist:

Learn your business. Higher education is a business and I say to my students, particularly my postgrads but I think it's applicable to early-career too, you need to know the system you're working in, inside out. If you don't, they'll tell you all sorts of things and you'll never get anywhere … that knowledge of the academy will help you navigate the obstacles because there will be people who will deliberately withhold information at best or give you misinformation at worst, just to hold you back.

The impacts of the neoliberal, hyper-competitive environment of HE to which Oliver refers, and of which we noted in the Introduction, are of course not felt exclusively by scholar-activists. Academics routinely speak of the 'dog eat dog' nature of their workplaces. But this environment can be particularly hostile for anti-racist scholar-activists, who already experience backlash because of their praxes, the subject matter of their work, and as a result of – or exacerbated by – their location within the matrix of domination. It is in this context that Oliver reflects on how we must protect ourselves against colleagues who may 'withhold information' or offer us 'misinformation'.

Reflecting on the key things that protect him within his institution, Elroy (Black, established academic) spoke about how he plays the system:

I know what I have to do as a minimum here to keep folks off my back, and we know about that. For me, it's writing. Now, I don't mind writing, so if I'm four papers for the REF and I'm engaged in ABCD, and I can get £10k off [a funder] to do the work into [anti-racist topic], how are you giving me fucking heat? You can't give me heat, can you?

Elroy's experience of working in HE for some time has enabled him to understand the priorities of the university. Whilst his own priorities are not the same as those of his institution, he is willing and able to 'tick the necessary boxes' – research output metrics, external funding, positive teaching evaluations – if it means that he is left alone to engage in anti-racist activism. Although many of us are pushing for change within our institutions to fundamentally reshape HE, the reality of our employment – and particularly those of us on precarious contacts – is that we are compelled to engage with the demands of the university, at least to some extent. With this in mind, we might exert our own backlash against our institutions in a range of ways, including by *struggling where we are* (see Chapter 5) or by building radical alternatives outside of the university, but we might also be strategic about what we push back against. Of course, there is an inherent danger to us complying with the governance structures and research frameworks of HE in that we risk giving legitimacy to those harmful processes. We risk becoming complicit, an idea we return to in Chapter 6.

Claudia (white, mid-career) shared a similar sentiment to Elroy in relation to strategic compliance:

> I would say my approach in academia is that I do completely play the game. So, I will get all my REF publications done, and I will publish in the most recognised journals, and I do that partly because actually I think that partly frees you up to do the other stuff. I know people who don't do that and then they don't actually have time to do a lot of other activism because they are chasing jobs or trying to get the next thing out. So, they've got like 20 publications, but they're not really recognised, and so they're still on that treadmill. Whereas, in a way, I feel if you can play the game within its limits then you've got over the bar and then you can do other stuff.

For Claudia, there is some sense in complying – albeit, in a critical fashion – with things like REF publication quotas (we could also think here of related pressures elsewhere: the tenure system in the United States, for example). Indeed, scholar-activists that achieve REF quotas may gain relative job security and financial stability, which may in turn enable them to engage in the anti-racist activism that matters to them. As Pulido puts it, a publication record can act as a 'shield of sorts', at least to a certain extent.[60] There is, however, an extremely difficult tension at play here in that our compliance reproduces the 'legitimacy' of metrics such as the REF, meaning that those who do not produce 'REF-able' publications or whose publications are undervalued within the structures of REF are potentially left with less job security. With this in mind, it is important that any compliance we give is not absolute – it is not an enthusiastic compliance, but rather a reluctant, cautious, and sceptical one. It is compliance to the extent that we keep the wolf from our door. It is the kind of critical compliance that we might engage in whilst simultaneously finding other ways to agitate against such metrics. These tensions point to the messy realities of anti-racist scholar-activism, and to the need for constant critical reflexivity around the gains and concessions of our actions.

Several of our participants also spoke about the importance of language in relation to playing the system, and here we return once again to Zami, who explained: 'You learn to be strategic. You learn how to package stuff. You learn how to mix the language of emancipation with bureaucratic language.' Framing the activist work we want to do through institutional language can offer some insulation against backlash, and help us to survive in the neoliberal-imperial-institutionally-racist university and under capitalism more broadly. Dez also reflected on his strategic use of language:

> In a lot of work on all the race equality stuff in the university, and I would tell people, and I did, I'd say, 'Man, I'm not talking about justice. I'm not doing the justice language. I'm dealing in institutional language. I'm talking about does diversity produce more rigorous knowledge, does it expand our knowledge base? Does diversity enable students to attain higher and not drop out, et cetera, et cetera?' I'm not going to confuse that arena with a justice thing. As soon as you start 'Ah, but it's justice for this, justice for that', it doesn't work in those settings because those settings aren't designed for that … I think part of it is, as well, is that we necessarily span and work in different environments. We're not the only ones who do that. There are other activists who do that in different capacities, but nonetheless, if we want to call ourselves activist scholars, we necessarily span different fora. It's our responsibility to understand what it is that we need to be doing in different fora.

Thus, whilst there is much scepticism amongst anti-racist scholars about the university equality and diversity agenda – not least because of its superficiality – Dez purports that one can strategically utilise the language of diversity to achieve one's own ends. The radical nature of Dez's work does not change; rather it is packaged in a way that is palatable or audible to the university: this is another example of strategic duplicity (also see Chapter 3). In this sense, we can avoid some of the backlash we might otherwise experience. Perhaps then, an ability to adapt to different environments should be a key skill of anti-racist scholar-activists. This might require us to adopt a different lexicon inside our institutions to that which we adopt outside; and, once again, we must remain reflexive about the costs of valorising the hollow language of diversity.

Conclusion

In this chapter, we have drawn upon a conceptualisation of backlash to explore the opposition that anti-racist scholar-activists face from colleagues and managers within our institutions, our academic disciplines, and the wider academy. Although we recognise that backlash is not confined to the academy – and often occurs, for example, through social and mainstream media – this chapter has focused on the academy specifically because of how central universities are in the daily lives of (university-based) scholar-activists. Although we have focused in part on experiences of *anti-anti-racist backlash*, we have argued that anti-racist scholar-activists experience backlash in a range of guises – not only because anti-racism can be considered subversive, but also because its subversion is enhanced by our activist orientations. We are, therefore, often positioned within our departments and broader institutions as simultaneously lacking (not theoretical enough, not objective enough, not intellectually competent, not nuanced) and excessive (too troublesome, too conspiratorial, too political, too threatening).

What is also clear is that those with marginalised positionalities experience intensified forms of backlash: backlash against their anti-racism, activist orientations, and as a result of their location within the matrix of domination. This attests to the heterogeneous nature of anti-racist scholar-activist experiences. We have also shown that scholar-activists do not passively accept the backlash exerted against them. Instead, they push back against it, developing strategies to mitigate, navigate, and overcome it, including by developing networks of support and by playing the university at its own games. In this regard, we exert our own backlash against the neoliberal-imperial-institutionally-racist university, using our collective power to enact positive social change within, as well as beyond, our institutions. With this in mind, we consider the university as a site of struggle in the next chapter.

5

Struggle where you are: resistance within and against the university

In the previous chapter, we considered how the neoliberal-imperial-institutionally-racist university constrains and lashes back against those engaged in anti-racist scholar-activism. Exploring how anti-racist scholar-activists find ways to survive and navigate the abrasive terrain of higher education (HE), we also insisted that the university is not a monolith but rather an assemblage of contradictory and competing forces which give rise to pockets of possibility that we might exploit.[1] Whether it be the British University and College Union (UCU) strikes,[2] student rent strikes, Rhodes Must Fall,[3] or Why is My Curriculum White?,[4] a litany of campus-based campaigns have shown that the university can be a site of resistance. Alongside these more high-profile examples are less visible forms of resistance that manifest through counter-hegemonic approaches to teaching and curricula development, speaking up in meetings, and challenging harmful institutional decisions. In this regard, we take seriously Stuart Hall's advice to *struggle where you are*[5] and suggest it can be an important guiding principle for the praxes of anti-racist scholar-activism.

In the first section of this chapter, we explicate the instruction to 'struggle where you are'. Thereafter, the chapter is split into two overarching sections. The first focuses on *the classroom and critical pedagogy*. We discuss resistance to the myths of objectivity and neutrality in relation to pedagogy;

the cultivation of critical thought; the potential for social transformation via, what we call, a *classroom-to-activism pipeline*; and the transformation of the classroom. The second section looks *beyond the classroom* to focus on wider acts of resistance in the university. Here, we focus on speaking up and pushing back in university meetings, and on labour union activism. In each section, we consider how those committed to anti-racist scholar-activism engage with the impetus behind struggle where you are, and the tensions it engenders.

Struggle where you are

We draw the idea of 'struggle where you are' primarily from the late public intellectual and cultural theorist Stuart Hall, who offered this brief comment as advice to a Black community group grappling with considerations of how best to engage in anti-racism.[6] A similar sentiment was expressed by the anti-colonial thinker and activist Walter Rodney, who argued that 'the first level of struggle for the intellectual is in his [sic] own sphere of operation'. He continued:

> The 'guerrilla intellectual' is one who is participating in this whole struggle for transformation within his [sic] own orbit. His or her [sic] task is to operate within the aegis of the institution and the structure and to take from it and transform it over time.[7]

Directing us to think about the foundations of the praxes of anti-racist scholar-activism, we argue that these teachings offer an important intervention in at least four interrelated ways. Firstly, the instruction to struggle where you are reflects a degree of pragmatism with regard to what is achievable. As Hall explained, 'you can't do everything, you fight the battles that you can fight'.[8] This is about how we, as individuals, can feed into a struggle that is necessarily vast and complex, against a system of racism that is vaster and more complex still. For those involved in activist movements, such wisdom will seem familiar. It is a necessary (though perhaps difficult) realisation in every activist's journey that one cannot do it all. This is important for managing expectations, for avoiding 'burnout', and for remembering that, as Angela Y. Davis reminds us in her book of the same title, 'freedom is a constant struggle'.[9]

Secondly, but relatedly, we also read struggle where you are to point to a movement that is bigger than the individual. The implication being that if we each struggle where we are, others will struggle where they are too and a collective struggle will grow. In Mouffe's terms, we can work towards a 'construction of the people' – a strong resistance movement to redress diverse forms of domination.[10] Under the hegemony of neoliberal capitalism, Davis warns, 'it has become especially important to identify the dangers of individualism', particularly within 'progressive struggles'.[11] To this end, she pronounces that 'it is essential to resist the depiction of history as the work of heroic individuals in order for people today to recognize their potential agency as a part of an ever-expanding community of struggle'.[12] In this community of struggle, university-based academics are just one group of actors amongst many others. This point is particularly apt given the concerns raised in earlier chapters around the dangers of academics being elevated or privileged within activist movements, and around the construction of the university as the site of 'legitimate' knowledge production.[13]

Thirdly, and despite the second point, we also understand struggle where you are to have a particular inflection for those of us working in powerful institutions, like the university. In previous chapters, we discussed the insistence of Cabral, Fanon, and others that petit bourgeois intellectuals have a particular role to play in betraying their class interests, or using their affiliation with power, in service to communities of resistance.[14] Through this lens, struggle where you are is an instruction with particular pertinence to those of us working in HE – one that, recalling our discussion in Chapter 3, implores us to repurpose the powerful machinery of the university to fuel the motors of resistance.

Fourthly, calls to struggle where you are also demand a degree of introspection, a notion of particular significance given our focus on *university-based* anti-racist scholar-activism. The hegemonic delusions that construct academia as a liberal space, detached from the racism and inequalities that characterise society,[15] mean that such introspection is generally as lacking as it is urgent. As Sara Ahmed shows us, 'the self-perception of being good blocks the recognition of racism'.[16] Thus for many academics, it is unthinkable that they, and the university more broadly, could be wrapped up in processes that maintain and perpetuate racism, and this is particularly so given that 'the face of racism' is often narrowly conceived as 'that of the moral degenerate, the hateful bigot'.[17] To struggle where you are in academia, therefore, is to break with the hegemony that sees the university as beyond reproach. As we began to argue in the book's Introduction, it involves recognising HE to be a site of historic and contemporary colonial injustice.[18] Nodding back to Chapter 3 on reparative theft then, and as Esther Stanford-Xosei warns,[19] the reparative work of universities and academics must resist the temptation to focus only on the external. Instead, it should contend with the internal need for institutional and educational repair. Once we recognise the university to be a key social institution in the production of contemporary inequality, it follows that it has to represent a key site of resistance.

Despite the potential for struggle in the university, it is also necessary – as the preceding chapter indicated and as we develop further in Chapter 6 – for us to take note of the limits of that potential. Darren Webb's work is particularly instructive in this regard. He argues that 'the university can be the site for fleeting, transitory, small-scale experiences of utopian possibility' but, given the predominance of 'corporate-imperial' interests, it 'cannot be the site for transformative utopian politics'.[20] Whilst we agree with Webb's conclusion that we must look to communities and movements outside of the academy if we seek to affect transformative social change, we argue in this chapter that if we take a pay packet and relative job security from our university employment, we have an obligation to also struggle where we are.

The classroom and critical pedagogy

The classroom (and/or lecture theatre) is central to what Rodney calls the 'sphere of operation'[21] of university-based scholar-activists; this view was reflected by several participants, including Khadija (Bangladeshi, early-career) who noted: 'I've always seen the classroom as the core space.' Pedagogy is, therefore, an important component of scholar-activist praxes.[22] As William D'Antonio wrote in an early piece on scholar-activism, 'activism begins in the classroom'.[23] Perhaps unsurprisingly then, participants articulated a range of points about pedagogy. These points help to map out a picture of what pedagogy might look like for those of us committed to anti-racist scholar-activism. As several participants noted, the picture that develops is one fundamentally influenced by traditions of *critical pedagogy*. Afterall, as Amara (South Asian heritage, mid-career) declared, 'if you are not talking about pedagogy and not thinking about pedagogy, then it's going to be just armchair intellectualism, like armchair activism'.

The tradition of critical pedagogy is generally traced to the seminal work of Paulo Freire in Brazil,[24] as well as to the Marx-influenced Frankfurt School and their development of critical theory. Whilst there is no single approach to critical pedagogy, there are some key elements to the tradition. With echoes of the fundamental tenets set out in the Introduction, critical pedagogy fundamentally problematises the myth of neutrality in education and is explicit about its aim of enacting positive social change.[25] Through both content and method, it seeks to encourage critical thinking, empower students, promote democratisation, and challenge the status quo both within the classroom and the wider social world. It attempts to break with top-down 'rote' learning and a 'just-the-facts' pedagogy,[26] to instead position students as active and equal participants in the learning process.[27]

Throughout this book, we have maintained that a critical (structural) understanding of racism and a commitment to anti-racism are fundamental to praxes of anti-racist scholar-activism. This continues into approaches to pedagogy too. Despite its usefulness, as Ereene (British Muslim, early-career) explained, 'critical pedagogy is often critiqued as [being] neglectful of race'. Indeed, Cann and DeMeulenaere have cautioned that critical pedagogy's 'historically class-based framework' has, at times, led to the elision of considerations of race and racism.[28] There is a need, therefore, to 'complicate critical pedagogy by centring race' and many scholars have done so.[29] Indeed, Ereene explained how she 'incorporates Critical Race Theory' into her pedagogy in order to realise the potential of critical pedagogy. Following Ereene and the numerous critical pedagogues who centre race – and in the spirit of anti-racist scholar-activism – we contend that there can be no critical pedagogy without a centring of race. For this reason, when we talk of critical pedagogy, the race (i.e. critical *race* pedagogy) is always already implied.

As should be clear from the book so far, and particularly from the tenets we set out in the introductory chapter, there are huge convergences between the critical pedagogy tradition and the ambitions and values underpinning scholar-activism. In what follows, we look in more detail at some of these elements, as raised by our participants. We begin by looking at the myth of neutrality and its relationship to *conscientisation*,[30] before we consider how anti-racist scholar-activists might cultivate critical thought, and build a *classroom-to-activism pipeline*. We then explore how we might work towards the transformation of classrooms.

Eschewing neutrality and engendering conscientisation

Critical pedagogues recognise that whilst dominant 'traditional' approaches to teaching masquerade as neutral, they work in actuality to 'sustain the interests of the dominant groups'.[31] This is not to say that (hegemonic) education merely reflects the status quo but rather that it actively constitutes it. Whether it maintains or disrupts the status quo, therefore, teaching is always a political act: it is never value-free.[32] Echoing broader points we have made about praxis throughout this book, such an understanding is central to critical pedagogy and informs the pedagogical praxes of many of our participants.

The importance of naming teaching as always partisan was conveyed by Dillon, a British Asian early-career academic:

> I'm very blunt in the sense that I tell students that I'm not neutral: there's no such thing as an objective sociologist. I tell them that I'm coming at this from a particular position. If you don't agree with it, well that's fine, you're more than welcome to question it and challenge it. One of my favourite writers is a guy called Howard Zinn and he says you can't be neutral on a moving train. To be neutral is to be complicit because social relations are structured in a particular way, and are moving in an unjust direction, and to be neutral is just to be a bystander and get swept along. So, you have to be actively resisting and actively pushing back, and I do that with my teaching and I'm very explicit about that.

Dillon's approach to pedagogy is based on an understanding that the university is unjust, much as the social world it constitutes, and it is constituted by, is unjust. As he explains, in such a context, teaching cannot be objective and non-partisan. Rather than maintaining the status quo, Dillon's approach is to actively resist and push back through pedagogy. By making this explicit to his students he undermines the fallacy of neutrality in teaching, and in so doing begins to reveal the mechanics of education: an act that is integral to critical pedagogy.[33] This work can alter the expectations of students, and create a precedent that encourages pedagogues to make clear the positions and assumptions that shape their teaching. In this way, Dillon contributes his small part to the wider project that Walter Rodney speaks of when he calls for a transformation of the institution.[34]

Eschewing neutrality creates the conditions for *conscientisation*, a concept Freire uses to describe the process through which we learn 'to perceive social, political, and economic contradictions, and to take action against the oppressive elements of reality'.[35] There are, therefore, two key elements to conscientisation that Freire encourages us to hold in tandem, elements that we try to convey through our use of the term 'praxis' in this book. The first refers to critical thought and the second to related action in pursuit of social change. These elements are evident in Jay's (Asian British, mid-career) reflections on the importance of teaching: 'I see teaching not just as imparting knowledge to students but also, encouraging an ethical stance in them. Not forcing one upon them but making them understand their role in broader society'. The significant point here is that understanding the social world should lead to taking a stance in relation to it: 'reflection leads to action', as Ereene put it. The 'action' element is often forgotten as 'critical thought' is prioritised and, with this in mind,[36] we want to now look at both elements in turn.

Cultivating critical thought

The cultivation of critical thought involves exposing students to critical understandings of the matrix of domination,[37] understandings that we have argued are fundamental to anti-racist scholar-activism. As Cann and DeMeulenaere contend, it is about pulling 'back the curtains on some of the greatest shows on earth – patriarchy, white supremacy, heteronormativity – and expos[ing] the make-up and the special effects that create the charade'.[38] The value in this work is not to be underestimated. As Khadija asserted: 'the classroom, for me, has been the most transformational space'. It was in a similar vein that Neville (white, mid-career) explained:

> If I think about what's the biggest impact that my own work has, it's probably not my research, it's probably talking to young people in the classroom, and getting them to think about stuff in a way that they haven't thought

about it before, and so I think as an academic you can still do stuff that's positive despite, rather than because of, the institution.

Given the centrality of the classroom to one's 'sphere of operation',[39] cultivating critical thought – through critical pedagogy – as Neville describes, is an opportunity to (begin to) put scholar-activism into practice. Neville's account illustrates an orientation that is oppositional to the systematic devaluing of teaching in the academy that arises, in part, from the hyper-competitive research culture and burgeoning workloads that are driven by neoliberalism.[40] It reflects a value system that is governed by a desire to influence social change (and a degree of pragmatism about where one is best able to do this), rather than by neoliberal metrics or individual careerism.[41] Neville's insistence that critical pedagogy occurs 'despite, rather than because of, the institution' also reminds us that in the classroom, as elsewhere, scholar-activism involves working within *and* against the university. Despite the neoliberal-imperial-institutionally-racist nature of HE, and the specific ways in which neoliberal metrics strangle the potential of critical pedagogy,[42] there remain pockets and spaces that constitute opportunities for resistance. The classroom is one such space.

The opportunities presented in the classroom for cultivating critical thought were acknowledged by many of those we spoke to, including Maria (white, mid-career) who reflected:

Teaching allows me a place where, even though I don't see immediate results with students, I do feel like the students are taking in tangible things from what's happening and they're being transformed by the experience and they're feeling empowered to do stuff that ends up being tied to activism.

In a similar vein, Elroy (Black, established academic) explained that the classroom is 'a space within which I can drop the fucking seed'. He continued:

I tell my students, 'You will be tomorrow's policymakers, and you will be tomorrow's academics, and you will be tomorrow's police officers, and I don't want you fucking up like these lot are doing at the moment.' So that's a space within which we can begin to have that conversation. So, the activism also takes place within the university. I don't see the space as divorced from activism. I don't see my students as insulated from the type of work I do outside.

These accounts both convey a sense that classrooms hold opportunities for cultivating more critical world views among students, and that the development of such critical thought can have a wider societal impact. Relatedly, like Neville's, these accounts reflect an orientation that is resistant to the systematic devaluing of teaching in the academy. This is perhaps reflective of a scholar-activist praxis that is governed by the notion of working *in service* to anti-racism (where teaching is seen to offer opportunities to bolster anti-racism), rather than in service to performance metrics (tools of neoliberalism), as we explored in Chapter 2.

Despite conveying an appreciation of opportunities for the cultivation of critical thought in the classroom, Maria and Elroy's accounts also caution against the assumption that the cultivation of critical thought is enough alone. Maria suggests that teaching can lead students to engage in activities that are 'tied to activism', which is perhaps different from saying that teaching (always) leads students to become activists. Elsewhere, she also noted that though teaching can be important, it is not something she thinks of as activism, in and of itself. Similarly, Elroy talks of teaching as a space in which we can '*begin* to have the conversation'. As such, although the engendering of a critical world view might be the first step – as the duality of critical thought and action in Freire's concept of conscientisation makes clear – there is more work to be done. The task, therefore, is for us to embolden students to *use* the critical thought generated in the classroom in order to effect change. Whilst Elroy talks of making sure students, as future academics and police officers, are not 'fucking up', there are questions over whether such teaching encourages students to transform the current system or merely helps them to operate within that system (albeit, from a more critical position): to be a better police officer, rather than to fight for the abolition of policing. This is a significant distinction. How do we create the conditions for students to act as agents of social transformation in the radical, rather than piecemeal, sense? How do we encourage students to become part of our communities of resistance?

Building a classroom-to-activism pipeline

If we are to encourage students to *act* on their critical thought in pursuit of radical social change, we need to facilitate possibilities for this to happen. As the critical pedagogue Henry Giroux explains, critical pedagogy has to involve the creation of 'opportunities to mobilize instances of moral outrage, social responsibility and collective action'.[43] Echoing this sentiment, Ereene explained: 'I want them [students] to be inspired and passionate and get involved in community organisations … and fight the battle as well.' Although the vision that Ereene articulates is an urgent one, the neoliberal contexts of our universities and the specific impact that student-centred performance metrics have on teaching means that it is a vision that is also deeply constrained.[44] With this in mind, and as Webb cautions, despite the allure of our classrooms, 'we should not overestimate their transformative potential'.[45] We might, therefore, be better thinking about how we make the most of these spaces in service to anti-racism, without mistaking critical approaches to teaching for the totality of the kinds of scholar-activist work we need to engage in.

We have written elsewhere about our own efforts to engage in teaching for social change.[46] In 2017, we taught sessions on the Grenfell Tower fire – a significant and devastating event in Britain, symbolic of deep-seated class and race inequalities[47] – in an attempt to cultivate critical thought and stimulate activism amongst our students. The sessions were emotionally moving, and we were left in little doubt that we had encouraged more critical world views and ignited a desire for social justice amongst our students. Upon reflection and an analysis of the surveyed views of our students, however, we realised that we had in fact failed to move beyond what we refer to as *bounded social change* – that is to say, despite developing politically charged sessions, students struggled to see how they could use their critical understanding beyond the immediate context of the neoliberal university.[48] We had not done enough to build *a classroom-to-activism pipeline*. We introduce the pipeline metaphor here to think about how our classroom praxes can create routes that enable students to move from the classroom into activism. In many cases, this pipeline is often blocked or poorly constructed. In the example of our own teaching, the pipeline failed to exit the university because, although our students wanted to 'do something' about the injustices of Grenfell, their imaginations – blunted as they were by neoliberal HE – could not see beyond writing a powerful essay. Of course, the current structure of the academy and its assessment processes mean that those essays have little, if any, real world utility.[49] In this regard, we were sharply reminded that conscientisation is not only about developing a critical understanding and a desire to act,[50] but about making that action imaginable and realisable. It is about enabling *freedom dreaming*,[51] which, in turn, helps students move 'from cynicism and despair to hope and possibility'.[52]

Some of our participants were deliberate in attempting to create pathways for action and social change, or in constructing a *classroom-to-activism pipeline*. For instance, Jay described to us a law course that trains students to investigate the cases of people who claim to have been wrongly convicted. This, he argued, allows activism to be tied into his academic role and to his classroom. Another example came from Aaliyah (Black, early-career):

> I suppose getting students to engage with local community projects and building relationships between the university and the community projects. I think that's really important because I think universities take a lot from community groups, don't they? So, it's about what we can give back. So, I

suppose the module that I'm teaching on, that I'm working on, is a way of
building relationships.

By forming links with community projects, Aaliyah creates opportunities
for students to imagine more socially just societies. In turn, students can
move beyond bounded social change towards forms of unbounded social
change that extend beyond the neoliberal university context. In the words
of Aronowitz and Giroux, she moves from the position of critical intellectual
to transformative intellectual – that is, 'beyond [an] isolated posture to
the terrain of collective struggle'.[53] A scholar-activist orientation is manifest
in Aaliyah's approach as there is a clear effort to place her teaching in
service to 'community projects' as a form of redistribution: as a way for
her to 'give back'. She points to how we might resource community groups
via the labour of students or via economic resources that we can leverage
from these sorts of courses. As Castle and McDonald make clear, 'there
must be some level of community engagement, or one has not moved
beyond ivory tower activism'.[54] We might add that such engagement must
be meaningful and beneficial to the engaged community, rather than the
extractive, short-lived and/or superficial community engagement that, in
the UK context, can be encouraged through frameworks such as the REF
Impact agenda.

Transforming our classrooms

As we have suggested, central to the idea of struggle where you are is a
recognition that it is insufficient to talk about power inequalities 'out
there' (in wider society), without paying attention to our 'own sphere of
operation'.[55] Taking this notion and the lessons of critical pedagogy seriously,
it is necessary for us to recognise the power dynamics that operate within
our own classrooms. In this regard, Ereene emphasised the need to create
'a space where everyone is a teacher, and everyone is a learner, and where
we together come up with actions for social change'. Echoing much of

this, Okoye – a Black, Muslim early-career woman – was also particularly thoughtful in this regard:

> Once I'm in that lecture, once I'm in that seminar, I'm on my own with the students and I feel like it's a space where we make the decisions of what takes place in that one hour, two hours that we have together. So, we set the tone together.

By positioning her students as co-decision makers within the classroom, Okoye attempts to pushback against, or transgress, traditional power dynamics that situate lecturers as service providers/knowledge givers and students as consumers/empty vessels. As Patricia Hill Collins acknowledges, when we 'set up our classes … social hierarchy is quite crucial to how students feel about learning, regardless of content'.[56] This subversion of classroom dynamics represents an attempt to build the Undercommons in the classroom,[57] to offer a 'place of refuge' or 'breathing space' from the wider university.[58] In turn, it creates an environment more conducive to critical consciousness raising and to anti-racist resistance.

There is more to this subversion though: it also undermines or pushes back against the hegemony of traditional pedagogy. Relatedly, it has the potential to push against the limiting imperatives of neoliberal education, operationalised in the UK primarily (though not exclusively) through 'student-centred' performance metrics such as the *Teaching Excellence Framework* and the *National Student Survey*. These tools have been noted to depoliticise the classroom, deter innovative teaching, prioritise metrics over real learning, and position students as consumers rather than active participants.[59] In this respect, the neoliberalisation of teaching makes critical pedagogy more challenging, but also more disruptive. As Okoye explained:

> if we were really having a dialogue there would be a sense right from the onset of students being partners in the classroom and that is a risk for any institution because the minute you make students partners and make them invested in their own learning you remove some of the power from yourself

and you legitimise knowledge that you don't always have control over, and that can dismantle the whole institution.

By undermining dominant logics of power in the classroom, Okoye attempts to weaken the university and the pervasive ideas it reproduces about 'legitimate' knowledge production. Anti-racist scholar-activists should, therefore, as Webb urges, adopt a 'dialogical pedagogy that prefigures in the very process of collaborative learning the kind of social relations that might characterize an alternative way of being.'[60] In this regard, we might also begin to transform student perceptions about what the university is or can be: we might encourage freedom dreaming.

Whilst Okoye's account may appear to hold some similarities with the institutional shift in recent years towards 'flipped classrooms',[61] it is in the underpinning anti-racist politics and commitment to social change that anti-racist scholar-activist approaches are defined and distinguished. As Okoye continued to explain, there are other factors that shape her approach to teaching:

> We have very uncomfortable conversations and we find ways to manage the cognitive requirements of it in terms of being able to critically think about some of the theories and unpack them. But also, the affective requirements. There's always an emotional, visceral response if somebody knows what they're talking about, how are we as a group going to manage that and work together to do that?

In this, Okoye shows a further break with hegemonic approaches as she places discomfort, affect, and emotion in the classroom. Taking us back to our earlier discussion of neutrality, mainstream educational discourse privileges the illusion of objectivity and rationality, and constructs emotion as lying 'beneath the faculties of thought and reason' and therefore as having no place in the classroom.[62] For Okoye and others, however, emotions do have a role to play in education and particularly in education for social change.[63] Emotions are relational[64] and, when directed in the pursuit of anti-racist social justice, an engagement with emotionality

– through pedagogies of discomfort[65] – can be productive. Making emotions present and visible in our classrooms can push back against academic convention and allow us to break with the norms of what is expected of an educator. To centre emotion in pedagogy, therefore, is to struggle where you are not only in the sense that it is a disruptive pedagogy, but also in its ability to create a classroom environment more conducive to the development of *communities* of resistance.

Whilst we have thus far emphasised the potential of the classroom and the importance of critical pedagogy, such teaching poses challenges that should be acknowledged too. Two related issues were highlighted by participants in particular: opposition from students; and how the matrix of domination, and specific tools of domination such as counter-terror as operationalised in the UK through Prevent,[66] shape classroom dynamics. Despite our optimistic tone regarding critical pedagogy, the strength of neoliberal logics of instrumentalisation and logics of white supremacy mean that not all students welcome counter-hegemonic and anti-racist approaches to teaching.[67] One way of working through this tension productively is to draw on the 'spectrum of allies' concept which, emerging out of the US civil rights context, has gained significant traction in recent years in social movement building and activism.[68] Employing this concept, we can see our aim as not being to win over all students but about engaging those who are within our spectrum of allies – that is, those who are open to being brought into our anti-racist movements.

There is, however, more at stake here than feeding the *classroom-to-activism pipeline*. The well-being of scholar-activists is also a vital consideration, particularly when we recognise that student hostility is especially pronounced when critical education is facilitated by teachers of colour.[69] Both Khadija (Bangladeshi, early-career) and Sara (British Muslim, early-career) illustrate this point:

> A classroom site is transformational, but also sometimes I get the impression some of the students don't necessarily want to be challenged or made too

uncomfortable either … We're both two women of colour teaching this course and it's been some of our white students who have been giving us a bit of a hard time because of how they've understood race (Khadija).

For me, racism [in the classroom], I cannot deal with it. I cannot just sit there and say that's fine, you know, homophobia, transphobia, Islamophobia, or whatever it is … that is something which I am very aware of, as a Muslim brown woman. I will not tolerate that … As a person of colour who was teaching, that is my body on the line that you are discussing … I have to be very strategic in who I am speaking to, about certain things that resonate with my own lived experience – its self-care (Sara).

As Khadija and Sara make clear, despite the promises of critical pedagogy, it is necessary to consider the threat of *backlash* (which returns us to the previous chapter) and the toll that critical teaching can take on academics, particularly those from minoritised communities.

Relatedly, whilst we hold that there is real value in making emotions visible in the classroom, there is also a need to be attentive to who is undertaking that emotional labour amidst the risk of reinscribing existing power imbalances. As Khadija and Sara make clear, classrooms are not immune from the matrix of domination. This is particularly manifest in the urgent need to think about how the Prevent duty, and counter-terror policy and Islamophobia more widely, curtail the potential of radical emotion-centred pedagogy. As Haytham (Pakistani, PhD researcher) explains:

Students are less willing to talk about their feelings and their positions within the classroom because they see it as a Police space now. They see it as a space that is potentially harmful to them in terms of their long-term aims and ambitions, right? So, it doesn't mean that they are not willing to be in that space, it just means that they have to alter themselves, they have to self-regulate based on this gaze that they are under.

Underpinning Haytham's account is a well-founded conviction that these issues of surveillance are specifically affecting students of colour, and particularly Muslim students.[70] What we see across the accounts of Khadija, Sara, and Haytham then is that structural issues pertaining to power and inequality have to be negotiated in the classroom, and threaten to limit the potential of critical pedagogy.

Another consideration regarding the limits of critical pedagogy has been highlighted by the onset of the COVID-19 pandemic and particularly the shift within HE institutions to online teaching (and related reliance upon digital technologies). These conditions have given rise to questions about how pedagogues can adapt, questions that are particularly pertinent given the likelihood that online teaching will become increasingly commonplace as a mode of delivery post-pandemic. Although our interviews took place well before the pandemic, such questions take on a particular inflection when we think specifically about scholar-activists and critical pedagogues. How do we build the community links that we describe in the previous section when we operate online? How do we engage students in online space in ways that inspire them to pursue anti-racist social justice? What does the *classroom-to-activism pipeline* look like when both the classroom and activist spaces are operating largely online? How do we manage emotion and difficult conversations in virtual classrooms? How do we break down hierarchies in the classroom when the classroom is digital? How do we manage racism in the online classroom? How do we take into account the particular forms of (digital) surveillance (and/ or dataveillance) that might encroach into online teaching? How do we respond to differential levels of access to digital technologies that are often reflective of (and will reproduce) racial and class inequalities? We are not suggesting, here, that the shift to online teaching makes anti-racist critical pedagogy insurmountable, but there are significant considerations with which we must grapple. Indeed, it would be naive to assume that methods of in-person teaching can be applied, without adaptation, to digital classrooms. There is a need, therefore, for those of us engaged in anti-racist scholar-activism to think about how we best adapt our methods to online spaces.

There are two more fundamental considerations here too. The first requires us to think more broadly about the implications of the pandemic. The question of how we consider all of the above, whilst also being attentive to the realities that our students are living through multiple crises and contending with a range of issues, becomes particularly pressing. The second consideration concerns the broader implications of the increasing reliance on digital technologies as tools for education. As Mirrlees and Alvi show, although digital technology is often uncritically celebrated for its capacity to revolutionise education, what they refer to as 'EdTech' acts to reproduce and exacerbate capitalist relations that are deeply unequal and imperial in nature.[71] There is a need to pay attention, therefore, to 'the real economic and political structures, institutions and interests that are shaping and attempting to benefit from EdTech's development, diffusion, application and impact in society'.[72] The point here is not to suggest that in-person teaching does not also reproduce inequalities (or to suggest that the use of digital technology in teaching is not without its benefits). Rather, there is a need to pay attention to the particular inequalities that can arise through the increasing reliance on digital technology in teaching and the wider web of vested interests that may drive and profit from such developments. For scholar-activists, this critical reading of digital technologies in education raises questions about the contradictions and complicities that can arise in our practice (an issue we return to in the next chapter), and highlights the need for forms of reflexivity that consider the wider implications and contexts of our work.

Notwithstanding the significant issues that threaten to constrain critical pedagogies, we have shown in this section that teaching presents opportunities for anti-racist scholar-activism. Nevertheless, we have also suggested that the transformative potential of teaching is curtailed by the institutional context, and specifically by the neoliberalisation of HE generally and the classroom particularly. Without wanting to diminish its value, our participants, like us, are clear that university-based critical pedagogy is not enough alone. As Webb aptly puts it, the university classroom is, at best, a 'bolt-hole' or a 'breathing space' in an otherwise 'suffocating environment'.[73] Whilst we have argued that we should create and exploit these pockets of possibility as much as possible, we should also look to build a pipeline out of the university and into communities of resistance. It is outside of the university where we can work most effectively in service to anti-racism. Knowing that our work is about more than teaching, and notwithstanding the dangers of focusing too much on struggle within the university setting, we now want to think about resistance that occurs elsewhere in the university.

Beyond the classroom: wider acts of resistance in the university

There is a need to look beyond the classroom in thinking about how we can struggle where we are. As Patricia Hill Collins states, critical pedagogy is not enough; rather 'teaching for a change involves struggling for institutional transformation so that we leave the social institutions that educated us better than we found them'.[74] Striking a similar chord, Giroux contends:

> it is crucial for progressive educators to wage battles over access for poor and minority students, shift power away from bureaucracies to faculties, and address the exploitative conditions under which many graduate students work – often constituting a de facto army of service workers who are underpaid, overworked, and shorn of any real power or benefits. Simply put, the what, how, and why of teaching cannot be separated from the basic conditions under which educators and students labour. This means rethinking how teaching functions as a form of academic labour within iniquitous relations of power.[75]

For Giroux and Collins alike, there is a need to ensure that one's praxis is not confined to critical pedagogy within the classroom, but that instead we consider other sites within the university where anti-racist resistance can be enacted. One such site might be the curriculum. Indeed, given that university curricula are so enduringly US-Eurocentric, and with student-led 'decolonise' movements demanding change, transforming the curriculum can be a way for critical scholars and anti-racist scholar-activists to struggle where we are. This work is key for challenging the coloniality of knowledge production, canonisation and discipline formation, and for feeding into critical consciousness raising. Whilst some of this work can occur in the classroom (as the previous section shows), it also needs to take place elsewhere in the university, particularly if change is to become institutionalised and embedded.[76] We can use university meetings and committees to effect change in relation to the curriculum, as well as for speaking up and pushing back against a range of other inequities and injustices.

Speaking up and pushing back in university meetings

The importance of meetings as sites of resistance was encapsulated by Sajid (British Pakistani, mid-career):

> If you're looking for a site of activism, staff meetings and team meetings, departmental meetings, are another way in which to bring your activism to bear because that's when we're talking about inequalities in the workplace. That's when workloads and deployment [is discussed] and [discussions are had] about student experience and about why Black and Asian students are much more likely to drop out. That is political, right, so I think it's about bringing the political into the meeting. That's activism.

Underpinning Sajid's account is a recognition of the harms caused by, and inequalities within, the university. Whilst staff meetings are perhaps not generally thought of as insurgent sites of activism, and without wanting to overstate their utility, Sajid emphasises their importance as a site for disrupting – or ameliorating – the harm caused by the university. This everyday disruptive work can sometimes be important. It holds potential for us to operate simultaneously in *and* against the university, providing an opportunity for us to seek to (partially) mitigate our own complicity in the inequalities reproduced in HE (see Chapter 6). As Amara reminded us, 'speaking up in meetings' can be one way of 'practising what you preach', or of engaging in the 'talk-plus-walk'[77] that we have suggested is integral to scholar-activism. We are not suggesting here that speaking up in meetings is unique to the praxis of scholar-activism (we are in no doubt that other academics engage in this work too), or that the act of speaking up constitutes scholar-activism, per se. Rather, we are suggesting that it may be one small part of an assemblage of practices that make up scholar-activist praxes.

Returning us to ideas developed in the previous chapter, capacity for speaking up is always mediated by a range of factors. The precarity of many academics, particularly those working at the margins, makes this kind of labour riskier for some than for others – that is to say, we do not always have the resources, power, or job security required to disrupt. Ironically, it is in fact often those with the most grievances that are situated in the weakest position from which to disrupt. Relatedly, rosalind hampton writes that 'university committees and the policies they produce and uphold are, by definition, intended to work for the university and protect its determined interests'.[78] There is a need, therefore, for scholar-activists to be 'critically selective' about this kind of disruptive work,[79] to recognise the limits of the university,[80] and to be cognisant of the profound challenges we might encounter when we try to talk back.[81] Vitally, we must also avoid being lulled into mistakenly seeing such meetings and committees as the only or even primary avenue for change, particularly in a context where the increasing neoliberal managerialism of HE means that such meetings are often merely a space through which participants 'go through the motions'. There is a danger here in becoming institutionalised – in developing a myopia that makes it difficult to see beyond institutional mechanisms and piecemeal reforms – and losing sight of our critical and radical visions.

Making a similar argument to Sajid, though pushing us to think more broadly about aspects of the university that too often go unchallenged, Galiev (person of colour, early-career) highlighted the need to:

> Always, always pull them up on everything that they're doing which is perpetuating inequality. If they're investing in the arms trade, if they're investing in Israeli military companies, if they're investing in fossil fuels, all that kind of stuff. Our job is to mitigate or ameliorate the fundamental, the systemic, the inequalities that the university engages in and to always hold them to account.

As Galiev points to the far-reaching ways in which the university reproduces (global) inequalities, he offers an important challenge to the irony that sees many academics writing about structures of inequality 'out there' without looking at the realities 'in here'.[82] Of course, recognising the backlash that might come from speaking truth to power, we should remember that this dissenting work is likely to be most effective in bringing about meaningful change 'when these goals are taken up as organizing and/or activist endeavours, with collective planning towards meeting clearly defined goals'.[83] As we suggested in the last chapter, protection can come (at least in part) from collectivisation.

These collectives can, and should, be formed with students too. Indeed, several participants spoke about the importance of building solidarity with students and offering (often behind the scenes)[84] support for students who may campaign on the types of issues that we (should look to) speak up about in meetings. Amara, for example, insisted on the importance of being led by students in such regards: 'I would not be a scholar-activist if I am not working with my students … I have become a radical because of my engagement with radical students.' Student campaigns are often able to have far more impact than would be possible were an academic to speak up in a meeting. In the spirit of struggle where you are, such work is also about having different actors and modes of influence in different spaces – that is both staff and students, as key constituents in the university, applying pressure to address particular issues.

Even with the relative protection and mutual support offered by collectives, holding the university to account is not without consequences. As discussed in the previous chapter, institutions exert backlash against anti-racist scholar-activists not only because anti-racism is considered subversive but because its subversion is enhanced by our activist orientations (and for some of us, our marginalised positionalities). In the context of his comments above, Galiev reflected on this issue:

> If you look at the people who are radical in what they say, who have reached the top, I'm not going to speak ill of these people because their scholarship has been really important to my work, but you may question whether or not they were scholar-activists. They're just maybe a radical public intellectual. As a radical public intellectual maybe it's easier to start from the bottom and get to the top. As a scholar-activist, I think the jury's out on that one as to whether or not they can make it to the top of their profession. I would be sceptical about that. If you've got someone who's been on the picket lines, who'd been at a senate meeting saying, 'we need to divest from x, y and z'. Who's been calling out the racism and sexism of their heads of department, I think they're going to find it very difficult to get to the top.

Here, Galiev articulates his sense that the praxes of scholar-activism have negative implications for career progression. As Sara Ahmed contends, 'when you expose a problem you pose a problem'.[85] For Galiev, this posing of problems is part of what defines anti-racist scholar-activist praxes and this creates a range of barriers over and above those faced by other kinds of academics, including public intellectuals.

Distinguishing this time between critical academics and scholar-activists, Alex (mixed-race, mid-career) made a similar point:

> I think it's definitely possible for a critical academic to have a quick career path to the top and to have a really high profile as an academic, writing Left-wing stuff, anti-racist stuff. I think there's a market for that, to be frank. I don't know, because I haven't worked in every institution and institutions are all different, but I think being a scholar-activist is different and yes, you will necessarily have a longer wait for promotion perhaps because you'll be involved in union organising that will make you unpopular with management and you won't be volunteering for managerial positions that you feel like you can't justify politically.

In both Galiev and Alex's accounts, the difficulties faced by scholar-activists can be understood as a consequence of, or as a part of, the *backlash* (see Chapter 4) against scholar-activists' attempts to struggle where they are. This is a struggle that, for Galiev, manifests in the speaking up and against the university's exploitative and extractive practices, and for Alex, in being part of union organising. In keeping with the accounts of Galiev and Alex, Patricia Hill Collins notes that confronting those that wield power within the university can result in scholar-activists being 'routinely passed over for cushy jobs' and 'fat salaries'.[86]

Galiev went on to explain that he is content to 'top out at a particular (academic job) level', if that enables him to maintain his commitment to working in service to communities of resistance. A similar perspective underscored Alex's account too, and both appear to share Cornel West's conviction that it makes little sense 'for somebody to have a radical sociological analysis with a neoliberal soulcraft'.[87] Whilst participants explained that the pursuit of 'cushy jobs' and 'fat salaries'[88] were not their motivators, there are at least two broader points worth making here. First, the difficulties one might encounter in gaining promotion as someone who speaks up and pushes back are manifestations of an institutional discouraging of – or backlash against – challenges to those in power (and perhaps discouraging of scholar-activist praxis more widely). Second, these difficulties are wrapped up with, and underpinned by, the same forces that create increased precarity and vulnerability to un(der)employ-ment. At the sharp end then, this is about far more than promotions and 'fat salaries' and, with this in mind, we must take heed of the imprisoned former Black Panther Mumia Abu-Jamal's reminder that 'even radical intellectuals must eat'.[89]

In the context of such challenges, many participants took self-preservation seriously. This takes us back to our framing of struggle where you are in the early parts of the chapter – notably, the importance of recognising that one cannot do it all. Okoye was one participant who exemplified this sentiment. Reflecting on her efforts to bring the 'decolonising style' of her community work into the university setting, she spoke of the challenges presented by the institution and her response to them:

> It is a lot more difficult to do it within the institution [than a community setting] because there are so many things that are confining you to a system of Eurocentric understandings around what objectivity is, the idea of universality, the idea of meritocracy, and you spend so much time fighting and fighting back that when you are the minority in terms of an academic, it is sometimes exhausting. So, I sometimes reconcile myself to the fact that, okay let me just get through today and I will be able to go back into the community and do some more meaningful work, which is not the ideal situation. But sometimes in terms of self-care you have to manage activism in that way, and just say let me just make a difference where I can, because it is too exhausting to try and fight a battle here. Sometimes it feels like it is a challenge worth taking and a fight worth fighting, but some weeks it is just like 'listen, the institution is too big for me to do on my own'. I just do what I need to do and then go.

Anti-racist work within the university is made more difficult by the institutional constraints that Okoye names, all of which are compounded for her because of her positionality as a Black hijabi woman – that is to say, as discussed in the preceding chapter, one's 'minority' status already creates conditions for exhaustion and this is exacerbated by backlash against anti-racist praxis, particularly when it comes from a scholar-activist orientation. For Okoye, this threat of exhaustion leads to a level of pragmatism: sometimes it is just necessary to 'get through the day' or, as Heidi Mirza puts it, to survive 'the sheer weight of whiteness'.[90] Not all battles can be fought, and as Okoye reminds us, self-care and self-preservation are vital. In some instances, therefore, Okoye chooses not to invest too heavily in (struggling against) the institution, in order to preserve herself for anti-racist resistance outside of the university, where the 'real work' gets done.[91] This serves as an important reminder of the diversity of approaches and perspectives of our participants, who, like us, vary in the extent to which they place their energies inside the academy. Whilst some expend significant energy struggling within their institutions, others place such struggle as secondary to their wider activist work outside of the university. Of course, the relative emphasis placed on sites of struggle can change over time too. It is impossible to do it all, and the decisions scholar-activists make, like activists more generally,[92] are often based upon strategic considerations of what will be most effective at that moment in time.

Okoye was not alone in placing limits on her engagement in struggle within the university setting. Abiola (African, PhD researcher) was even more forthright in waging his resistance outside of the academy:

> I'm quiet in the academy. I just like to get on with stuff, head down into my work and let my activism take place outside the academy, or through my academic writing, but not in my physical reality, that's my persona. But whenever something happens on campus that's an injustice, and I realise it's an injustice, there is this internal monologue that's going, 'Oh God, you're going to have to get up. You're going to have to expose yourself. You're going to have to take the mask off. You're going to have to deal with it.' And, as much as I don't have a problem doing that, I don't always welcome it because when I'm working and thinking like an academic, I sometimes like that space the academy provides just to think, to be able to creatively imagine and consider theory without always being on defence from the State. Not always be having to confront. But it's part and parcel of the job.

I don't think you can be a scholar-activist without being prepared for that eventuality.

Abiola is a well-known community activist who has had longstanding involvement in a range of anti-racist social justice campaigns and community education. For him, the university is not the site for his activism. Rather, it is a space in which he prefers to keep his 'head down', to take a step back, to think, and to rest. It provides respite from the need to be defensive and reactive, and this respite serves an important function in allowing him to 'creatively imagine' – a key but undervalued component in activist praxis.[93] As he acknowledges, though, there are situations in which he feels it necessary to speak up – that is, there are certain injustices that simply cannot be ignored. Placing Abiola's approach in contrast to those who are involved in union activism (which we discus below), or those who otherwise resist on campus, underscores the need to remember that scholar-activism is heterogeneous (there is no 'right way').

The union as a site of struggle

As many participants explained, another way we can seek (partial, not absolute) preservation comes via participation in the union. The interviews for this book took place in the midst of 'unprecedented levels of strike action' from the main academic union in the UK, the UCU, with major strikes held in 2018, 2019, and 2020.[94] The strikes initially and primarily centred on pensions, but also focused on cuts to pay, racial and gender discrimination in pay, working conditions, and the casualisation of labour. These disputes therefore shaped the backdrop of many of the discussions we had with participants related to the union and working conditions in HE.

The long and damning history of racism within trade unions has been widely recognised.[95] This history led Ambalavaner Sivanandan to trouble, and Paul Gilroy to write off, the potential for effective interracial class solidarity within trade unionism. Satnam Virdee has suggested, however, that this writing off was somewhat premature, pointing to a flurry of efforts within trade unionism to build interracial class solidarity in the 1970s, perhaps best encapsulated by the Grunwick strike.[96] Notwithstanding some of the criticisms raised by Sivanandan, Gilroy, and others, the importance of trade unionism has been well documented within anti-racist movements. From C.L.R. James and Martin Luther King Jr, to John La Rose and Angela Y. Davis, trade unions have been understood, despite their problems, to be spaces from which we can build collective resistance and class-based solidarity. The value attributed to unions is not only reflective of the importance of organising blocs, but also of the inextricable ties between capitalism and racism, or the reality that anti-racist resistance must be anti-capitalist. In this regard, and in the context of sometimes hostile unions, Black Worker Committees have often constituted communities of resistance *within* unions. As such, they have been of vital importance in fighting for anti-racism within unionism.[97]

Whilst racism endures in trade unions today,[98] and the UCU Black Members and others continue to have to highlight that many union issues are impacted by race and migration,[99] a number of our participants emphasised the importance of the union and of union activism (though many noted the union's limitations too). Rosa (white, mid-career), for example, exemplified this:

> without my union activism I would be, perhaps, more involved in the productivism of the careerist. Whereas, because of my activism in the union and then recently also the strike – which was super-engaging, and physically and mentally involving – I mean, it's a matter of fact, you just take time out from writing articles, networking, advertising yourself, because now it's all about how you market yourself. So, in practice, if you decide to become active in your workplace, to fight the terms and conditions of your own employment, and to help colleagues with casework and support others, your time becomes limited. So, you make a choice, and automatically you stop being that perfect, productivist, neoliberal university worker.

For Rosa – an academic who migrated to Britain – being an active part of the union is not only an important way to effect change in our workplaces, but it also acts to underscore one's orientation. It renders one 'in but not of' the university: it locates one in the margins.[100] This positioning ensures that we are located not on the side of the employer – or the neoliberal-imperial-institutionally-racist university – but on the side of workers' struggle. To be engaged in the union offers an anchoring, or grounding, that runs counter to the hegemonic logics of the academy. It involves taking time out from being the 'perfect, productivist, neoliberal university worker' and redirects your time to struggling where you are. As Tanzil Chowdhury notes, and as we discussed briefly in Chapter 3, '[t]he fight over the working day is a fight over the marketization of higher education.'[101] Thus, the struggle over time within the neoliberal university is a key battleground, and to disrupt the logic of 'accelerated capitalist time' can be a political act.

The importance of supporting union strike action was highlighted by other participants too, but the significance of the strikes was particularly great for Sajid:

> for me, being on strike is one of the few ways in which a person is almost stripped naked and all you can see are their politics, right? … For me that is a moment where somebody's politics are laid bare … It's much more disappointing when somebody [crosses a picket who] claims to have progressive values and claims to have progressive credentials. I gave you one example earlier and actually there were a couple of examples … [of people] who would identify as Critical Race scholars who have crossed the picket line. That doesn't compute for me. It doesn't correspond, you can't do that, it's a contradiction and it comes back to what scholar-activist means and this distinction between actually practising activism and just simply writing critically. I think that there's a distinction there and I think strikes are a perfect way to gauge how somebody is willing to respond.

Sajid sees engagement with strikes as a way in which critical scholars must move beyond *talking the talk* to *walking the walk* of their criticality.

It is an opportunity to put one's critical credentials into action. As Sajid sees it, for critical scholars not to support the strike or wider workplace/sectoral struggle creates a contradiction between their writing/teaching and their wider practice; or perhaps it merely highlights – as we suggested in the Introduction – the distinction between critical scholarship and scholar-activism. Scholar-activism, Sajid avows, requires a degree of consistency between one's scholarship and one's actions (though perhaps such consistency should be, and for many is, an inherent feature of critical scholarship too). As we show in Chapter 6, whilst we are all inescapably wrapped up in contradictions that make us complicit in reproducing inequities in the academy, there are some contradictions that simply cannot hold.

For many of those we interviewed, crossing a picket line was one such contradiction. Galiev echoed this sentiment:

> you've got loads of armchair radicals who are happy to profess all of these ideas of structural inequalities and all these problems which are systemic, but because often these people are in positions of power, these strikes might strike at the heart of the privilege from which they benefit. Yes, I don't think it's unusual to have people who are scholar-activists … Again, *I* won't call them scholar-activists, but people who are self-proclaimed radicals that would then engage in the very structural abuses and inequalities that are producing these pension changes, the increasing precarity within Higher Education.

Like Sajid, Galiev positions the strikes as an opportunity to practise the talk-plus-walk[102] of scholar-activism. He suggests that too many academics are concerned with the protection of their own privileges. This exposes the hollowness of some claims of being radical and to being engaged in scholar-activism. In the first chapter, we discussed how there is often an overclaiming of the anti-racist scholar-activist label. Here, Galiev's account implies that this overclaiming is embodied by the 'armchair radicals' who write about structural inequality, whilst crossing the picket lines of strikes against those very conditions. Giroux holds that 'a radical pedagogy as a form of resistance should, in part, be premised on the assumption that educators vigorously resist any attempt on the part of liberals and conservatives to reduce them to the role of either technicians or multinational operatives'.[103] For Sajid and Galiev, the vigorous resistance that Giroux refers to is realised on the picket line.

Earlier in this chapter, and in the preceding chapter too, we noted the potential costs of speaking up. Despite the relative power of trade unions, participants made clear that similar costs can also be suffered through union activism. In the following account, Sajid recalls an experience on the picket line that had serious ramifications:

> I can almost guarantee you that in one of my previous jobs my contract wasn't renewed because I confronted the Head of Department who was crossing the picket line … And I was on a fractional contract, right? Like a temporary contract. And I'm out with not many colleagues. There are many full-time permanent staff members that aren't even on strike. Either they're sat at home or they're crossing the picket lines. And so, the Head of Department comes up, right, to cross the picket line, and I confronted him … I asked him 'Are you a member of UCU?' He said 'yeah', and I said 'well UCU have passed a democratic vote to support this strike'. And he said 'well, if you want to grass me up to UCU, that's fine, you can do that …' So anyways, he crossed the picket line, but I pissed him off. I could see that I'd pissed him off, and lo and behold a few months down the line my contract isn't renewed and I'm basically out of a job.

There is a cost to speaking up. In this case and others,[104] that cost is one's employment. Just how high the stakes are was highlighted in late 2020 when news broke that Gargi Bhattacharyya, a leading anti-racist scholar and activist, was facing redundancy from her position at the University of East London in what appeared to be a targeting of union activists. As the former president of the National Union of Students Malia Bouattia contends, 'it is clearly because of what Bhattacharyya represents and the threat she poses, that the university is attempting to get rid of her'.[105] Like

Sajid's account, events like these reflect a wider picture in which university-based scholar-activists operate at the juncture of complex tensions – that is to say, they may be 'critiquing the power structure on one hand, while on the other depending on it for their livelihood'.[106] Notwithstanding this point about livelihoods, as Bhattacharyya defiantly put it, 'if you're a union rep and your employer hates you, you should always think that means you're doing something right. Tattoo it on your heart and be proud.'[107]

Although the union was generally regarded as a vehicle through which we, as anti-racist scholar-activists, can struggle where we are, there are two points of critique worth reiterating here. Firstly, the UCU – like all unions – is imperfect, particularly when it comes to issues of 'race', racism, and migration.[108] Indeed, the UCU has often failed to prioritise anti-racism and the experiences of academics of colour, non-British academics, and others working in the margins. Second, there is an urgent need to better establish the links between campus-based activism and wider struggles beyond the ivory tower. Galiev recalled his attempts, via a letter to his colleagues, to urge them to collectively address the two issues:

> I said, 'It's really important that we support the strike, and this is brilliant', but then I was saying, 'We've got to link this to precarity. We've got to link this to wider struggles, man, because as bad as it is that they're trying to reform our pension, this is a bourgeois struggle, man.' Do you know what I mean? We've got to talk about the people on the frontline who are the most vulnerable which are people like TAs, people on precarious contracts, with it disproportionately obviously, affecting women, scholars of colour et cetera, et cetera. That was rebuffed.

As Galiev explains, whilst strikes and the work of the union are important in their own right, there is vital work to be done in thinking about whose needs get centred in those strikes, and how we situate the strikes in a broader context of resistance. With this in mind, although it is important to struggle where you are, this should not be myopic and should not be the end point. It should be understood, instead, alongside notions of working in service (see Chapter 2) and reparative theft (see Chapter 3), which maintain the scholar-activist orientation as prioritising anti-racist resistance *outside* of the academy.

Conclusion

In this chapter, we have taken up the instruction given by Stuart Hall to struggle where you are, in order to illustrate that it is an important component in the praxes of many anti-racist scholar-activists. As well as prioritising a movement over individualism, to struggle where you are implores us (collectively) to look inwards at the university. In this sense, it offers a break with the all too common understanding of the university as sitting outside of, rather than constitutive of, inequality and injustice. As we have shown, there are many opportunities for resistance within the academy. Indeed, notwithstanding the challenges engendered by the logics of neoliberalism and institutional racism, the classroom can offer opportunities to 'drop the seed' and raise anti-racist critical consciousness amongst students. We might go a step further, as some of our participants did, in fostering a *classroom-to-activism pipeline*; a vital step if we are to address how marketisation and instrumentalisation blunts the imaginations of students and prevents us all from freedom dreaming.[109] We might also seek to transform the dynamics of the classroom, subverting teacher/student hierarchies as a political act that pushes against established norms within HE. Ultimately, we have shown that pedagogy is one way in which university-based scholar-activists can embrace calls to struggle where you are.

Recognising the need to operate not only within but also beyond the classroom, participants spoke about the importance of speaking up and pushing back in staff meetings and/or in wider institutional interactions, to hold the university to account. Notwithstanding the importance of this work, not all battles can be fought, such is the inequitable distribution of power and precarity in the academy. For some scholar-activists this means waging resistance within the university; however, for others, there is a need to be selective and strategic in what they take on: in this respect, self-care becomes a key consideration. A further site of activism might lie in engagement with the trade union. Such engagement, we argue, ensures that we are *struggling where we are* over workplace conditions. It is an opportunity for us to walk-the-walk of our critical writing: it is, in Ruth Wilson Gilmore's terms, talk-plus-walk.[110] Engagement with union activities provides an anchoring that pushes back against the neoliberal logics of the university and, by prioritising union work, we often come to deprioritise academic productivity. We reclaim our time.

Despite the virtues in struggling where you are, at several junctures in this chapter we also noted the dangers of our activism being constrained by the institution, and becoming myopic or reformist. We must remain attentive to avoiding praxis – and freedom dreaming – that is restricted to tweaking the system, whilst also (perhaps inadvertently) maintaining that very system. That said, we maintain that as long as we are accepting a pay check from a university, we have some obligation to exploit the pockets of possibility for dissent and transformation that arise from our positions, no matter how 'fleeting, transitory [and] small-scale' they may be.[111] In the next chapter, we build upon these discussions as we look at the complicities that arise from operating within the university, alongside practices of dissent.

6

Uncomfortable truths, reflexivity, and a constructive complicity

Throughout this book, we have shown that the dominant logics of the neoliberal-imperial-institutionally-racist university are often antithetical to anti-racist scholar-activism – that is to say, higher education (HE) institutions are active reproducers of the very inequalities and injustices that scholar-activists seek to challenge. Despite our dissent both inside and outside of the university, our employment and participation within the academy means that we are implicated in those injustices: we are complicit. This may be an uncomfortable 'truth' but it is one with which we must grapple. As Chandra Talpade Mohanty argues, 'the social organization of knowledge in the academy, its structures of inquiry, and discipline-based pedagogies are inevitably connected to larger state and national projects, and engender their own complicities as well as practices of dissent'.[1] With this in mind, in this chapter, we develop Gayatri Chakravorty Spivak's passing reference to the notion of 'constructive complicity'[2] in order to explore how anti-racist scholar-activists navigate their complicity in HE. Ultimately, we ask, given our complicities, why do we stay in the academy? We offer no easy answers in response, but rather seek to capture the messiness of, and contradictions inherent within, anti-racist scholar-activism.

We begin by explicating the idea of constructive complicity.[3] We do so to show the duality of complicity and dissent, and to show how reflexivity is integral to navigating that duality. Drawing on the accounts of participants, we then explore how anti-racist scholar-activism involves working to minimise and offset complicity in (re)producing inequalities. Next, we think about the limits of the university as a site from which we can enact social change, before considering the compromising nature of university employment alongside other forms of wage labour under capitalism. Finally, we examine the uncomfortable 'reality' that those of us engaged in scholar-activism benefit on an individual level from the knowledge and practices of the communities of resistance that we work within.

Moving towards a constructive complicity

Despite their construction as spaces of enlightenment, HE institutions have never been truly open or levelling spaces.[4] Rather, they are active (re)producers of the unequal power relations that make up the matrix of domination and are a key element of the racial State apparatus.[5] By the very virtue of our presence, and regardless of how committed we might be to radical alternatives, those of us working in the academy are implicated in a range of harms that are antithetical to our utopian visions or to, what Robin D.G. Kelley refers to as, our *freedom dreams*.[6] Indeed, although we have argued throughout this book that our university positions enable pockets of possibility for anti-racist scholar-activism, complicities also arise from 'affiliating with aggregates of intellectual organization and power'.[7] For example, although we might champion the principle of free education and organise against economic inequality, our university employment means that we play a role in maintaining and legitimising a neoliberal system that extorts huge fees from students and saddles them with staggering debt.[8] We are implicated too in the commodification of knowledge, the construction of the university as *the* site of knowledge production, and the reproduction of inequalities through the privileging of accreditation. Whilst many of us may be concerned about housing and homelessness, we work in institutions that gentrify the neighbourhoods and displace the communities that we claim to work in service to. Our employers often hold ties to multinational arms companies and military projects that undermine peace.[9] Moreover, although some of us are committed to the abolition of policing, the criminologists among us often find themselves working in departments that hold direct (including financial) ties to police forces, offer a home to former police officers, train future police recruits, and produce research for the benefit of the police.[10]

Despite 'widening participation' initiatives aimed at bringing more people of colour into HE, university policies, academic cultures, and wider agendas enacted through the university (such as Prevent and the hostile environment)[11] all operate to make our institutions hostile spaces for people of colour.[12] Staff and students of colour are forced to contend with a range of issues, including: underrepresentation and stifled progression, an awarding gap,[13] ethnocentric curricula, and everyday racism. Many HE institutions are direct – financial and material – beneficiaries of the transatlantic trafficking and enslavement of African people.[14] We are left in little doubt, therefore, that HE must be a site of anti-racist dissent. As Mohanty urges, we need to take up an anti-racist, anti-imperialist, anti-capitalist, multiply gendered feminist praxis in order to carry out the necessary work of disrupting, rather than reproducing, systems of domination.[15] Yet, even if scholar-activists adopt these dissenting positions, can we ever be free from implication and complicity? It seems clear to us that complicity and dissent operate within scholar-activism simultaneously: we can at the same time be engaged in the dismantling of intersecting structures of oppression and be tainted ourselves – to varying degrees and in different ways – by those very same structures.

Recognition of complicity therefore necessitates meaningful reflexivity. As de Jong insists, given that 'there is no outside of the power structure, one needs to act critically and reflexively from within'.[16] This urges us to be attentive both to how power structures influence our praxis, and the relational aspects of our praxis (our positionality). Of course, it is not only scholar-activists who are concerned with reflexivity,[17] but as should be clear throughout this book, and as we assert in our closing chapter, reflexivity is no doubt a key constitutive element of anti-racist scholar-activism. For those engaged in anti-racist scholar-activism, meaningful reflexivity is integral to the navigation of the dual position of 'insider' and 'outsider' – that is, of 'holding commitments and allegiances that are grounded 'outside' while working in, or engaging with, 'insider' positions,'[18] and crossing the in–out border in ways that are productive of social change, at the same time also looking to break down that very notion of a border. It is this reflexivity that allows us to be 'in but not of' the university (see Chapter 3) and to work in service to anti-racism (see Chapter 2).

Reflexivity can, however, become a proxy for the 'real work'. As Sara Ahmed explains, reflexivity has the potential to foster a 'politics of declaration', in which academics '"admit" to forms of bad practice and the "admission" itself becomes seen as good practice.'[19] This politics of declaration manifests in particularly raced and gendered ways too, whereby white people and men of colour are often rewarded for declarations, whilst Black women's declarations are far less celebrated or are ignored. For anti-racist scholar-activists, recognising complicity to be something more than a declaration of privilege involves shifting away from thinking about self-reflexivity, which inherently centres the Self. Instead, our primary concerns lie at the structural level. This framing can help us to avoid the paralysis that comes with focusing on how we, as individuals, contribute to the (racist, classist, sexist, disablist, heteronormative) status quo. Avoiding this paralysis allows us to strive for what Gayatri Chakravorty Spivak refers to as 'a constructive rather than disabling complicity.'[20] This *constructive complicity* resonates with Sandra Harding's concerns around that passivity of guilt.[21] Guilt – whether that be generated by racialised or other forms of privilege – cannot come in the way of putting our constructive complicity to work in the pursuit of anti-racist social change. Although Spivak's work speaks to the relationship between the researcher and the subaltern Other, she nonetheless teaches us that it is not simply enough to recognise our complicity in structures of oppression within the academy, though this is an important step. We must manipulate those very structures, put power to work, and exploit the (institution's) contradictions for the benefit of anti-racism.[22] This is an advantage, and an obligation, that comes from affiliating with power.[23]

In this context, we conceive of constructive complicity – a concept that has been developed little since Spivak made passing reference to it back in 1999 – as comprising three overlapping steps. Firstly, it refers to the ways in which we can recognise the contradictions and problematics of the space in which we operate (the university). Secondly, it involves a subsequent recognition of how we are wrapped up in (or complicit in) the injustices of the university, and thirdly it involves us working within and against the university to ensure our complicity is constructive – that is, that we are in the university in order to subvert it. This can take on various forms, ranging from the more reactive/defensive – which involves challenging the harms caused by the university directly – and the more proactive/ offensive, in which we leverage resources to do more radical and critical work (that might run counter to the dominant forces in the university) in service to communities of resistance and anti-racism. An example might help to illustrate what we mean here. On the one hand, defensive dissent might involve speaking up and pushing back in meetings – where possible[24] – to challenge the introduction of 'policing studies' degrees in our departments. On a more offensive note, we might access resources to bolster the work of community groups working towards police abolition. These two registers are not mutually exclusive; both can be important and can feed in, in different ways, to our anti-racist resistance.

Ultimately, the pertinent question might be *are we doing more harm than good?* Whilst immeasurability might render this question unanswerable in any concrete sense, and this messiness and contradiction is part of anti-racist scholar-activism, the question can still be generative as we reflect on the extent to which our complicity is constructive. Having laid the theoretical groundwork, we begin in the next section to explore participants' accounts of how they navigate complicity.

Recognising and minimising complicity

Across our conversations, participants reflected on how the university (re)produces unequal power relations and thus how they, by virtue of being a university employee – an affiliate of power, in Mumia Abu-Jamal's terms[25] – are complicit in those processes. Galiev (person of colour, early-career), for example, noted that:

> The university doesn't sit above the social structure inequities, right? So, it's necessarily constituted by them. Therefore, we occupy a position of contradiction. Maybe it's not a fundamental contradiction, but there is a contradiction there to a degree and because of that we are part of a system that necessarily perpetuates the very inequalities that we're trying to ameliorate and mitigate and fundamentally get rid of.

Here, Galiev begins by acknowledging the normative assumption that the university is a progressive and liberal space, a myth that he and other participants are keen to dispel. As Galiev continues in his critique of this construction of the university, he highlights that it does not exist in a vacuum, but rather is both constituted by and constitutive of broader socio-structural inequities. In this sense, those of us engaged in scholar-activism inevitably occupy positions of implication. Although we aim for our work to challenge social inequalities inside and outside of the academy, we operate within a system of HE that (re)produces the very oppressions we seek to address. The aim of our work may be to make racism visible and to pursue an anti-racist agenda but, as an employee of an institution central to the maintenance of white supremacy,[26] we will always be complicit in the re-enactment of white dominance. It is only by radically reimagining and reshaping (perhaps even dismantling) the university that we can move beyond this complicity.

Yet, Galiev also begins to speak to Spivak's notion of constructive complicity when he suggests that the contradiction may not be a fundamental one. In doing so, he implies that the contradictory position of anti-racist scholar-activists should not lead to resignation – it should not immobilise us[27] – but rather, by acknowledging complicity (by seeing it and understanding it), one can take a step towards diminishing it. Indeed, Galiev makes explicit reference to what he sees as the obligation of anti-racist scholar-activists to 'ameliorate and mitigate' structural inequalities. Quite rightly, therefore, he points to how it is not simply enough to recognise complicity. In order to work in service to anti-racism (see Chapter 2), we must minimise and challenge the harms caused by the university, whilst – in the spirit of Chapter 3 – extracting all of the power and resources that we can in service to anti-racism.

Galiev was not the only interviewee to note how recognising both the university's centrality to the maintenance of white supremacy, and one's own complicity within those processes, is fundamental to anti-racist scholar-activist praxis. Reflecting on her own positionality, Malaika (Black, early-career) noted:

> I don't know if I can reconcile and I think it's important not to reconcile some things because this creates some kind of a comfort zone or a stopping, and this inertia can be very dangerous … we're going to have to learn how to survive with these contradictions.

Not only does Malaika acknowledge her complicity but she also points to how her consciousness brings with it discomfort. In this sense, she recognises the productivity of discomfort: its transformative potential.[28] For Malaika, the position of scholar-activists within the university *should* be an uncomfortable one; one that she warns should not be easily reconciled.

It was clear from Malaika's account then that she engages in meaningful reflexivity. She does not simply engage in a politics of declaration,[29] highlighting the problem as a way to quickly move past it. Rather, by suggesting that we should never reconcile our implication, she points to how the constructive acknowledgement of complicity should – like anti-racist scholar-activism – remain an unfinished, open-ended project.

Recognition of this complicity cannot, however, be allowed to immobilise us or as Malaika says, cause 'a stopping' of our scholar-activist work, an 'inertia'. Instead, as Rosa (white, mid-career) explained, complicity and dissent operate simultaneously in the work of those engaged in scholar-activism:

> I believe that we're full of ambivalences. That we are not these kind of pure subjects that either we do truly radical research or we are incorporated into the neoliberal university. I believe that all of us operate in contradictory spaces.

Rosa cautions us against viewing 'radical research' and the 'neoliberal university' as binary opposites, and encourages us instead to recognise our contradictory practices and the contradictions of the university. In doing so, she implies that complicity is not absolute: we are not totally 'incorporated into the neoliberal university'. Indeed, as this book shows, it *is* possible – at least to some extent – to engage in radical anti-racist work within HE, to be 'in but not of' the university.[30] For that reason, we must not allow our concerns over our complicity with the neoliberal-imperial-institutionally-racist university to lead to a passivity of guilt. Nonetheless, Rosa is also clear that none of us, no matter how radical our research, are 'pure subjects'. Put another way, the radical nature of our work does not protect us from the implication that comes from affiliating with power. Engaging in even the most counter-hegemonic praxis does not fully negate the role we play in furthering the hegemonic power structures that underpin and are fed by HE. To this end, it is important that we recognise that complicity is constant and universal; although, there are of course degrees of complicity and, if we remain cognisant, ways of minimising complicity, including by *struggling where we are* (see Chapter 5). The (perhaps unanswerable) question we should ask ourselves once again is, do the benefits we accrue in service to anti-racism outweigh the negative effects of our complicity?

A similar sentiment was shared by Amele (Indian heritage, mid-career), who also reflected on the inescapability of complicity: 'the thing is, living in the world that we live in and the university system out of which we're being produced, you can't be in it and be pure, it's impossible'. Recognising that it is impossible to avoid being tainted both by the university system and the social world around us, Amele questions the construction of the university as a radical space that sits apart from wider society and/or exists to challenge the State. Instead, she insists, the university reproduces the same inequalities found in the broader social world. This argument is reminiscent of the work of Suryia Nayak, who observes that regardless of 'the political positions we adopt, it is an inescapable fact that we are all always implicated'.[31] With this in mind, thinking reflexively about the Self in relation to power structures is not enough. We must act. We must dissent. We can do this by exploiting the contradictions of the system in service to communities of resistance, and anti-racism more broadly.

The contradictory nature of university-based scholar-activist work was something most participants grappled with and, although some had considered leaving the university (and some since have), there was an abiding sense that ultimately there were few better alternatives for enacting social change at the present moment. It was perhaps Zami (person of colour, established academic) who articulated this most clearly:

other than flying off to planet Mars and being an anarchist, what else are you going to do? And that has its drawbacks, actually. You don't reach anyone doing that. So yeah, we're implicated, it's hard, we're reproducing stuff we don't want to and we have to – I mean, I suppose all I can do is

> just be really rigorous in trying to track that layer by layer. But it's a slow, hard, painful process. It's hard to know you're replicating the very thing that squashes you down. It's very difficult.

Like Amele above, Zami first reflects on the impossibility of being absolved from implication in (re)producing inequalities, a sentiment also present in the words of Ali (Arab, early-career), who argued that 'contradiction is sort of the colour of life … it's not only about Higher Education'. As both Zami and Ali intimate, some complicity is inevitable, even for those engaged in anti-racist dissent; but, for Zami, disengaging is not an option. Instead, it is being conscious of, but also acting on, our complicity that is important. It is clear that Zami employs a deeply reflexive approach to 'tracking' her complicity, and here, once again, she shares similarities with Ali, who said that 'what is definitely necessary … which is often lacking in academia and in general, is reflexivity'. As we have argued, Paulo Freire speaks of a dialectic between reflection and action – that is, that both 'reflection and action upon the world' are needed 'in order to transform it'.[32] This is *praxis*, and praxis can enable anti-racist scholar-activists to operationalise constructive complicity: we can move from a recognition of the problematics of the university and our implication in those problematics (reflection), to using our 'in but not of'[33] status in service to anti-racism (action).

What Zami also reflects on is how painful it can be for one to know they are complicit in perpetuating inequality as someone who works hard to challenge oppression through their own work. In doing so, she not only reflects on how HE – across much of the world – (re)produces inequality in the broad sense, but also how it (re)produces the very oppressions that squash *her* down. Zami thus hints at the uncomfortable position she occupies as a Black feminist working to dismantle the matrix of domination, whilst simultaneously perpetuating and legitimising the intersecting racialised, gendered, classed, heteronormative oppressions that push against her and (other) Black women and women of colour within the academy.

Zami's notion of 'flying off to planet Mars' is worth pausing to consider here, too. The need to earn a wage (for our very survival), and the relative economic security of working in the academy (at least for those in more senior and/or less precarious roles), can make radical alternatives seem as far away as planet Mars. We can return to Robin D.G. Kelley. Kelley emphasises the importance of *freedom dreaming* and imagining alternative utopias. Relatedly, Lipsitz observes that 'domination produces resistance, and resistance plants the seeds of a new society in the shell of the old'.[34] Thought of in this way, the 'anarchist Mars' of Zami's rendering might be closer than we think, particularly given the unsustainability of the current model of HE across much of the Global North and of capitalism more broadly, and the unfolding impact the pandemic-induced economic recession might have on HE. Perhaps the seeds of 'anarchist planet Mars' exist in the self-organisation and autonomous efforts to build free universities and community education,[35] or in other spaces where radical alternatives and experimentation might take place. These radical alternatives might include: projects committed to the opening up of knowledge through free online resources;[36] community-based reading groups;[37] anarchist publishing houses; community theatre and art;[38] or – more widely – the threat that squatting poses to neoliberal hegemony, and the building of cooperatives and alternative communities.[39] Part of our constructive complicity might, therefore, involve working outside of the university to help build such projects and the infrastructure to sustain them. Thus, through *freedom dreaming* and/or *utopian pedagogy*,[40] we can begin to see the potential for such spaces to ring the death knell for the university as we currently know it.

In a similar way to how Zami is 'rigorous in trying to track' her own complicity 'layer by layer', Abiola – an African community activist in the final stages of a PhD – also noted the importance of not only recognising one's role in perpetuating oppression, but working actively to minimise complicity:

Now I'm in the university, do I feel tainted by it? There's an element of that. But that's like a baseline thing. I live in a capitalist society. I live in a patriarchal society. I'm an anti-capitalist and I am, for want of a better word, a womanist. So, I'm against the patriarchy, I'm against capitalism. But if I want to eat in a capitalist society, I have to pay in cash … So, some level of compromise is inevitable, but that doesn't put me off. So, for me, the question isn't can I avoid being tainted by this corruption? It's what do I do, knowing that this corruption exists to mitigate the damage? Am I making things better or am I making things worse? Now, ideally, of course, I'd just leave it. But at the same time, if I am able to understand it, to be able to utilise it [position in the university] and actually weaponise it in favour of the interests that I believe in, I would. I would. So, I don't lose sleep over that.

Here, Abiola shifts the emphasis from the 'tainting' effects of the university to those of broader capitalist and patriarchal forces. For him, the scholar-activist's implication in these structures is inevitable and thus the question should not be *Are we complicit?* Rather, it ought to be: *Given that we are complicit in affiliating with power, how can we exploit that complicity for the benefit of communities of resistance and in pursuit of anti-racism?* Or, more simply, as he puts it, how do we make sure we are 'making things better' rather than 'making things worse'. Recognising the need to earn a wage prevents him from leaving academia, he hints at a notion discussed in Chapter 4 – that is, one well-versed in the bureaucratic processes and 'legitimate language'[41] of the university, and cognisant of its values and agendas, may use those tools against the university. One can 'weaponise in favour of the interests that [they] believe in', or in service to anti-racism. Whilst Audre Lorde may be right – the master's tools will never dismantle the master's house – intimate knowledge of how institutions oppress, perhaps through lived experience, can form part of the broader arsenal of those engaged in anti-racist scholar-activist work.[42] As Abiola indicates, this approach to damage mitigation must, however, extend beyond the university setting. Indeed, aware of the impossibility of non-complicity in an unequal society, a key concern of those engaged in (scholar-)activism must therefore be how we can deploy the pockets of possibility presented to us as university employees in service to anti-racism.

Despite acknowledging that the university and university-based scholar-activists are deeply implicated within structures of unequal power, many participants did return to the notion that the university holds a range of opportunities for anti-racist scholar-activism: the pockets of possibility that we have discussed throughout the book. As Dillon put it: 'I still think the university is something to be cherished, I still think it's something we need to fight for, but … it's becoming increasingly compromised.' Although clearly of the opinion that the university still holds some value for anti-racist scholar-activism, what Dillon begins to do here is reflect on its limits. If we recognise that our institutions are complicit in upholding unequal power relations within wider society – and by association, we too are complicit, even if we attempt to use the complicity in a constructive manner – it brings us to a place in which we are cognisant of the limits of the university. This recognition was key for those that we spoke to.

Recognising the limits of the university

Neville (white, mid-career), like many of our participants, understood the university to be a space that is limited in the social change it can, or is willing, to facilitate:

> I think if you're looking at where social change is going to come from, I don't think it's really higher education. I think it's movements outside of university, really. So, for me, I feel like it's definitely not sufficient just to research and write and teach about society. I feel like it's my duty as a human being to be involved in activism as well, even if it's not related to my research.

It is clear that Neville's criticality of HE has shaped his praxis as a scholar-activist, leading him to look beyond the academy – and sometimes even his own research – to effect change. As Neville points out, despite the importance of *struggling where you are* (see Chapter 5), the university is not the centre of the struggle: it is not the only, or for many even the main, site of resistance. Thinking back to Zami's notion of 'anarchism on Mars', Neville's account perhaps reiterates the case for building radical educational alternatives outside of the institution. Notwithstanding his earlier comments about the value of teaching (see Chapter 5), he does not believe it is simply enough to engage in teaching and writing about the social world: the 'traditional' work of the academic. In this sense, and with echoes of the tenets of anti-racist scholar-activism that we set out in the Introduction, Neville rejects the notion that the academic should remain detached, objective, and apolitical. In fact, reminiscent of several accounts in Chapter 2, he not only views activism as part of his role as an academic but as his 'duty as a human being'. He reflects the Freirean notion that we each have the right and the *duty* to change the world.[43] Perhaps then, we might conceive of constructive complicity as a recognition of the limits of the university and a subsequent commitment to operating outside of it to bolster anti-racist resistance.

The view that the academy holds limited potential for transformative change was also shared – more forcefully, this time – by Dez, an established Black professor:

> For me, if we are choosing to be in the institution, then the one thing we need to be very, very clear about is that the institution will never change because of us alone … What I'm saying is that the project is bigger than academia. The project is bigger than an academic … Plenty of people go around talking as if they're going to lead a revolution, but not from the academy, I'm sorry!

Dez points to how the project of social change extends far beyond academia – that is to say, the changes sought under an anti-racist agenda are far greater than can be achieved by academics alone, even those engaged in dissenting and/or scholar-activist work. Indeed, his reference to 'us alone' implies that – as we argued in Chapter 2 – those engaged in scholar-activism must work within wider *communities of resistance* in order to achieve social change. We must become part of what Mouffe calls 'a people' that form 'a collective will', one that 'results from the mobilization of common affects in defence of equality and social justice'.[44] At the same time, Dez disavows the academic as the leader of the 'revolution',[45] troubling the power structures and classed relationalities that too often position academics as more knowledgeable than other activists.

Dez's reflections may also be taken as a reminder, once again, that the university does not exist in a vacuum. It is itself part of a 'project [that] is bigger'. The university's capacity for transformative change will always be curtailed because it is itself woven into the very fabric of a deeply inequitable social structure. It is constituted by and constitutive of white supremacy.[46] We might, therefore, conceptualise 'the project' to which Dez refers in two ways. On the one hand, we can imagine 'the project' as one that we are involved in: the anti-racist project. On the other hand, however, we should not lose sight of the university's own project – that is, its contribution to the project of white supremacist capitalist patriarchy. In this sense, Dez reminds us that scholar-activism involves recognition of the limits of one's own location – that is, the university. In a similar way, and reflective of how scholar-activism is not experienced by all in the same way, we might also think about the particular raced, gendered, or classed limits of our own position. This recognition helps us to remain cognisant of how our dissent – and thus mitigation of complicity – can be most effective.

Participants also reflected on the slow and unresponsive nature of universities. Even though they often found ways to be strategic in how they use the university system to work in service to anti-racism – for example, by engaging in *reparative theft* (see Chapter 3) – Zami reflected on how slow university processes can be oppositional to the more urgent work of scholar-activists:

I do most of my work under the radar because otherwise you're not going to be able to be as responsive as you want to a community group. In other words, community groups aren't going to wait nine months, ten months, or two years whilst you get a bit of bureaucracy through. But you learn to be strategic, you learn how to package stuff. You learn how to mix the language of emancipation with the bureaucratic language. But there'll always be a compromise.

Here, Zami nods to how the different pace at which the university operates can act as a barrier to the urgency with which she must respond to the needs of community groups. The need to be responsive was noted time and time again by participants. Of course, there is much to be said too about the merits of 'slow academia',[47] 'slow scholarship',[48] and 'slow knowledge',[49] and perhaps what is most important is not whether we engage in slow or urgent research as scholar-activists but that it is anti-racist movements and not universities that set the pace. Given the importance Zami places on being responsive, and the university's unwillingness to accommodate urgent research agendas,[50] she must, like Harney and Moten's fugitive,[51] conduct 'most of [her] work under the radar'. This approach was enabling for Zami and for others, and suggests that there are pockets within the system, in spite of itself, where radical work can be done. Nevertheless, there are also a set of challenges that emerge from working under the radar that can increase precarity, limit capacity for career progression, and limit the time available for such work. So, whilst such clandestine work can be productive (and can, as in Zami's case, be the only way to serve the needs of communities of resistance),[52] there is also a larger task of legitimising such work within the academy or challenging the pace and rhythm of the institution,[53] which is also a task of reimagining the university with anti-racist scholar-activism at its heart.

Galiev also commented on the importance of not only reflecting on the university's limits but then taking action – or dissenting – to reshape institutions in light of those limits:

there are limits to what we do and the kinds of interventions that we make. Then you could just say, 'Well, fuck it then. What's the point of engaging?' This is where I think that we can draw from Angela Davis' analysis when she talks about the prison-industrial complex, and about non-reformist reforms. What does an intervention look like that isn't just legitimating the system, but is trying to fundamentally change it?

Like Zami's earlier reflections on 'anarchism on Mars', Galiev suggests that rather than disengaging from the academy because of its limitations, there is value in remaining inside it in order to radically change it. Pointing to the distinction between 'reformist reforms' and 'non-reformist reforms',[54] Galiev encourages us not simply to pursue reforms within the existing framework of HE, but rather to imagine a radically different alternative. At the same time we must, as Angela Y. Davis urges, strive towards abolitionist ends.[55] In this context we must ensure that, as far as possible, any reforms we advocate do not legitimise the matrix of domination that both underpins and is fed by the academy. Instead, we should endeavour to use our dissenting praxes to dismantle the unequal university and rebuild it in our utopian vision, and/or develop and extend radical alternatives to the university. Of course, reflective of the interconnectedness of the unequal university and the unequal society, we must look beyond the compromised and compromising nature of HE to also consider how *all* wage labour (in a capitalist and structurally unequal system) makes anti-racist scholar-activists complicit in affiliating with power.

All wage labour is compromised

Several interviewees spoke about how the university is not unique in engendering complicity, but rather how related work outside of academia is likewise compromised. Alison (white, mid-career), for example, said:

If you want to keep doing research then maybe go with the more risky consultancy type work. But again, the people that can afford to contract research generally tend to be those who are attached to more normative or powerful agendas.

Alison points to how the most immediately related alternatives to working in a university can also be compromised. Organisations that can afford consultancy are usually those that benefit from the status quo. It follows then that such organisations are generally more interested in perpetuating, rather than challenging, hegemonic ideas and practices. As Alison's account indicates, there are perhaps no easy solutions, or magic bullets, for avoiding complicity. Consultancy research can be as implicating as research carried out within the university, but may not offer the same opportunities; for example, the opportunities offered through teaching (see Chapter 5), access to resources (see Chapter 3), or (relative) job security, which Alison intimates through her description of such alternatives as 'risky'. Indeed, although short-term and temporary contracts are prevalent within the HE sector,[56] it remains for many people a more stable form of employment relative to much research work outside of the university. As Aaliyah explained, whilst the prospect of becoming an 'independent scholar-activist' is an appealing one, this is difficult when cast against 'the reality of coming from a working-class background' and needing the 'stability' that comes with 'a stable wage'.

Building upon Alison's argument about related forms of labour, some participants, such as Claudia (white, mid-career), reflected on the importance of recognising *all* wage labour as compromised, making us complicit in upholding racial capitalism and the injustices we seek to work against:

> There isn't anything pure, because if I think about what I can do that would be socially engaged and more progressive or more transformative than academia, it's pretty hard to think of anything that's not going to compromise that. Like, NGOs are usually compromised. If you work in a school, you can really make a difference in kids' lives, but they are reproducing loads of stratification and particular social relations. So, I think treating it like a job and recognising it as wage labour is quite important.

Claudia offers a useful reminder that the university should not be set apart from wage labour more broadly. Whilst there is value to be drawn from this perspective, we also want to complicate it slightly by suggesting that although 'there isn't anything pure', there are differences in manifestations and degrees of complicity. Put crudely, it is hard to make a case that the baker is as complicit in injustice as the arms dealer. Indeed, this differentiation is implied in Claudia's suggestion that other roles would compromise the capacity for social transformation that derives from her role in academia – that is to say, although she recognises that all wage labour is compromised under capitalism, Claudia operates from the academy based on a 'cost–benefit' analysis of the opportunities it enables for social justice versus complicity in the harms caused. A similar calculation, including a consideration of job security, can be observed in Alison's account above. An awareness of these differences in manifestation and degrees of complicity encourages an attentiveness to where we each sit within such calculations, or along the hypothetical spectrum of the baker and the arms dealer. Such reflexive attentiveness – embodied in our earlier question of whether we are doing more harm than good – can leave us open to the possibilities that we might be able to operate more effectively from outside of the academy.

Claudia's framing of working in the university as simply one of many possible forms of wage labour is a generative one. It points to a critical detachment from the university and a recognition of how activism necessarily extends beyond one's employed work. It also implies that more radical work may take place in the spaces outside of wage labour generally, and outside of the university specifically. Indeed, for Claudia, her university employment resources the 'real work': her activism. The more imaginative amongst us may be able to envisage radical alternatives to university-based scholar-activism that can still sustain us economically – in fact, some of our participants have since left the academy – and those of us that cannot imagine, might look to nurture and cultivate such an imagination. To do so, we might need to look to activism outside of wage labour, away from *Bullshit Jobs*,[57] in order to engage in far less compromised and compromising work than that of our current employment. As we noted in relation to Neville's emphasis on operating outside of the institution, such work allows us to begin to build the alternatives that can offer sites of hope beyond what is commonly imaginable. This is the task of *freedom dreaming*,[58] or realising 'anarchism on Mars' in Zami's earlier words, that is part of offsetting our complicity in the harms of the university. In this regard, Claudia's framing is helpful in ensuring our complicity is constructive – that is, that we recognise the limits of the university and wage labour more broadly, and engage in work outside of those structures. It also leaves scope, however, for us to recognise the (relative) benefits and resources that derive from our university employment, which we can put to work in service to communities of resistance.

Alex (mixed-race, mid-career) shared Claudia's understanding of the compromised nature of all work by also suggesting that other forms of wage labour reproduce the structural inequalities she tries to redress:

> Whatever field you go into, in a capitalist world, it's going to be compromised. If I was working as a Legal Aid lawyer, I would also be deeply frustrated and I would be perpetuating many of the major structural inequalities that I would be attempting to also fight, the same with everything else that I can think of that I could do. Within the constraints of having to have a salaried job in a capitalist economy, academia at least gives me the freedom to be in the classroom and to design my own courses, to a large extent, and to have freedom with what I write. Then the other thing is that because our working conditions are quite flexible, I do have time to do activism because I don't have to be in an office from eight to six or whatever. If I do need to take three or four days off to write a blog, I can do it, and if I need to go to a protest at four in the afternoon on a Wednesday, I can do it, whereas [other] jobs, I think, don't give you that flexibility.

As Alex suggests, anti-racist scholar-activists are implicated in the inequalities we seek to fight, by virtue of having to live – to exist – within a capitalist system. As university employees, we are implicated, for example, by working in and drawing a wage from institutions that burden students with debt (a difficult contradiction with which we must tarry).[59] It is in this context that Alex reflects on how she can work within 'the constraints of having to have a salaried job in a capitalist economy' and considers the academy to offer some advantages – in terms of pedagogic opportunities (see Chapter 5) and flexible working (albeit a privilege not afforded to everyone within HE) – that can enable scholar-activism. The reflexive cost-benefit calculations that we saw in Claudia and Alison's accounts are evident in Alex's reflections too. We might understand constructive complicity then to involve us seeking to (partially) mitigate, offset, and exploit complicity by seizing the privileges afforded to us through our university employment for the benefit of anti-racist movements. We want to re-emphasise how important freedom dreaming can be here. Whilst some of our arguments could be read as suggesting that the university is simply viable because it is less bad than other bad options, freedom dreaming encourages us to continue to imagine possibilities beyond what is right in front of us (that is, those options that might exist on *anarchist planet mars* or, in embryonic form, within resistance movements).

Mutual benefit

Part of pursuing a constructive rather than immobilising complicity involves a repudiation of the passivity of guilt, which in turn necessitates that scholar-activists become accustomed to the uncomfortable realities of their affiliation with power. A key source of discomfort for some participants lay in the benefit one accrues from working within communities of resistance. This uncomfortable 'truth' was one that Okoye (Black, early-career), for example, reflected on:

there's always going to be some sort of mutual benefit. You're not working passively with the community, there's always got to be something in it for both of you.

Although it is often assumed (via a romanticised conception) that activism is characterised by altruism, some mutual benefit or self-interest – albeit, when it is not a key motivator – can be an important organising tool.[60] One may be motivated to pursue social change, for example, because of lived experience; relationships with others; by a desire to live up to how one views oneself or believes others to view them; and/or because of the relationship between one's organising and one's role as an academic. The framing of activism as entirely self-sacrificing can, therefore, be deeply problematic in many respects, not least because its unrealisability can lead to inertia, the passivity of guilt to which de Jong refers.[61] Self-interest, and a love for and solidarity with others, are not mutually exclusive. Indeed, although we have suggested that the primary goal of those engaged in anti-racist scholar-activism is not the pursuit of their own academic careers, the careers of some individuals – particularly those occupying positions of structural advantage – may nonetheless benefit from their engagement within communities outside of the academy. In the UK context (though with similarities elsewhere), this may be the case, particularly, in the context of the university's agendas around 'Impact', 'social responsibility', and 'public engagement'. As mentioned earlier, some of our participants have in fact won awards from their institutions for their 'Impact',[62] which makes clear that whilst scholar-activist understandings of impact are fundamentally different to notions of REF Impact (see Introduction), interests can at times converge. This might mean that scholar-activism is merely 'accommodated within the institutional imperative of the marketized university',[63] but it does also reflect contradictions in the system that anti-racist scholar-activists can exploit in pursuit of constructive complicities.

Discomfort with the mutuality of benefit was felt acutely by Barry (person of colour, early career) who asked: 'If I produce a book, there might be money, there's stuff like that which is like how do you – what do you do about that?' This question reflects Barry's sense of discomfort that he might benefit financially from authoring a book based on the views and experiences of the people he has met, spent time with, built friendships with, and interviewed as part of his research. This is a 'reality' of most academic publications: we benefit financially or in other ways – such as via career progression or in building our reputation – by reproducing the voices of, or writing about issues that affect, others. Of course, the benefits that individual academics accrue are nothing compared to the big business of academic publishing, which in large part is built on the shoulders of the (often) free labour of academics. Yet nonetheless, financial benefit may be a particularly discomforting notion for scholar-activists who are often reproducing the voices of marginalised people: people who may themselves be in financially challenging situations, with precarious immigration status, or systematically denied a platform from which to voice their own perspectives. That Barry grapples with this issue points to a theme that we flagged in the Introduction, and that has since run throughout this book – that is, that reflexivity is, and should be, common practice amongst those engaged in anti-racist scholar-activism. This reflexivity does not end at the point of 'declaration'[64] – an acknowledgement of complicity is not enough – but rather, our participants *act* on their discomfort by putting it to work in service to communities of resistance.

Barry's unease resonates with us strongly. Whilst donating our book royalties to the *Northern Police Monitoring Project*[65] means that we will not personally benefit financially from this book (at least not in the immediate sense), Barry's concerns run deeper than a point about book royalties, and so do ours. Indeed, the irony of writing a book about anti-racist activism, most likely read by a largely academic audience, has not passed us by. Although our intention is to offer a fervent critique of the hegemonic traditions within HE, and to encourage academics to take up anti-racist dissenting positions that operate within and beyond the bounds of the academy, the book will still be subject to many of the processes that we critique within it. It will, for example, still likely be entered into the REF where no doubt it will be judged within the context of the *institutional backlash* documented in Chapter 4 – that is, it will likely be seen as not objective enough, or too political. But that is not what we are uncomfortable about. We are uncomfortable that our academic profiles may grow as a consequence of this book; certainly, our publication list will. In turn, the book might contribute to a future promotion or a new appointment. On the other hand, if we were struggling from elsewhere, without the university's vested interest, it would be very difficult for us to carve out the time to produce such work. It is clear that we are operating from a position of contradiction, and although that position is discomforting, we should not shy away from such discomfort, as Malaika urged earlier in this chapter. Nor should we let the 'academic treadmill' stymie our freedom dreaming any further.

Conclusion

In this chapter, we have explored the uncomfortable 'truth' that our proximity to power, as university employees, makes us complicit in reproducing and legitimising the very systems of domination we work against as anti-racist scholar-activists. At the beginning of the chapter, we posed the question: given our complicities, why do we stay in the academy? Rather than offer a simple answer, which would belie the complexities and heterogeneities of anti-racist scholar-activism, we have pointed to the messy contradictions inherent within such praxes. In doing so, we have extended Spivak's notion of constructive complicity[66] in order to show that the university is a limited space from which to resist, but that it nonetheless presents pockets of possibility that anti-racist scholar-activists can exploit for the benefit of communities of resistance. This is the duality of complicity and dissent to which Chandra Talpade Mohanty refers.[67] The navigation of this duality requires meaningful reflexivity: it is not simply enough to recognise the problematics of HE and one's implication in them, or in Ahmed's terms, to declare our complicity as a means of quickly moving past it.[68] Instead, anti-racist scholar-activism puts our complicity *to work* in service to anti-racism.

University employment is of course not unique in engendering complicities. As our participants noted, all wage labour is compromised under capitalism, and as the imprisoned former Black Panther Mumia Abu-Jamal's puts it, 'even radical intellectuals must eat; and to eat means to affiliate with aggregates of intellectual organization and power'.[69] We are clear, though, that there are differences in manifestations and degrees of complicity. This recognition takes us to a place in which we must reflect on whether we are doing more harm than good as university-based scholar-activists. For most of our participants (three have since left academia), their cost-benefit analysis leads them to remain in the academy; although, their 'in but not of' status enables them to maintain a critical detachment that sets the stage for freedom dreaming, or at least has the potential to do so. If we allow ourselves to *freedom dream*,[70] we quickly realise that the 'anarchist Mars' to which Zami refers may be closer than we think and, as such, we might need to leave the university to develop existing, and build new, radical anti-racist alternatives.

A manifesto for anti-racist scholar-activism

Whilst this book has shown that there is no *one* way to engage in anti-racist scholar-activism, we have highlighted a number of themes that might be understood as broad, guiding principles. These ideas build on the tenets we set out in the Introduction as informing our vision of anti-racist scholar-activism, and they also inform our own praxes. More importantly, though, they are recurrent across the accounts of participants. In some ways, this chapter shares similarities with a traditional conclusion, in that it offers a recapitulation and distillation of the key arguments we make in the book. Yet in other ways we depart with convention and, instead, the chapter assumes the guise of a ten-point manifesto. We adopt this form to invoke a spirit that is explicitly political, and emblematic of a desire to see and feed into anti-racist social change. We hope that the ten points are broad enough so as not to be too reductive to reflect the messy and contradictory praxes we have described in the preceding chapters. Some of the points we offer emerge particularly from a specific chapter; others are more cross-cutting, emerging in various sections across the chapters. Others still manifest more as undercurrents, popping up explicitly only on occasion, but always lying just beneath the surface of our arguments.

Like the book at large, this manifesto should not be read as definitive or static; instead, we offer it as a resource to be adapted, contested, and developed. Our hope is that it can serve as a primer for thinking about, and working towards, anti-racist scholar-activism. We hope too that these ideas will be shared and discussed widely, both inside and outside of the academy. This manifesto is best read, therefore, as a *live* text, a springboard for *collective* reflection, conversation, and praxes. We would like to see its margins filled with 'intelligent graffiti'.[1] Some of the principles we outline will resonate with some readers more than others, some are not unique to scholar-activism but crosscut with other approaches within academia, and some will be practised by some readers more than others. Regardless, we hope this manifesto distils some of the wisdom of those with whom we spoke as part of this research project.

1 A critical understanding of (anti-)racism

Fundamental to the praxis of anti-racist scholar-activism must lie a critical understanding of racism. It seems obvious that we should comprehensively understand that which we seek to fight. After all, as the early proponent of Critical Race Theory Derrick Bell argues, 'we can only delegitimate it if we can accurately pinpoint it'.[2] Despite its apparent obviousness, this is a vital point. In the words of Ruth Wilson Gilmore, we 'have to figure out what makes oppressive and liberatory structures work and what makes them fall apart'.[3] It is from a critical understanding of racism that we begin to develop our perspectives on, and approaches to, anti-racism.[4] Undoubtedly, there are variances in understandings of racism between our participants, and among anti-racist scholars and activists more broadly. It is evident too that our understandings are always developing, but there are some key elements to a critical understanding of racism that should not be compromised within anti-racist scholar-activism.

Following the more radical tradition of anti-racism we outlined in the Introduction, racism has to be understood as an institutional, structural, systemic, and historically rooted phenomenon. It is State-driven, but also extends beyond any one State. It is global. For the anti-racist, to understand it as such is to grapple with the enormity of the task at hand. Popular liberal understandings construct racism (where it is recognised to exist at all) as something that is experienced only at the interpersonal level, as the fault of individual racists and as confined to a particular event.[5] Such misdiagnoses are shown to be ineffective and lead to misguided interventions that tackle symptoms but not causes.

There is an urgent need to reach beyond liberal analyses to more radical understandings of racism. It was in this regard that Sivanandan noted the important distinction between 'the racism that discriminates and the racism that kills'.[6] It was, by and large, the latter that provided an organising principle for his work and continues to inform the praxes of many anti-racist scholar-activists today. Indeed, liberal misunderstandings of racism provide inadequate foundations for building anti-racist responses. As Gargi Bhattacharyya states:

> as long as we think that racism happens between you and me – and it's because I didn't know enough about what you like to eat for your dinner, and what your mum liked to wear at home – our responses to racism can't go much beyond, 'well can I just train you about what I like to eat for dinner, or can I train you to be nicer'. Now all of that is a liberal capture of something that is much more entrenched and endemic in the capitalist societies we've seen so far, and [it] could not be addressed like that.[7]

Whilst individual racial prejudice may provide a way into thinking about racism, we must, as we develop more critical understandings, move beyond micro-level analyses. We must grasp at the root.[8]

It is also necessary to recognise that racism interlocks with other systems of oppression, as part of what Patricia Hill Collins refers to as a matrix of domination.[9] Understood in this way, racism is recognised to be intimately tied to capitalism, as well as heteropatriarchy and ableism. Understanding that racism is mediated by, and mediating of, other systems of oppression reveals that racism cannot be tackled without reckoning simultaneously with these other systems. Recognising this enables us to consider how some within the 'ranks of the disenfranchised'[10] are rendered more vulnerable than others and to think carefully about the approaches we adopt to tackling oppression. Moreover, this critical framing of racism sees us work from an understanding that anti-racist scholar-activism must also involve anti-capitalist, anti-imperialist, anti-ableist, multiply gendered feminist praxis.[11] This takes us to a place where solidarity sits at the centre of our anti-racist scholar-activism. Such solidarity is premised on cognisance of the contextualised and contextually specific ways in which racism can manifest. Moreover, it can and should enable us to recognise the importance of a plurality of anti-racist praxes. The understanding we are describing here is one that is forged through critical engagement with theory, with history, and through reflexive praxes alongside *communities of resistance*.[12]

2 An expansive understanding of (scholar-)activism

Developing an expansive understanding of what constitutes activism and, therefore, scholar-activism, is a vital task. We began this project with much narrower ideas about what 'activism' and 'scholar-activism' entail than we have now. Whilst our initial conceptions were shaped by popular imaginaries of 'idealised' forms of activism, the accounts of participants included in this book implore us to look beyond more masculine and confrontational 'frontline' styles.[13] Thus, we want to nurture an appreciation of the full range of approaches people take to their scholar-activism and to recognise some of the less visible work that can be both effective and sustainable, even if less celebrated.

Although this book has focused on the experiences and perspectives of anti-racist scholar-activists working in universities, it bears repeating that not all scholar-activism is university-based. There are many scholar-activists operating outside of the academy, and their contributions to knowledge and resistance should be recognised and valued highly. That the work of Ambalavaner Sivanandan – who never worked in a university – underpins much of this book, underlines the necessity of seeing scholar-activism as not confined to university spaces. Understanding this not only enables us to appreciate the organic forms of knowledge that develop outside of universities but it also helps us to see how the neoliberal-imperial-institutionally-racist university can impede more radical research, particularly that which responds to the needs of marginalised communities.[14] Recognising that scholar-activism is not the preserve of university-based academics, and that the most radical and urgent thought will likely come from outside of the ivory tower, is part of the urgent task of decentring the university as *the* site of knowledge production;[15] a task for which there is much at stake.

An expansive definition of anti-racist scholar-activism also encourages us to be attentive to the ways in which scholar-activism overlaps with a range of other practices including public intellectualism, critical pedagogy, and engaged and applied approaches to research. Whilst others have drawn distinctions between activist-scholars and scholar-activists,[16] we have used the term scholar-activist throughout this book in its broad sense, to encompass the different approaches and identities of our participants; the varying emphasis they place on the constituent parts of scholar-activism; and ultimately, to demonstrate the heterogeneous nature of scholar-activist praxes. In this sense, although we do not intend the 'scholar' in scholar-activism to have any prominence over the 'activism', we have emphasised the importance of meticulous scholarship and (as discussed in the previous principle) a critical understanding of the problem(s). Although some participants felt that the raced, classed, and elite nature of the term 'scholar' made it ill-fitting and others noted how they are often constructed within the academy as unscholarly – with the explicitly political nature of their work framed as biased and 'anti-intellectual' – participants placed significant emphasis on the value of intellectual thought and academic rigour. This is particularly pertinent for our discussion of scholar-activism, but it also challenges the construction of activism (more generally) as being bereft of theory and careful consideration – a construction that massively belies the reality.[17] In the words of the Black Power activist Kwame Ture, 'one must study … you can't be a revolutionary off the top of your head'.[18]

3 Doing the doing, walking the walk

Several participants lamented how academics talk the talk of scholar-activism, without walking the walk. This point might seem to be in tension with our call above for a more expansive definition of scholar-activism, but this is a productive tension: a necessary counterbalance. Whilst more expansive understandings of what constitutes scholar-activism are welcome and necessary, it is also vital that we demand forms of anti-racist scholar-activism that move beyond mere performance to recognise that 'oppositional work is talk-plus-walk'.[19] In a context where terminologies are routinely hollowed of their radical potential – as we have seen with 'decolonisation'[20] – there is a need to be attentive to the danger that scholar-activism suffers the same fate, if it has not already. Despite the many challenges that anti-racist scholar-activists face by virtue of their praxes – articulated as backlash in Chapter 4 – it is clear that there is some currency in the scholar-activist identity. This currency makes the identity susceptible to institutional co-optation and easy to overclaim which, in turn, dilutes its meaning and utility. In the UK, this is apparent in the limited and superficial overlap between scholar-activism and institutionalised notions of 'Impact'. As Aziz Choudry reminds us, neoliberal institutional cultures mean many working within the university are more likely to *perform* public engagement and embeddedness, rather than actually do the time-consuming and labour-intensive work of scholar-activism.[21] After all, it is typically only the performance that is needed to reap the institutional rewards.

In this context, one useful step is to insist on thinking more of scholar-activism as praxis: something that one *does*, rather than something that one is (in any fixed sense). By placing the emphasis on *doing*, scholar-activism can be understood as always incomplete. It is an unfinished project, something to which we must strive. Like the pursuit of freedom, scholar-activism is – and should be – *a constant struggle*.[22] If scholar-activism is conceived of as walking the walk, then the walk is unfinished. This is not to contend that there is no utility in identifying as a scholar-activist or that identifying as a scholar-activist necessarily forecloses the possibility of seeing this work as always ongoing. Rather, if we understand our existence as always incomplete,[23] then it remains possible to identify as a scholar-activist whilst also recognising this as constituting an ongoing process – that is to say, 'to do' and 'to be' are not necessarily at odds. Put another way, even if we understand a scholar-activist identification to be part of who we are, we can understand our existence as something fluid and forged through praxis: we are always engaged in a process of *becoming*.

Focusing on praxis also enables us to appreciate the work of those that are reluctant to embrace a scholar-activist identity or those who identify in another way, perhaps – and without wanting to completely erase the different inflections of these terms[24] – as an activist-scholar; an academic activist; an activist academic; an intellectual activist; a subversive intellectual; or as a troublemaker. It also enables an appreciation of those that *walk the walk* but outright reject the imposition of such labels. What is important here is not semantic differences but the *doing*. Ultimately, focusing on the doing implores us to decentre ourselves as individuals, in favour of the broader project of anti-racism.

4 Working in service

In Chapter 2, we introduced the idea of working in service to communities of resistance, and to anti-racism more broadly – although, it is an idea that runs throughout the book. Sivanandan powerfully and repeatedly used the servicing metaphor in relation to anti-racist resistance (or Black

Liberation) during his transformation of the radical think tank, the Institute of Race Relations.[25] His work influenced and inspired many of our participants, with some drawing explicitly on his thinking around working in service. This notion of service is apparent elsewhere, too. Steven Osuna, for example, traces it through the *Black Radical* tradition, and specifically the works of Walter Rodney, Frantz Fanon, Cedric Robinson, and Amílcar Cabral.[26] Patricia Hill Collins has expressed that the notion of working in service is foundational to what she refers to as intellectual activism,[27] and the phraseology is taken up by many scholar-activists in their writing and praxis.[28]

The crux of the matter lies in the question of to whom or to what we are in service. Although the dominance of neoliberal technologies of higher education (HE) threaten to see academics work in service to performance metrics (such as the Research Excellent Framework (REF) in the UK), a scholar-activist orientation highlights the importance of breaking with this norm. Anti-racist scholar-activism involves working within (formal and informal) anti-racist groups in service to the dispossessed – that is, working in service as *a duty* to those who bear the brunt of racism's effects, and to those who seek to resist racism and its intersections with other systems of oppression. Thus, anti-racist scholar-activism invokes a radical reorientation that is forged collectively through study,[29] praxis, reflection, and involvement within communities of resistance. To borrow from Harney and Moten, crucially, this positions anti-racist scholar-activists as being 'in but not of' the university.[30] It also opens us up to the possibilities of needing – through a Black feminist *practice of refusal*[31] or through *freedom dreaming*[32] of something better – to leave the university. The in service orientation, therefore, provides an anchoring that informs all aspects of our anti-racist scholar-activist praxes.

A commitment to working in service should not impair criticality or blunt reflexivity. Whilst it is necessary to subvert logics that elevate academics over community groups and organisers, we must also avoid positioning activist and community groups as immune to or above questioning. Like many of our participants, our own experiences tell us that community groups are imperfect, as we all are. Thus, we must not work impetuously and unquestioningly in service to groups that are, quite simply, getting it wrong. In this regard, we would suggest that it is more useful to conceive of ourselves as working in service to social justice and anti-racism (understood through principle 1), rather than to particular anti-racist organisations. This is vital given the range of institutions and organisations that perpetuate racism, under the cover of hollow anti-racist declarations. Through our service to anti-racism, we will of course, and necessarily, work within – and in service to – *communities of resistance*.

5 'Being there': embeddedness in communities of resistance

Clarke, Chadwick and Williams state that *being there* is a key principle for 'critical social research as a site of resistance'.[33] On the one hand, participants emphasised the importance of being there and, on the other, the undervalued nature of such work within the neoliberal academy. Being there – as we have articulated it in this book – involves moving beyond superficial and purely instrumental interactions with individuals, groups, and communities outside of the academy to building meaningful relationships. As others have written, this can manifest in a range of ways, from being a shoulder to cry on, to stacking chairs at or buying pizza for community meetings.[34] It is about *bearing witness*[35] to injustices and the pursuit of justice. It needs to be recurring and meaningful – which is to say, being there as a form of meaningful engagement is about something more than mere proximity. As our participants attest, it is about much more than what is required to fulfil the hollow performance required for the REF. In sum, being there is the unglamorous and often unseen work that will not be institutionally rewarded. This work requires a degree of humility that recognises our academic 'expertise' is not always what is needed or what we are best placed to provide to communities of resistance.

Through being there, anti-racist scholar-activists can strive to be embedded in communities of resistance, and it is from this embeddedness that research needs can be identified. In this sense, we should resist academic conventions that stipulate that research should derive from and work to fill 'gaps in the literature', and the attempts by funders to influence our research priorities. Whilst research may serve a purpose in our service to anti-racism, we can also recognise the need to look beyond research and to consider forms of praxis – protest, organising, solidarity-building, for example – that our university training does not prepare us for. Scholar-activism, therefore, requires us to understand that we need to 'study' much more than the academy offers.[36] This study can occur through our embeddedness in communities of resistance or, in Harney and Moten's terms, in *The Undercommons*.[37]

Additionally, and vitally, embeddedness enables us to derive a sense of accountability and a grounding that sees us emulate something akin to Walter Rodney's *guerrilla intellectual*.[38] Although the task of being there might at first glance seem simple, the challenges involved in being there should not be underestimated since, in the neoliberal context of HE, it engenders a battle over time. Against a backdrop in which workload pressures are increasing – thereby making engaged and activist work more difficult to squeeze in – using our time to build meaningful relationships and embed ourselves in communities of resistance involves swimming against the neoliberal tide.

6 Reparative theft

Harney and Moten contend that, in the modern university, the task of the subversive intellectual (or anti-racist scholar-activist, in our terms) is to 'sneak into the university and steal what one can': the 'only possible relationship to the university today is a criminal one'.[39] Conceived of in this way, the (significant) resources of the university present opportunities for anti-racist scholar-activists to leverage those resources in service to anti-racism. That universities are largely unwilling to relinquish that wealth and status, particularly for more counter-hegemonic ends, makes the redistribution of resources an act of subversion: an act of 'theft'. That the university is not a monolith, but rather an assemblage of contradictory and competing forces, creates possibilities for such theft.[40]

As participants explained, theft from the university is entirely justifiable. This framing is based upon a recognition that the imperial university's wealth is ill-gotten, amassed in part through the exploitation of minoritised groups, particularly people of colour. Many HE institutions in the UK and elsewhere are the direct beneficiaries of transatlantic trafficking and enslavement, and colonialism,[41] and continue to build on the shoulders of overworked and disproportionately underpaid staff of colour,[42] all the while treating students as 'cash cows'. It is in this context that we suggest that placing the idea of theft in conversation with a reparations discourse can be generative. Crudely, but sufficiently for our purposes, reparation invokes an imperative to seek repair to redress harms.[43] Thus, whilst it is true that subversion and subterfuge (or theft) may be necessary,[44] and the act of redirecting resources is fraught with difficulties reflecting this framing, it is also true that those acts of theft are a small part of a wider process of repair (which is to acknowledge that, though important, these largely individual acts are not enough to achieve full reparative justice; instead, they work towards those ends). Our concept of *reparative theft* therefore encapsulates the nuance of these dynamics.

There are a range of resources that anti-racist scholar-activists can look to redistribute to communities of resistance. Most obviously, there are those that are immediately economic in nature – that is, those that derive from our access to university research funding or community engagement and Impact streams. As key actors in the reparations movement make clear, however, repair is about more than the purely financial.[45] Stealing 'work time' to work on activist projects is another form of reparative theft that moves against the neoliberal forces of academic productivity. Through printing, sharing resources such as (paywalled) reading materials, and providing spaces for community meetings, there are a whole host of ways (some requiring more subterfuge than others) that we can, with a clear conscience, steal from the university for the sake of communities of resistance. The ultimate theft may involve us taking the education we have gained in the institution and using it, or repurposing it, to work outside of the university. Put another way, the ultimate theft may be the theft of ourselves: our leaving HE to take up radical community alternatives.

7 Teaching anti-racism

Teaching constitutes a key part of much academic employment in Britain and elsewhere, and, as our participants made clear, the classroom can be a site for the pursuit of anti-racism. This is reflected in Walter Rodney's conviction that the intellectual's primary site of struggle is within their 'sphere of operation'.[46] Whether it be the work of Paulo Freire, bell hooks, Henry Giroux, or others,[47] critical pedagogy holds many lessons for anti-racist scholar-activists. Such critical thought can inform our pedagogy as well as our wider scholar-activist praxes. The endeavour of engaging students in anti-racist *conscientisation*, or in cultivating an anti-racist imagination in the classroom, disrupts the hegemony of the university. It involves us eschewing the facade of political neutrality and detachment, and making it quite plain that we are on the side of marginalised communities. The rejection of neutrality also holds more fundamental significance than the cultivation of consciousness in any one classroom. It pushes against the norms of pedagogy, and through practice – both in terms of how we teach and what we teach – advocates for more engaged forms of teaching and learning. In this sense, it shows that university classrooms can not only be spaces of transformation but also spaces that can be transformed.

For anti-racist scholar-activists, transforming the classroom into radical anti-racist spaces, or at least 'breathing spaces',[48] is buttressed both by efforts to break down the power dynamics that separate teachers and learners (or consumers and providers), and by rejecting the process of rote learning. This might involve bringing difficult knowledge and emotion into the classroom in ways that are oppositional to mainstream educational discourses that privilege rationality; discourses that urge us to leave our feelings (and politics) at the door. By channelling emotion in the classroom in a direction that challenges social inequalities – as they operate in the classroom, as well as in wider society – we can, as Karl Marx urged, encourage students not simply to interpret the world but to change it.[49] Whether through more creative and active assignments or creating substantive links with activist community groups we can – and must – open up pathways for students to put that learning into practice. We must build a robust and sustainable *classroom-to-activism pipeline*.[50] Of course, this work is disincentivised by the neoliberal imperatives of the Teaching Excellence Framework and the National Student Survey in the UK context, and similar 'student-centred' performance metrics elsewhere in the world, which depoliticise the classroom and deter innovative teaching. In addition, the structures of academia now mean that research is often incentivised over teaching (one's career is far more likely to be judged on research excellence than on teaching).[51] Nevertheless, teaching remains an important site for scholar-activism, and one from which we can take seriously Stuart Hall's instruction to *struggle where you are*.

At the same time, however, we have to recognise the limits of the university, and cling on to a conception of resistance that does not become confined to the 'ivory tower'. We must therefore take radical pedagogies outside of the university, reaching 'beyond the boundaries of the classroom into communities, workplaces, and public arenas'.[52] Ultimately, we must realise that though it is important, critical pedagogy within the university is not enough on its own.

8 Building and being part of networks

We have already highlighted the importance of engagement within communities of resistance outside of the academy. This is integral to the notion of working in service (principle 3) and is manifest in the act of being there (principle 4). Here, however, we want to emphasise the need for building networks of scholar-activists within, across, and outside universities. Such networks have sustained, nourished, and inspired us, and were mentioned numerous times by participants. The importance of such supportive networks has also been noted in wider writing on scholar-activism and in work that centres the experiences of academics of colour.[53] In no small part, the need for such networks is a result of, and is underlined by, the nature of the (neoliberal-imperial-institutionally-racist, heteropatriarchal and ableist) university; which is to say, for those doing subversive work, such networks – which are largely but not exclusively, informal – offer a support mechanism and a defence against the *backlash* of the university. These networks can also be a site for strategising, drawing inspiration, and for forming collectives that enhance our power within institutions, including with students, whilst also enabling us to work collectively in service to communities of resistance outside of the academy. Key to anti-racist scholar-activism, therefore, is the process of building networks able to bring about the types of transformation we would like to see. A key task for us is ensuring that these networks extend beyond national borders and, for those of us in the Global North, that we build solidarity with colleagues in the Global South. This solidarity needs to be protected by reflexivity about the emergence of unequal power dynamics.

In addition to the more informal networks that we build, there are also more established networks, including the Universities and College

Union in the UK context. Although levels of labour union engagement varied somewhat between our participants, there was general consensus over the need to support struggles over working conditions through industrial action and union organising. A structural analysis of racial capitalism, combined with a degree of pragmatism about how the university works and recognition of the relative power of unions, make unions an important network for many scholar-activists. Unions are not without their problems, of course, particularly in terms of race and migration, and this is not to be glossed over. For anti-racist scholar-activists, to be engaged with the union requires us to recognise not only its potential but also its limits. Moreover, it requires us – as individuals and through the anti-racist blocs that we form – to push those limits, and to bring issues of race and migration from the margins to the centre. We must take care not to underestimate the work involved in crafting the union in a more anti-racist vision, or the need to engage in work beyond the union (and the university), but it is clear that unions – like teaching – continue to hold opportunities to *struggle where we are.*

9 Being strategic

Being strategic is an essential component of activism generally,[54] and of scholar-activism specifically. Although the principle of being strategic appears in the book explicitly only on occasion, it is an undercurrent that runs throughout. Whilst activists and scholar-activists are often constructed as acting on whim or impulse, the evidence presented in this book shows that strategy is at the heart of anti-racist scholar-activism. This principle reflects a more expansive understanding of what constitutes scholar-activism (principle 2), and is governed by a comprehensive and complex understanding of racism and the matrix of domination (principle 1). It is also reflective of a commitment to working in service (principle 4) and being embedded in communities (principle 5), and it enables us to think carefully about our approach to reparative theft (principle 6). Moreover, as so many of our participants explained, the strategies that we adopt are formed, constructively challenged, and refined within the networks that we build (principle 8). Evidently then, although all of the principles outlined in the chapter are interconnected, *being strategic* is particularly fundamental.

Being strategic also involves a degree of subterfuge, or *strategic duplicity*. As we discussed in Chapter 4, anti-racist scholar-activism can often involve switching between registers and performances in order to bring about the greatest benefit for communities of resistance. This might involve, as Abiola recalled, the need to 'wear a suit and tie'. It might require that we learn to speak the 'legitimate language' of our institutions, or that we become well-practised in navigating institutional processes and governance structures, including the REF in the UK context. It might also involve performing the role of the 'neutral evidence producer', as Alison put it. These decisions should always be based on a strategy that is reflexive about the potential pitfalls (or drawbacks) of such engagements, including the ways in which we perpetuate hegemonic myths about knowledge production and make ourselves complicit in institutional harms. Perhaps most importantly, being strategic implores us to think critically about when to speak up and when to preserve ourselves. This latter point, of course, encourages us to reflect upon our positionalities and how – along lines of race, class, gender, disability, sexuality, nationality, migration status, and more – some of us are rendered more vulnerable than others. Recognising our positionality and being part of networks of support (as per the previous principle) enable us to think carefully about who is best placed to speak up and when, as well as who steps back and when.

10 Being reflexive

In a similar way to the principle of being strategic, being *reflexive* undergirds the preceding principles we have put forward in this manifesto. In the first instance, it encourages us to reflect on the extent to which we are fulfilling our commitments to each of the principles set out above: it involves us reflecting on and refining our strategy, not as individuals but as collectives. It also involves us reflecting on the extent to which our work is in service to anti-racism, and the vested self-interests we might hold. This is the 'continual cycle of action and reflection'[55] that we, following Freire,[56] have sought to capture in referring to 'praxis' rather than practice. The process of reflection, however, is never finished, and we must take great care to avoid what Sara Ahmed calls, a politics of declaration: where the simple admission of privilege or poor practice is mistaken as the end point.[57]

Given our affiliation with institutional power, the principle of being reflexive also implores us to grapple with the inevitable complicities and contradictions that arise through our work. There is no escape from complicity under capitalism and there is certainly no escape from complicity in the neoliberal-imperial-intuitionally-racist academy. 'The multifarious trappings of academia' and its deep implication in the reproduction of unequal power structures 'mean that we must always be cognisant of the question: are we doing more harm than good?'[58] This uncomfortable question should be one that we return to time and time again. Central to being reflexive is this praxis of questioning both ourselves and the power structures that we maintain. With this in mind, we should consider, as Cornel West asks, are we governed more by 'ruthless ambition than [we] are [by] moral conviction'? Are we 'tied to a *we* consciousness [or] … an *I* consciousness'?[59] Similarly, as Cann and DeMeulenaere encourage us to ask, are we being 'coopted by the system. Selling out'?[60] To reflect seriously on these questions requires that we think about our own relative positions of power, be they attributable to race, class, gender, disability, sexuality, or any other stratifier. Reflexive positionality has to be at the heart of anti-racist scholar-activism. Ultimately, reflexivity urges us to always consider our role in the academy, to never become too comfortable, and be attentive to the possibility that we might be more effective from elsewhere – that is to say, we may in the future need to enact a practice of refusal[61] and leave the university. This must form part of our *freedom dreams*.[62]

Anti-racist scholar-activist futures

The principles that we have presented here, like the book at large, are in no way exhaustive. We know that there are a range of other principles that other anti-racist scholar-activists will identify, and perhaps some scholar-activists will want to discuss, adapt, or correct the principles we have offered here. Like all books, this work is inevitably incomplete: as are we, as anti-racist scholar-activists. We hope, however, that by drawing upon the wisdom of our participants, and that of the co-conspirators and comrades that we work and organise with, this manifesto – and the book more broadly – offers a springboard from which we can better think about the role and duties of academics in the contemporary university. We hope that it can serve as a catalyst to encourage more people to take up the praxes of anti-racist scholar-activism and for us, together, to move scholar-activism from margin to centre. We hope too that it can enable us, collectively, to refine and sharpen that praxes, so that they better service communities of resistance and broader anti-racist movements.

HE is fraught with problems, many of which are deep-rooted. Despite all of this, and notwithstanding the institutional backlash we face as anti-racist scholar-activists, we have shown in this book that the university presents a range of opportunities – pockets of possibility – to those of us who are committed to anti-racism specifically and social justice more generally. With such enduring racial injustices nationally and globally, it is vital that those of us within the academy find ways to contribute to anti-racist resistance; all the while, we must struggle where we are to reshape, or rather radically overhaul, the contemporary university in our collective vision. Moreover, we must continue to bring our *freedom dreams* into being by bolstering existing, and building new, alternatives to the university. The accounts in this book show that there *are* academics working in universities who are deeply committed to forms of anti-racist resistance. We hope that many more will join us, and that this book inspires and informs bright anti-racist scholar-activist futures.

Notes

Introduction: anti-racist scholar-activism and the neoliberal-imperial-institutionally-racist university

1 Following Sivanandan, we use 'communities of resistance' throughout this book to capture the agentic nature of 'marginalised communities'; see Ambalavaner Sivanandan, *Communities of Resistance: Writings of Black Struggles for Socialism* (London: Verso, 2019).

2 Though commonly regarded more as a public intellectual than a scholar-activist, Karim Murji advances a compelling argument for seeing Hall as a 'theorist-activist' – a concept he perceives to 'overlap with ... [but] carries a different inflection from both' public intellectual and scholar-activist; see Karim Murji, 'Stuart Hall as a criminological theorist-activist', *Theoretical Criminology*, 24:3 (2020), 447–460.

3 We are very deliberate in referencing extensively throughout. This book builds upon a wide range of works that have come before, and so our interventions are born out of this wider scholarship. As such, and taking a politics of citation seriously, we hope that a further contribution we make is to draw attention to many of the important works that we cite. We therefore encourage readers to follow up and engage with the citations that we draw upon. As Sara Ahmed argues, 'Citation is how we acknowledge our debt to those who came before.' See Sara Ahmed, *Living a Feminist Life* (London: Duke University Press, 2017), p. 17.

4 The dictum 'pessimism of the intelligence, optimism of the will' was first coined by Romain Rolland and later developed by Gramsci, to whom it is most commonly attributed, before it was then later picked up by Hall; see

Notes

Stuart Hall, 'The great moving right show', *Marxism Today*, January 1979, available at: https://mronline.org/wp-content/uploads/2019/06/79_01_hall.pdf [accessed 4 June 2021].

5   We return to the concept of freedom dreams throughout the book because, as well as influencing the spirit with which we have written the book, we argue that freedom dreaming is also an important component of anti-racist scholar-activist praxes; see Robin D.G. Kelley, *Freedom Dreams: The Black Radical Imagination* (Boston, MA: Beacon Press, 2002).

6   Deborah Gabriel and Shirley Anne Tate, *Inside the Ivory Tower* (London: Trentham Books, 2017); Jason Olsen, Miro Griffiths, Armineh Soorenian, and Rebecca Porter, 'Reporting from the margins: Disabled academics reflections on higher education', *Scandinavian Journal of Disability Research*, 22:1 (2020), 265–274; Michael Seal, *The Interruption of Heteronormativity in Higher Education* (London: Palgrave, 2019); Katy Sian, *Navigating Institutional Racism in British Universities* (London: Palgrave, 2019).

7   Les Back, *Academic Diary: Or Why Higher Education Still Matters* (London: Goldsmiths Press, 2016); Mark Olssen, 'Neoliberal competition in higher education today: Research, accountability and impact', *British Journal of Sociology of Education*, 37:1 (2015), 129–148.

8   Henry Giroux, 'Do hope and critical pedagogy matter under the reign of neoliberalism?', in *Issues in Art and Design Teaching*, ed. by Nicholas Addison and Lesley Burgess (London: Routledge Falmer, 2003), 167–177, p. 173.

9   Scarlett Harris, 'Islamophobia and anti-racism in two british cities: Place, theory and practice'. PhD thesis, University of Glasgow, 2020, p. 5.

10 David Gillborn, 'Anti-racism: From policy to praxis', in *Routledge International Companion to Education*, ed. by Miriam Ben-Peretz, Sally Brown, and Bob Moon (London: Routledge, 2000), 476–488.

11 Alana Lentin, *Racism and Anti-Racism in Europe* (London: Pluto Press, 2004), p. 1.

12 Alastair Bonnett, *Anti-Racism* (London: Routledge, 2000), p. 3.

13 Adam Elliott-Cooper, 'The struggle that cannot be named: Violence, space and the re-articulation of anti-racism in post-Duggan Britain', *Ethnic and Racial Studies*, 41:14 (2018), 2445–2463.

14 Lentin, *Racism and Anti-Racism in Europe*, p. 6.

15 As a concept, political Blackness points to the existence of a shared experience 'of colonial rule and subsequent state racism' that unites people from 'African, Caribbean and Asian migrant communities as Black peoples'; see John Narayan, 'British black power: The anti-imperialism of political blackness

and the problem of nativist socialism', *The Sociological Review*, 67:5 (2019), 945–967, p. 946.

16 Jenny Bourne, 'The life and times of institutional racism', *Race & Class*, 43:2 (2001), 7–22, p. 12.

17 Narayan, 'British black power', p. 945.

18 Paul Gilroy, *There Ain't No Black in the Union Jack* (London: Routledge, 2002 [1987]), p. 177.

19 For a critical analysis of the limits of seeing racism as confined to the far-Right, see Aurelien Mondon and Aaron Winter, *Reactionary Democracy: How Racism and the Populist Far Right Became Mainstream* (London: Verso, 2020).

20 Bourne, 'The life and times of institutional racism', p. 12.

21 Paul Gilroy, 'The end of anti-racism', *Journal of Ethnic and Migration Studies*, 17:1 (1990), 71–83, p. 71.

22 For a searing critique of these trends, see Benjamin Zephaniah, *The Race Industry*, available at: https://benjaminzephaniah.com/rhymin/talking-turkeys-2/ [accessed 4 June 2021].

23 Lentin, *Racism and Anti-Racism in Europe*.

24 Ibid.

25 Liz Fekete, 'Reclaiming the fight against racism in the UK', *Race & Class*, 61:4 (2020), 87–95, p. 90.

26 For example, the Sewell Report has been criticised for its lack of 'intellectual rigour, academic credibility and stakeholder engagement', and its gross and disingenuous misrepresentation of evidence; see Runnymede Trust, *Sewell Reports: Runnymede Responds*, available at: www.runnymedetrust.org/sewell [accessed 4 June 2021].

27 Adam Forrest, 'Who are the authors behind government's race report?', *The Independent*, 31 March 2021, available at: www.independent.co.uk/news/uk/politics/race-commission-report-uk-racism-b1824922.html [accessed 4 June 2021].

28 Institute of Race Relations, *IRR: Sewell Report Seeks to Sideline Structural Factors Attached to Racism*, available at: https://irr.org.uk/article/irr-responds-to-commission-race-ethnic-disparities-report/ [accessed 4 June 2021].

29 Jasbinder S. Nijjar, 'Echoes of empire', *Social Justice*, 45:2/3 (2018), 147–162.

30 Gilroy, 'The end of anti-racism', p. 71.

31 Lentin, *Racism and Anti-Racism in Europe*, p. 129.

32 Fekete, 'Reclaiming the fight against racism in the UK'; also see Narayan, 'British black power'.

33 Initially introduced through a set of policies in 2012, the hostile environment describes a set of measures, policies, and a wider culture that seeks to make

life in the UK as hostile as possible for those without 'leave to remain'. It has had a chilling – sometimes fatal – effect on the lives of migrants and people of colour in the UK; see Maya Goodfellow, *Hostile Environment: How Immigrants Became Scapegoats* (London: Verso, 2018).

34 Prevent is one of four policy strands of the UK government's counter-terrorism strategy: CONTEST. It was launched in 2003 by the New Labour government with the supposed purpose of countering terrorist ideology by supporting people vulnerable to radicalisation. Its remit was extended in 2015 by the Conservative–Liberal Democrat Coalition government to place a statutory duty on certain institutions (including educational institutions) to report 'at risk' individuals. It has been widely condemned for its Islamophobic underpinnings and outcomes; see, for example, Fahid Qurashi, 'The Prevent strategy and the UK "war on terror": Embedding infrastructures of surveillance in Muslim communities', *Palgrave Communications*, 4:17 (2018).

35 Paul Routledge and Kate Driscoll Derickson, 'Situated solidarities and the practice of scholar-activism', *Environment and Planning D: Society and Space*, 33:3 (2015), 391–407; Susan A. Tilley and Leanne Taylor, 'Complicating notions of "scholar-activist" in a global context: A discussion paper', *Journal of the International Society for Teacher Education*, 18:2 (2014), 53–62.

36 Kate Driscoll Derickson and Paul Routledge, 'Resourcing scholar-activism: Collaboration, transformation, and the production of knowledge', *The Professional Geographer*, 67:1 (2015), 1–7.

37 Autonomous Geographies Collective, 'Beyond scholar activism: Making strategic practices inside and outside the neoliberal university', *ACME: An International E-Journal for Critical Geographies*, 9:2 (2010), 245–274; Ruth W. Gilmore, 'Public enemies and private intellectuals: Apartheid USA', *Race & Class*, 35:1 (1993), 65–78.

38 Patricia Hill Collins, *On Intellectual Activism* (Philadelphia: Temple University Press, 2013).

39 Walter Rodney, *Walter Rodney Speaks: The Making of an African Intellectual* (Trenton, NJ: Africa World Press, 1990).

40 Stefano Harney and Fred Moten, *The Undercommons: Fugitive Planning and Black Study* (Brooklyn, NY: Minor Compositions, 2013).

41 Corinne Lennox and Yeşim Yaprak Yildiz, 'Activist scholarship in human rights', *International Journal of Human Rights*, 24:1 (2020), 4–27.

42 Catherine Eschle and Bice Maiguashca, 'Bridging the academic/activist divide: Feminist activism and the teaching of global politics', *Millennium: Journal of International Studies*, 35:1 (2006), 119–137.

Notes

43 Colette Cann and Eric DeMeulenaere, *The Activist Academic: Engaged Scholarship for Resistance, Hope and Social Change* (Gorham, ME: Myers Education Press, 2020); Sandra Grey, 'Activist academics: What future?', *Policy Futures in Education*, 11:6 (2013), 700–711.

44 David Croteau, 'Which side are you on? The tension between movement scholarship and activism', in *Rhyming Hope and History: Activists, Academics and Social Movement Scholarship*, ed. by David Croteau, William Hoynes, and Charlotte Ryan (Minneapolis: University of Minnesota Press, 2005), 20–40; Kristin Reynolds, Daniel Block, and Katharine Bradley, 'Food justice scholar-activism and activist-scholarship', *ACME: An International Journal for Critical Geographies*, 17:4 (2018), 988–998.

45 Derrick P. Aldridge, 'W.E.B. Du Bois in Georgia', *New Georgia Encyclopedia*, available at: www.georgiaencyclopedia.org/articles/history-archaeology/w-e-b-du-bois-georgia [accessed 4 June 2021].

46 Our use of 'ignorance' here seeks to capture something more than the common usage of the term, and instead draws upon Charles Mills's concept of *white ignorance* to refer to active forms of ignorance that are historically, structurally, and ideologically produced, and productive of white supremacy; see Charles Mills, 'White ignorance', in *Race and Epistemologies of Ignorance*, ed. by Shannon Sullivan and Nancy Tuana (Albany, NY: SUNY Press, 2007), 13–38.

47 Phil Scraton, *Power, Conflict and Criminalisation* (Abingdon: Routledge, 2007), p. 11.

48 Ambalavaner Sivanandan, 'Catching history on the wing', speech given at the Institute of Race Relations 50th celebration conference (2008), transcript available at: www.irr.org.uk/news/catching-history-on-the-wing/ [accessed 4 June 2021].

49 Frantz Fanon, *Black Skin, White Masks* (London: Pluto, 2008), p. 8.

50 bell hooks, *Teaching to Transgress: Education as the Practice of Freedom* (London: Routledge, 1994); bell hooks, *Feminist Theory: From Margin to Center* (Boston, MA: South End Press, 1984).

51 Paulo Freire, *Pedagogy of the Oppressed* (London: Continuum, 2005 [1970]), p. 51.

52 Walter Rodney, *The Groundings with My Brothers* (London: Verso, 2019).

53 Antonio Gramsci, *Selections from the Prison Notebooks*, ed. and trans. by Quintin Hoare and Geoffrey Nowell-Smith Hoare (New York: International Publishers, 1971).

54 Henry Giroux, David Shumway, Paul Smith, and James Sosnoski, 'The need for cultural studies: Resisting intellectuals and oppositional public spheres', *Dalhousie Review*, 64:2 (1984), 472–486, p. 479.

55 Orlando Fals-Borda, *Knowledge and People's Power: Lessons with Peasants in Nicaragua, Mexico and Columbia* (New Delhi: Indian Social Institute, 1988); Orlando Fals-Borda and Luis E. Mora-Osejo, 'Context and diffusion of knowledge: A critique of eurocentrism', *Action Research*, 1:1 (2003), 29–37.

56 hooks, *Teaching to Transgress*; hooks, *Feminist Theory*.

57 Cited by Claire Alexander (via Lawrence Grossberg) in 'Stuart Hall and "race"', *Cultural Studies*, 23:4 (2009), 457–482.

58 Alexander, 'Stuart Hall and "race"'.

59 C.L.R. James, *The Black Jacobins* (New York: Random House, 1964); Cedric Robinson, *Black Marxism* (London: Zed Press, 1983).

60 Robinson, *Black Marxism*.

61 Robin D.G. Kelley, 'Foreword: Between home and street: Andaiye's revolutionary vision', in *The Point is to Change the World: Selected Writings of Andaiye*, ed. by Alissa Trotz (London: Pluto, 2020), xxii–xxvii.

62 Patricia Hill Collins, *Black Feminist Thought* (London: Routledge, 1991), p. 554.

63 Ibid., p. 222; also see Kimberlé Crenshaw, 'Mapping the margins: Intersectionality, identity politics, and violence against women of colour', *Stanford Law Review*, 43:6 (1991), 1241–1299; Heidi Safia Mirza, 'Plotting a history: Black and postcolonial feminisms in "new times"', *Race, Ethnicity and Education*, 12:1 (2009), 1–10.

64 Ann Phoenix and Pamela Pattynama, 'Editorial: Intersectionality', *European Journal of Women's Studies*, 13:3 (2006), 187–192.

65 Adam Elliott-Cooper, '"Our life is a struggle": Respectable gender norms and black resistance to policing', *Antipode: A Radical Journal of Geography*, 51:2 (2009), 539–557.

66 Alexander, 'Stuart Hall and "race"'; Murji, 'Stuart Hall as a criminological theorist-activist'.

67 Patricia Hill Collins, 'Truth telling and intellectual activism', *Contexts*, 12:1 (2013), 36–41, p. 37.

68 Ibid., p. 38.

69 Harney and Moten, *The Undercommons*.

70 la paperson, *A Third University is Possible* (Minneapolis: University of Minnesota Press, 2017).

71 Harney and Moten, *The Undercommons*, p. 26.

72 Steven Osuna, 'Class suicide: The Black Radical tradition, radical scholarship, and the neoliberal turn', in *Futures of Black Radicalism*, ed. by Gaye Theresa Johnson and Alex Lubin (London: Verso, 2017), 10–21.

73 Gilmore, 'Public enemies and private intellectuals', p. 71.

Notes

Notes

74 Lennox and Yildiz, 'Activist scholarship in human rights'; Murji, 'Stuart Hall as a criminological theorist-activist'.

75 rosalind hampton, *Black Racialization and Resistance at an Elite University* (Toronto: Toronto University Press, 2020).

76 Osuna, 'Class suicide'.

77 David Harvey, *A Brief History of Neoliberalism* (New York: Oxford University Press, 2005), p. 3.

78 Wendy Brown, *Undoing the Demos: Neoliberalism's Stealth Revolution* (New York: Zone Books, 2015), p. 175.

79 Alpesh Maisuria and Mike Cole, 'The neoliberalization of higher education in England: An alternative is possible', *Policy Futures in Education*, 15:5 (2017), 602–619.

80 Zeena Feldman and Marisol Sandoval, 'Metric power and the academic self: Neoliberalism, knowledge and resistance in the British university', *Triple C*, 16:1 (2018), 214–233; Olssen, 'Neoliberal competition in higher education today'.

81 John Holmwood, 'Race and the neoliberal university: Lessons from the public university', in *Decolonising the University*, ed. by Gurminder K. Bhambra, Dalia Gebrial, and Kerem Nişancıoğlu (London: Pluto, 2018), 37–52.

82 Margaret Thornton, 'The mirage of merit', *Australian Feminist Studies*, 28:76 (2013), 127–143.

83 Darren Webb, 'Bolt-holes and breathing spaces in the system: On forms of academic resistance (or, can the university be a site of utopian possibility?)', *Review of Education, Pedagogy and Cultural Studies*, 40:2 (2018), 96–118, p. 96.

84 Liz Morrish, 'The accident of accessibility: How the data of the Teaching Excellence Framework creates neoliberal subjects', *LSE Blogs*, 24 September 2019, available at: https://blogs.lse.ac.uk/impactofsocialsciences/2019/09/24/the-accident-of-accessibility-how-the-data-of-the-teaching-excellence-framework-creates-neoliberal-subjects/ [accessed 4 June 2021].

85 Erin Sanders-McDonagh and Carole Davis, 'Resisting neoliberal policies in UK higher education: Exploring the impact of critical pedagogies on non-traditional students in a post-1992 university', *Education, Citizenship and Social Justice*, 13:3 (2018), 217–228.

86 Morrish, 'The accident of accessibility'.

87 Sanders-McDonagh and Davis, 'Resisting neoliberal policies'.

88 Feldman and Sandoval, 'Metric power and the academic self'.

89 The funding councils of the devolved nations are: the Higher Education Funding Council for England (HEFCE), the Scottish Funding Council (SFC),

Notes

the Higher Education Funding Council of Wales (HEFCW), and the Department for the Economy (DfE) in Northern Ireland.

90 Feldman and Sandoval, 'Metric power and the academic self', p. 219.

91 John O'Regan and John Gray, 'The bureaucratic distortion of academic work: A transdisciplinary analysis of the UK Research Excellence Framework in the age of neoliberalism', *Language and Intercultural Communication*, 18:5 (2018), 533–548.

92 Olssen, 'Neoliberal competition in higher education today'.

93 Tom Murphy and Daniel Sage, '"Perceptions of the UK's Research Excellence Framework 2014: A media analysis', *Journal of Higher Education Policy and Management*, 36:6 (2014), 603–615.

94 Olssen, 'Neoliberal competition in higher education today', p. 135.

95 Liz Morrish, *Pressure Vessels: The Epidemic of Poor Mental Health Among Higher Education Staff*, HEPI number Occasional Paper 20, available at: www.hepi.ac.uk/wp-content/uploads/2019/05/HEPI-Pressure-Vessels-Occasional-Paper-20.pdf [accessed 6 June 2021].

96 UKRI, *REF Impact*, available at: https://re.ukri.org/research/ref-impact/ [accessed 6 June 2021].

97 'Gaming' refers to the ways in which institutions artificially optimise their chances in the context of the high-stakes Research Excellence Framework. An example of this is the process by which universities designate (or do not designate) staff as 'research active' and therefore enterable into the REF.

98 John Horton, 'For diffident geographies and modest activisms: Questioning the anything-but-gentle academy', *Area*, Special Section (2020), 1–6.

99 Vik Loveday, 'The neurotic academic: How anxiety fuels casualised academic work', *LSE Blogs*, 17 April 2018, available at: https://blogs.lse.ac.uk/impact ofsocialsciences/2018/04/17/the-neurotic-academic-how-anxiety-fuels-casualised-academic-work/ [accessed 6 June 2021].

100 Olssen, 'Neoliberal competition in higher education today', p. 140.

101 O'Regan and Gray, 'The bureaucratic distortion of academic work'.

102 Webb, 'Bolt-holes', p. 96.

103 Ibid., p. 97.

104 Gurminder K. Bhambra, Kerem Nişancıoğlu, and Dalia Gebrial, 'Decolonising the university in 2020', *Identities*, 27:4 (2020), 509–516.

105 Gurminder K. Bhambra, Dalia Gebrial, and Kerem Nişancıoğlu, 'Introduction: Decolonising the university?', in *Decolonising the University*, ed. by Gurminder K. Bhambra, Dalia Gebrial, and Kerem Nişancıoğlu (London: Pluto, 2018), 1–16, p. 5.

106 Edward Said, *Orientalism* (New York: Pantheon Books, 1978).

Notes

107 Bhambra, Gebrial, and Nişancıoğlu, 'Introduction: Decolonising the university', p. 5.

108 Linda Tuhiwai Smith, *Decolonizing Methodologies*, 2nd ed. (London: Zed Books, 2018), p. 1.

109 Ibid., p. 63.

110 Estelle H. Prinsloo, 'The role of the humanities in decolonising the academy', *Arts and Humanities in Higher Education*, 15:1 (2016), 164–168.

111 Piya Chatterjee and Sunaina Maira, 'Introduction: The imperial university: Race, war, and the nation-state', in *The Imperial University: Academic Repression and Scholarly Dissent*, ed. by Piya Chatterjee and Sunaina Maria (Minneapolis: University of Minnesota Press, 2014), 1–50.

112 Kristi Carey, 'On cleaning: Student activism in the corporate and imperial university', *Open Library of Humanities*, 2:2 (2016), unpag.

113 Heidi Safia Mirza, 'Racism in higher education: "What then, can be done?"', in *Dismantling Race in Higher Education: Racism, Whiteness and Decolonising the Academy*, ed. by Jason Arday and Heidi Safia Mirza (London: Palgrave, 2018), 3–23; Sian, *Navigating Institutional Racism*.

114 Nijjar, 'Echoes of empire'.

115 Stokely Carmichael (Kwame Ture) and Charles Hamilton, *Black Power: The Politics of Liberation in America* (New York: Random House, 1967), p. 4.

116 Campaign Against Racism and Fascism, *What is Institutional Racism?*, Institute of Race Relations website, 1 October 1998, available at: https://irr.org.uk/article/what-is-institutional-racism/ [accessed 6 June 2021].

117 Andrew Pilkington, 'The rise and fall in the salience of race equality in higher education', in *Dismantling Race in Higher Education: Racism, Whiteness and Decolonising the Academy*, ed. by Jason Arday and Heidi Safia Mirza (London: Palgrave, 2018), 27–45.

118 UCU, *Black Academic Staff Face Double Whammy in Promotion and Pay Stakes*, 14 October 2019, available at: www.ucu.org.uk/article/10360/Black-academic-staff-face-double-whammy-in-promotion-and-pay-stake [accessed 6 June 2021].

119 The 'awarding gap' refers to the 13% difference between the likelihood of white students and students from Black, Asian, and Minority Ethnic backgrounds getting a First or a 2:1 degree classification. The gap widens further (24%) when we focus on the differences in awarding between white and Black students only; see Universities UK and National Union of Students, *Black, Asian and Minority Ethnic Student Attainment at UK Universities: #Closingthegap* (London: UUK and NUS, 2019).

Notes

120 UKRI is an organisation that brings together the seven disciplinary research councils in the UK, as well as Research England (which supports knowledge exchange in HE) and Innovate UK (the UK's innovation agency).

121 Paulette Williams, Sukhi Bath, Jason Arday, and Chantelle Lewis, *The Broken Pipeline: Barriers to Black PhD Students Accessing Research Council Funding* (London: Leading Routes, 2019).

122 Sian, *Navigating Institutional Racism*, p. 72.

123 David Theo Goldberg, *Are We All Postracial Yet?* (Cambridge: Polity Press, 2015).

124 Mirza, 'Racism in higher education', p. 4.

125 Shaun R. Harper, 'Race without racism: How higher education researchers minimize racist institutional norms', *Review of Higher Education*, 36:1 (2012), 9–29.

126 The Australian Research Council is responsible for administering its research evaluation framework: *Excellence in Research in Australia (ERA)*. *FOKUS* is used by the Swedish Research Council as a model for 'quality based research allocation'. There are similar examples in places like Canada, and there are parallels too with the tenure system in the United States. More broadly, metric culture dominates much of the Western HE.

127 Azeezat Johnson, 'An academic witness: White supremacy within and beyond academia', in *The Fire Now: Anti-Racist Scholarship in Times of Explicit Racial Violence*, ed. by Azeezat Johnson, Remi Joseph-Salisbury, and Beth Kamunge (London: Zed, 2018), 15–25; Smith, *Decolonizing Methodologies*.

128 Sivanandan, *Communities of Resistance*.

129 Harney and Moten, *The Undercommons*.

130 The International Network of Scholars and Activists for Afrikan Reparations (INOSAAR), *Global Report*, available at: www.inosaar.llc.ed.ac.uk/sites/default/files/atoms/files/inosaar_global_report_sept_2019_final.pdf [accessed 6 June 2021].

131 Bonnett, *Anti-Racism*; Anoop Nayak, '"White English ethnicities": Racism, anti-racism and student perspectives', *Race, Ethnicity and Education*, 2:2 (1999), 177–202; George Yancy, *Backlash: What Happens When We Talk Honestly About Racism in America* (London: Rowman & Littlefield, 2018).

132 David Gillborn, 'White lies: Things we're told about race and education that aren't true (Part 2)', *Leeds Beckett Annual Race Lecture 2016*, available at: www.youtube.com/watch?v=4Ma7oM46b2g&t=475s [accessed 6 June 2021].

133 Gayatri Chakravorty Spivak, *Critique of Postcolonial Reason* (Cambridge, MA: Harvard University Press, 1999).

Notes

134 Sara Ahmed, 'Declarations of whiteness: The non-performativity of anti-racism', *Borderlands*, 3:4 (2004), unpag.

135 Back, *Academic Diary*.

Chapter 1 – Problematising the 'scholar-activist' label: uneasy identifications

1   Carol L. Glasser and Arpan Roy, 'The ivory trap: Bridging the gap between activism and the academy', *Counterpoints*, 448 (2014), 89–109.

2   Sara Ahmed, 'The non-performativity of anti-racism', *Meridians*, 7:1 (2006), 104–126.

3   Judith Butler, *Bodies that Matter: On the Discursive Limits of Sex* (London: Routledge, 1993), p. 2; also see Bridget Byrne, 'Troubling race: Using Judith Butler's work to think about racialised bodies and selves', *Queering Development, IDS Seminar Series*, available at: www.ids.ac.uk/download.php?file=files/dmfile/byrne.pdf [accessed 6 June 2021].

4   Tilley and Taylor, 'Complicating notions of "scholar-activist" in a global context'.

5   Sivanandan, *Communities of Resistance*.

6   Chris Bobel, '"I'm not an activist, though I've done a lot of it": Doing activism, being activist and the "perfect standard" in a contemporary movement', *Social Movement Studies*, 6:2 (2007), 147–159, p. 148.

7   Tammy Castle and Danielle McDonald, 'Intellectual activism and public engagement: Strategies for academic resistance', *Justice, Power and Resistance*, 1:1 (2017), 127–133.

8   Reynolds, Block, and Bradley, 'Food justice scholar-activism'.

9   Jason Arday, *Exploring Black and Minority Ethnic (BME) Doctoral Students' Perceptions of an Academic Career* (London: UCU, 2017), available at: www.ucu.org.uk/media/8633/BME-doctoral-students-perceptions-of-an-academic-career/pdf/JA_BME_doc_students_report_Jun17.pdf [accessed 6 June 2021].

10 Sian, *Navigating Institutional Racism*; Nicola Rollock, *Staying Power: The Career Experiences and Strategies of UK Black Female Professors* (London: UCU, 2019), available at: www.ucu.org.uk/media/10075/Staying-Power/pdf/UCU_Rollock_February_2019.pdf [accessed 6 June 2021].

11 We introduce the concept of a matrix of domination in the book's Introduction. The matrix of domination captures how systems of oppression – such as race, class, gender, sexuality, disability, nationality, and others – interlock to form an overarching system of domination; see Collins, *Black Feminist Thought*.

12 Whilst this framing might be troubled by the professionalisation of many contemporary activisms, we assume that Barry is deploying a narrower and more idealistic definition of who and what constitutes an activist. It is worth noting, though, that there is often a classed aspect to who is able to do 'shit for free'.

13 Ana Lopes and Indra Dewan, 'Precarious pedagogies? The impact of casual and zero-hour contracts in higher education', *Journal of Feminist Scholarship*, 7:8 (2014), 28–42; UCU, *Precarious Work in Higher Education: A Snapshot of Insecure Contracts and Institutional Attitudes* (London: UCU, 2016), available at: www.ucu.org.uk/media/7995/Precarious-work-in-higher-education-a-snapshot-of-insecure-contracts-and-institutional-attitudes-Apr-16/pdf/ucu_precariouscontract_hereport_apr16.pdf [accessed 6 June 2021].

14 Madeline Bodin, 'University redundancies, furloughs and pay cuts might loom amid the pandemic, survey finds', *Nature*, 30 July 2020, available at: www.nature.com/articles/d41586-020-02265-w [accessed 6 June 2021]; Anna McKie, 'UK universities cutting jobs accused of exploiting pandemic', *Times Higher Education*, 1 February 2021, available at: www.timeshighereducation.com/news/uk-universities-cutting-jobs-accused-exploiting-pandemic [accessed 6 June 2021].

15 Unis Resist Border Controls, *The Hostile Environment Policy has Extended the Border into UK universities* (no date), available at: www.unisresistbordercontrols.org.uk/facts/ [accessed 6 June 2021]; see note 33 in the Introduction for a brief description of the hostile environment.

16 Emma Craddock, 'Doing "enough" of the "right" thing: The gendered dimension of the "ideal activist" identity and its negative emotional consequences', *Social Movement Studies*, 18:2 (2019), 137–153.

17 Lara Coleman and Serena Bassi, 'Deconstructing militant manhood', *International Feminist Journal of Politics*, 13:2 (2011), 204–224; Abigail Bakan, 'Marxism, feminism, and epistemological dissonance', *Socialist Studies*, 8:2 (2012), 60–84.

18 Jonathan Dean and Bice Maiguashca, 'Gender, power, and Left politics: From feminization to "feministization"', *Politics & Gender*, 14:3 (2018), 376–406.

19 Collins, *On Intellectual Activism*; Remi Joseph-Salisbury, 'Confronting my duty as an academic: We should all be activists', in *The Fire Now: Anti-Racist Scholarship in Times of Explicit Racial Violence*, ed. by Azeezat Johnson, Remi Joseph-Salisbury, and Beth Kamunge (London: Zed, 2018), 44–55.

20 Leon Sealey-Huggins, 'Depoliticised activisms? Ambivalences and pragmatism at the COP16', *International Journal of Sociology and Social Policy*, 63:9/10 (2016), 695–710.

21 Osuna, 'Class suicide'.

22 W.E.B. Du Bois, *The Talented Tenth*, Teaching American History website, available at: https://teachingamericanhistory.org/library/document/the-talented-tenth/ [accessed 6 June 2021], unpag.

23 Kehinde Andrews, *Back to Black: Retelling Black Radicalism for the 21st Century* (London: Zed Books, 2018).

24 Juan Battle and Earl Wright II, 'W.E.B. Du Bois's talented tenth: A quantitative assessment', *Journal of Black Studies*, 32:6 (2002), 654–672, p. 656.

25 Collins, *Black Feminist Thought*.

26 Aziz Choudry, 'Reflections on academia, activism, and the politics of knowledge and learning', *International Journal of Human Rights*, 24:1 (2020), 28–45, p. 31.

27 Ibid.

28 Ahmed, 'The non-performativity of anti-racism'.

29 There are a wider set of issues surrounding the co-optation of decolonization, particularly due to the erasure of its historical invocation to refer to indigenous struggles over land, sovereignty, and livelihoods; see Eve Tuck and K. Wayne Yang, 'Decolonization is not a metaphor', *Decolonization: Indigeneity, Education & Society*, 1:1 (2012), 1–40.

30 Sadhvi Dar, Angela Martinez Dy, and Jenny Rodriguez, *Is Decolonizing the New Black?*, Sisters of Resistance website, 12 July 2018, available at: https://sistersofresistance.wordpress.com/2018/07/12/is-decolonizing-the-new-black/ [accessed 6 June 2021], unpag.

31 Ibid.

32 Ibid.

33 Ahmed, 'The non-performativity of anti-racism', p. 117.

34 As we explore more in Chapter 4, for some academics the scholar-activist identity is far from desirable. Indeed, some 'traditional' academics view those engaged in scholar-activism as not being objective enough, being too political and/or too emotional, leading to a hostile experience of academia.

35 Kayla Abrams, Jemima Fregene, and Lana Awadallah, 'Discourse and debate: Is performative activism inherently bad?', *Columbia Spectator*, 26 March 2019, available at: www.columbiaspectator.com/opinion/2019/03/27/discourse-and-debate-is-performative-activism-inherently-bad/ [accessed 6 June 2021], unpag.

36 Ahmed, 'The non-performativity of anti-racism'.

37 Rodney, *The Groundings*.

38 Dar, Dy, and Rodriguez, *Is Decolonizing the New Black?*

39 Bakan, 'Marxism, feminism, and epistemological dissonance'.

40 Gilmore, 'Public enemies and private intellectuals', p. 71.

41   Kevin Hylton, 'Talk the talk, walk the walk: Defining Critical Race Theory in research', *Race, Ethnicity and Education*, 15:1 (2012), 23–41, p. 28.

42   Bobel, '"I'm not an activist"', p. 153.

43   Myfanwy Taylor, '"Being useful" after the ivory tower: Combining research and activism with the Brixton Pound', *Area*, 46:3 (2014), 305–312; Craddock, 'Doing "enough"'.

44   Taylor, '"Being useful" after the ivory tower', p. 307.

45   Bobel, '"I'm not an activist"'; Danielle K. Cortese, 'I'm a "good" activist, you're a "bad" activist, and everything I do is activism: Parsing the different types of "activist" identities in LBGTQ organizing', *Interface*, 7:1 (2015), 215–246.

46   Whilst many of us engaged in scholar-activism experience a relative lack of surveillance and criminalisation compared to non-academic activists, it is essential that we continue to be attentive to the heterogeneity in our experiences. Mediated by the matrix of domination, as well as the nature and approach of our scholar-activism, there are examples of participants in this project and beyond who, through things like counter-terrorism policy, are the subject of significant surveillance and who face the threat of criminalisation.

47   Taylor, '"Being useful" after the ivory tower'.

48   Bobel, '"I'm not an activist"', p. 154.

49   Ibid.

50   Daiyu Suzuki and Edwin Mayorga, 'Scholar-activism: A twice told tale', *Multicultural Perspectives*, 16:1 (2014), 16–20, p. 17.

51   See Boaventura de Sousa Santos, *Epistemologies of the South* (London: Routledge, 2014).

Chapter 2 – Working in service: accountability, usefulness, and accessibility

1   Sivanandan, *Communities of Resistance*; Sivanandan, 'Catching history on the wing'; Arun Kundnani, 'Introduction', in *Communities of Resistance*, by Sivanandan, xiii–xxii.

2   Sivanandan, *Communities of Resistance*.

3   For a discussion of the history of IRR, and specifically its transformation, see Liz Fekete, 'A brief history of the Institute of Race Relations', *Surviving Society Podcast*, available at: https://soundcloud.com/user-622675754/s1e1-liz-fekete-a-brief-hsitory-of-the-institute-of-race-relations [accessed 6 June 2021].

4   Sivanandan, *Communities of Resistance*.

5   Ibid., unpag [emphasis added].

6   Sivanandan's position outside of the university is worth noting here because it underlines how academics can and should learn lessons from those operating outside of academia. This point is particularly salient because many of our respondents noted that Sivanandan influenced their own praxis. It is also worth noting this point because the context of the university may raise particular questions for what it means to work in service – that is to say, we do not want to take for granted the applicability of Sivanandan's words to other contexts. With this in mind, we draw upon the insights of our participants later in the chapter (and elsewhere in the book) to consider how the notion of working in service can apply to those employed by universities.

7   Gargi Bhattacharyya, Satnam Virdee, and Aaron Winter, 'Revisiting histories of anti-racist thought and activism', *Identities*, 27:1 (2020), 1–19.

8   Sivanandan, *Communities of Resistance*.

9   Frantz Fanon, *The Wretched of the Earth* (New York: Grove Press, 2004 [1963]), p. 1.

10   Walter Rodney cited by Osuna, 'Class suicide', p. 37.

11   Osuna, 'Class suicide'.

12   Collins, *On Intellectual Activism*, p. ix.

13   Horton, 'For diffident geographies and modest activisms'.

14   Olssen, 'Neoliberal competition in higher education today'.

15   Dave Beer, *Metric Power* (London: Palgrave Macmillan, 2016).

16   Osuna, 'Class suicide'.

17   Fekete, 'A brief history of the Institute of Race Relations'.

18   Alvaro Huerta, 'Viva the scholar-activist', *Inside Higher Ed*, 30 March 2018, available at: www.insidehighered.com/advice/2018/03/30/importance-being-scholar-activist-opinion [accessed 6 June 2021], unpag.

19   Osuna, 'Class suicide', p. 38.

20   Ibid., p. 24.

21   Ulrich Oslender and Bernd Reiter, 'Introduction', in *Bridging Scholarship and Activism: Reflections from the Frontlines of Collaborative Research*, ed. by Bernd Reiter and Ulrich Oslender (East Lansing, MI: Michigan State University Press, 2019), ix–xx.

22   Harney and Moten, *The Undercommons*, p. 26.

23   Ibid.

24   Osuna, 'Class suicide'; Amílcar Cabral, *Unity and Struggle: Speeches and Writing of Amílcar Cabral* (New York: Monthly Review Press, 1979).

25   Laura Pulido, 'Frequently (un)asked questions about being a scholar activist', in *Engaging Contradictions: Theory, Politics, and Methods of Activist Scholarship*,

ed. by Charles R. Hale (Berkeley and Los Angeles, CA: University of California Press, 2009), 341–366.

26 Mark Deuze, 'Journalism in liquid modern times: An interview with Zygmunt Bauman', *Journalism Studies*, 8:4 (2007), 671–679, p. 674.

27 Kelley, *Freedom Dreams*.

28 We argue elsewhere that, given that the expansion of policing and prisons in recent years has not improved community safety, we should defund the police and invest instead in community infrastructure and education, health and social care; see Remi Joseph-Salisbury, Laura Connelly, and Peninah Wangari-Jones, '"The UK is not innocent": Black Lives Matter, policing and abolition in the UK', *Equality, Diversity and Inclusion*, 40:1 (2021), 21–28.

29 Pulido, 'Frequently (un)asked questions', p. 357.

30 Feldman and Sandoval, 'Metric power and the academic self'.

31 Morrish, *Pressure Vessels*; Loveday, 'The neurotic academic'.

32 Horton, 'For diffident geographies and modest activisms'.

33 Pulido, 'Frequently (un)asked questions', p. 251.

34 Collins, *On Intellectual Activism*, p. 43 [emphasis in original].

35 Gramsci, *Prison Notebooks*, p. 10.

36 Becky Clarke, Kathryn Chadwick, and Patrick Williams, 'Critical social research as a "site of resistance": Reflections on relationships, power and positionality', *Justice, Power and Resistance*, 1:2 (2017), 261–282, pp. 266–267.

37 Choudry, 'Reflections on academia, activism', p. 35.

38 Ornette Clennon, 'Scholar activism as a nexus between research, community activism and civil rights via the use of participatory arts', *International Journal of Human Rights*, 24:1 (2020), 46–61; Maria do Mar Pereira, 'Struggle within and beyond the performative university: Articulating activism and work in an "academic without walls"', *Women's Studies International Forum*, 54 (2016), 100–110.

39 Choudry, 'Reflections on academia, activism', p. 42; also see Clennon, 'Scholar activism as a nexus'; Julia Sudbury and Margo Okazawa-Rey, 'Introduction: Activist scholarship and the neoliberal university after 9/11', in *Antiracism, Feminism, and Social Change*, ed. by Julia Sudbury and Margo Okazawa-Rey (London: Routledge, 2009), 1–14.

40 Smith, *Decolonizing Methodologies*.

41 Choudry, 'Reflections on academia, activism', p. 42.

42 Osuna, 'Class suicide', p. 36.

43 Fals-Borda, *Knowledge and People's Power*; Fals-Borda and Mora-Osejo, 'Context and diffusion of knowledge'; Rodney, *The Groundings*.

44 Osuna, 'Class suicide'.

45 Choudry, 'Reflections on academia, activism', p. 36.

46 Olssen, 'Neoliberal competition in higher education today'.

47 Benedict Anderson, *Imagined Communities* (London: Verso, 1983); Sivanandan, *Communities of Resistance*.

48 João H. Costa Vargas, 'Activist scholarship: Limits and possibilities in times of black genocide', in *Engaging Contradictions: Theory, Politics and Methods of Activist Scholarship*, ed. by Charles R. Hale (Berkeley and Los Angeles, CA: University of California Press, 2008), 164–182, p. 166.

49 Andreas Wimmer and Nina Glick Schiller, 'Methodological nationalism and beyond: Nation-state building, migration and the social sciences', *Global Networks*, 2:4 (2002), 301–334.

50 Carmichael and Hamilton, *Black Power*, p. xi.

51 Narayan, 'British black power'.

52 Collins, *On Intellectual Activism*.

53 Grey, 'Activist academics'.

54 What, How & For Whom, *Really Useful Knowledge* (Madrid: Museo Reina Sofía, 2014), available at: https://monoskop.org/images/9/94/Really_Useful_Knowledge_2014.pdf [accessed 6 June 2021], p. 19

55 Richard Johnson, '"Really useful knowledge", 1790–1850', in *Culture and Processes of Adult Learning*, ed. by Richard Edwards, Ann Hanson, and Mary Thorpe (London: Routledge, 1993), 17–29.

56 Tunde Adeleke, 'Guerilla intellectualism: Walter A Rodney and the weapon of knowledge in the struggle for black liberation', *Journal of Thought*, 35:1 (2000), 37–59, pp. 41–42.

57 Thomas Mathiesen, *Silently Silenced: Essays on the Construction of Acquiescence in Modern Society* (Winchester: Waterside, 2004), p. 78.

58 Lennox and Yildiz, 'Activist scholarship in human rights', p. 8.

59 George Yancy, 'Afterword', in *The Fire Now: Anti-Racist Scholarship in Times of Explicit Racial Violence*, ed. by Azeezat Johnson, Remi Joseph-Salisbury, and Beth Kamunge (London: Zed, 2018), 266–274, p. 271.

60 Joy James, 'Academia, activism, and imprisoned intellectuals', *Social Justice*, 30:2 (2003), 3–7, p. 5.

61 Routledge and Derickson, 'Situated solidarities', p. 396.

62 See Robinson, *Black Marxism*; Gargi Bhattacharyya, Adam Elliott-Cooper, Sita Balan, Kerem Nişancıoğlu, Kojo Koram, Dalia Gebrial, Nadine El-Enany, and Luke de Noronha, *Empire's Endgame: Racism and the British State* (London: Pluto Press, 2021).

63 Michael Flood, Brian Martin, and Tanja Dreher, 'Combining academia and activism: Common obstacles and useful tools', *Australian Universities Review*, 55:1 (2013), 17–26.

Notes

64 Kwame Ture, *Stokely Speaks: From Black Power to Pan-Africanism* (Chicago: Chicago University Press, 2007); Angela Y. Davis, *Freedom is a Constant Struggle* (Chicago: Haymarket Books, 2016); Josh Virasami, *How to Change it* (London: Merky Books, 2020); Freire, *Pedagogy of the Oppressed*.

65 Collins, *On Intellectual Activism*, p. 42.

66 Choudry, 'Reflections on academia, activism', p. 29.

67 Ibid.

68 Alexander, 'Stuart Hall and "race"'.

69 Castle and McDonald, 'Intellectual activism and public engagement'.

70 Derickson and Routledge, 'Resourcing scholar-activism'; Choudry, 'Reflections on academia, activism'; Clarke, Chadwick, and Williams, 'Critical social research'.

71 Gargi Bhattacharyya, 'How can we live with ourselves? Universities and the attempt to reconcile learning and doing', *Ethnic and Racial Studies*, 36:9 (2013), 1411–1428.

72 Castle and McDonald, 'Intellectual activism and public engagement', p. 128.

73 Gurminder Bhambra, *Connected Sociologies* (London: Bloomsbury Academic, 2014); Sujata Patel, 'Is there a "South" perspective in Urban Studies?', in *Routledge Handbook on Cities of the Global South*, ed. by Sue Parnell and Sophie Oldfield (London: Routledge, 2014), 37–47.

74 Theresa Lillis and Mary Jane Curry, *Academic Writing in a Global Context: The Politics and Practices of Publishing in English* (New York: Routledge, 2010); Patel, 'Is there a "South" perspective'; Smith, *Decolonizing Methodologies*.

75 Asit K. Biswas and Julian Kirchher, 'Prof, no one is reading you', *The Straits Times*, 11 April 2014, available at: www.straitstimes.com/opinion/prof-no-one-is-reading-you [accessed 6 June 2021].

76 Collins, *On Intellectual Activism*, p. 41.

77 Barder cited by Duncan Green, 'Whatever happened to the Academic Spring? Publishing academic work behind paywalls is more than an inconvenience', *LSE Blogs*, 12 August 2013, available at: https://blogs.lse.ac.uk/impact ofsocialsciences/2013/08/12/whatever-happened-to-the-academic-spring-green/ [accessed 6 June 2021].

78 Collins, *On Intellectual Activism*, p. xiii.

79 Ibid.

80 Bhattacharyya, 'How can we live with ourselves?', pp. 1425–1426.

81 Sivamohan Valluvan, *The Clamour of Nationalism* (Manchester: Manchester University Press, 2019), p. 26.

82 Glenn Jordan, 'Stuart Hall as a public intellectual', *Institute of Welsh Affairs*, 27 October 2013, available at: www.iwa.wales/agenda/2013/10/stuart-hall-as-a-public-intellectual/ [accessed 6 June 2021].

Notes

83   Jessie Daniel and Polly Thistlewaite, *Being a Scholar in the Digital Era: Transforming Scholarly Practice for the Public Good* (Bristol: Bristol University Press, 2016); Michael Eric Dyson, 'Thinking out loud', *New Republic*, 10 September 2015, available at: https://newrepublic.com/article/122756/think-out-loud-emerging-black-digital-intelligentsia [accessed 6 June 2021]; Stephen J. Quaye, Mahauganee D. Shaw, and Dominique C. Hill, 'Blending scholar and activist identities: Establishing the need for scholar activism', *Journal of Diversity in Higher Education*, 10:4 (2017), 381–399; Collins, *On Intellectual Activism*.

84   Dyson, 'Thinking out loud', unpag.

85   Kelley, *Freedom Dreams*.

86   Collins, *On Intellectual Activism*, p. x.

87   Natalie Fenton, *Digital, Political, Radical* (Cambridge and Malden, MA: Polity, 2016), p. 127.

88   Bhattacharyya et al., *Empire's Endgame*, p. 15.

89   Richard Seymour, 'We are witnessing the end of the "Twitter Revolution"', *New Statesman*, 27 November 2019, available at: www.newstatesman.com/science-tech/social-media/2019/11/we-are-witnessing-end-twitter-revolution [accessed 6 June 2021].

90   Casey Brienza, 'Opening the wrong gate? The Academic Spring and scholarly publishing in the Humanities and Social Sciences', *Publishing Research Quarterly*, 28:3 (2012), 159–171, p. 168; Tanner Mirrlees and Shahid Alvi, *EdTech Inc.: Selling, Automating and Globalizing Higher Education in the Digital Age* (London: Routledge, 2020).

91   George Lipsitz, 'What is this black in the Black Radical tradition?', in *Futures of Black Radicalism*, ed. by Gaye Theresa Johnson and Alex Lubin (London: Verso, 2017), 108–119.

92   Jeffrey Ghannam, *Social Media in the Arab World: Leading up to the Uprisings of 2011* (Washington: Center for International Media Assistance, 2011).

93   Zeynep Tufekci and Christopher Wilson, 'Social media and the decision to participate in political protest: Observations from Tahrir Square', *Journal of Communication*, 62:2 (2012), 363–379.

94   Kaitlynn Mendes, Jessica Ringrose, and Jessalynn Keller, '#MeToo and the promise and pitfalls of challenging rape culture through digital feminist activism', *European Journal of Women's Studies*, 25:2 (2018), 236–246; Alison Phipps, *Me, Not You: The Trouble with Mainstream Feminism* (Manchester: Manchester University Press, 2020).

95   Monica Anderson, Skye Toor, Lee Rainie, and Aaron Smith, 'Activism in the social media age', *Pew Research Center*, 11 July 2018, available at: www.

pewresearch.org/internet/2018/07/11/activism-in-the-social-media-age/ [accessed 6 June 2021].

96 Mendes, Ringros, and Keller, '#MeToo'; Remi Joseph-Salisbury, '"Does anybody really care what a racist says?" Anti-racism in "post-racial" times', *Sociological Review*, 67:1 (2019), 63–78.

97 Cathy O'Neill, *Weapons of Math Destruction: How Big Data Increases Inequality and Threatens Democracy* (New York: Crown Publishers, 2016); Safiya Noble, *Algorithms of Oppression: How Search Engines Reinforce Racism* (New York: NYU Press, 2018); Yarden Katz, *Artificial Whiteness: Politics and Ideology in Artificial Intelligence* (New York: Columbia University Press, 2020); Ruha Benjamin, *Race After Technology: Abolitionist Tools for the New Jim Code* (Medford, MA: Polity Press, 2019).

98 Michael Kwet, 'Digital colonialism: US empire and the new imperialism in the Global South', *Race & Class*, 60:4 (2019), 3–26, p. 3.

99 Collins, *On Intellectual Activism*, p. xiii.

Chapter 3 – Reparative theft: stealing from the university

1 Sivanandan, *Communities of Resistance*.

2 By way of illustration, the University of Manchester had an annual income of more than £1 billion in 2018–19, not far short of the *combined* revenues of the two major sporting brands of the same city, Manchester United and Manchester City football clubs; see Rowan Moore, 'The free-market gamble: Has Covid broken UK universities?', *Observer*, 17 January 2021, available at: www.theguardian.com/education/2021/jan/17/free-market-gamble-has-covid-broken-uk-universities [accessed 6 June 2021]; University of Manchester, *Financial Statements 2019*, available at: https://documents.manchester.ac.uk/display.aspx?DocID=46451 [accessed 6 June 2021], p. 31.

3 John D. McCarthy and Mayer N. Zald, 'Resource mobilization and social movements: A partial theory', *American Journal of Sociology*, 82:6 (1977), 1212–1241.

4 Harney and Moten, *The Undercommons*.

5 Ibid., p. 26.

6 Ibid., p. 26.

7 Janet Newman, *Working the Spaces of Power: Activism, Neoliberalism and Gendered Labour* (London: Bloomsbury, 2012).

8 Harney and Moten, *The Undercommons*, p. 26.

9 Lennox and Yildiz, 'Activist scholarship in human rights', p. 8.

Notes

10   Harney and Moten, *The Undercommons*, p. 26.

11   Ibid., p. 33.

12   Davarian Baldwin, 'Scholars for social justice – Reparations in higher education part 1', *Scholars for Social Justice*, available at: http://scholarsforsocialjustice.com/the-university-as-neighbor/ [accessed 6 June 2021]; Adom Getachew, 'Reparations 2020?' *Scholars for Social Justice*, available at: https://scholarsforsocialjustice.com/__reparations/ [accessed 6 June 2021]; hampton, *Black Racialization and Resistance*.

13   Nathaniel Tobias C̶o̶l̶e̶m̶a̶n̶, 'Eugenics: "The academy's complicity"', *Times Higher Education*, 9 October 2014, available at: www.timeshighereducation.com/comment/opinion/eugenics-the-academys-complicity/2016190.article [accessed 6 June 2021]; Robbie Shilliam, 'Behind the Rhodes statue: Empire and the British Academy, *Race Ed*, available at: www.race.ed.ac.uk/recorded-events/ [accessed 6 June 2021].

14   Collins, *Black Feminist Thought*, p. 222.

15   Christina Sharpe, *In the Wake: On Blackness and Being* (London: Duke University Press, 2016).

16   Harney and Moten, *The Undercommons*, p. 31.

17   INOSAAR, *Global Report*, pp. 4–5.

18   Ibid.; whilst this short definition suffices for our purposes in this chapter, INOSAAR's report, and their wider activities, provide a useful starting point for those interested in the rich history and present of the movement for African reparations.

19   Despite welcoming 'reparation' initiatives, critics have quite rightly problematised the parameters of the 'reparations' that Glasgow are offering. Heuchan, for example, notes that the development of a research centre is 'unlikely to do any tangible, material good in the lives of people who are still harmed by the legacy of the transatlantic slave trade'; Claure Heuchan, 'If Glasgow University is serious about slavery reparations, it would pay those still affected', *HuffPost*, 23 August 2019, available at: www.huffingtonpost.co.uk/entry/university-glasgow-reparations-slave-trade_uk_5d5fdea1e4b0dfcbd48c3065 [accessed 6 June 2021].

20   la paperson, *A Third University*.

21   INOSAAR, *Global Report*, p. 12.

22   Andrews, *Back to Black*.

23   Harney and Moten, *The Undercommons*; la paperson, *A Third University*; Osuna, 'Class suicide'.

24   Baldwin, 'Reparations in higher education'.

25   Harney and Moten, *The Undercommons*.

26 As Walter Rodney pronounced, the 'guerrilla intellectual' must rid themselves of the 'Babylonian captivity of bourgeois society'; see Adeleke, 'Guerilla intellectualism', p. 41.

27 Freire, *Pedagogy of the Oppressed*.

28 Bhattacharyya, 'How can we live with ourselves?', p. 1471.

29 Webb, 'Bolt-holes', p. 99.

30 Derickson and Routledge, 'Resourcing scholar-activism', p. 2.

31 Grey, 'Activist academics'; McCarthy and Zald, 'Resource mobilization'.

32 As discussed in earlier chapters, through its Impact Agenda, the UK Research Excellence Framework's exercise attempts to measure the impact of research outside of academia. The REF defines Impact as 'an effect on, change or benefit to the economy, society, culture, public policy or services, health, the environment or quality of life, beyond academia'; see UKRI, *REF Impact*. We discussed the limits and problems with the REF Impact agenda in the Introduction.

33 Laura Connelly and Teela Sanders, 'Disrupting the boundaries of the academe: Co-creating knowledge and sex work "academic-activism"', in *The Emerald Handbook of Feminism, Criminology and Social Change*, ed. by Sandra Walklate, Kate Fitz-Gibbon, JaneMaree Maher, and Jude McCulloch (Leeds: Emerald, 2020), 203–218. Similar issues can arise with other marginalised groups too, such as those whose migration status renders them vulnerable to the nationalist whims of the State.

34 See note 33 in the Introduction for a brief description of the hostile environment.

35 Grey, 'Activist academics'.

36 Of course, many of those we spoke to engaged in activism in addition to their academic work, regardless of whether the two were tied.

37 O'Regan and Gray, 'The bureaucratic distortion of academic work'; Murphy and Sage, 'Perceptions of the UK's Research Excellence Framework'; Nicholas Stern, *Research Excellence Framework Review (Stern Review)* (London: Department for Business, Energy & Industrial Strategy, 2016).

38 la paperson, *A Third University*.

39 Webb, 'Bolt-holes'.

40 Noam Chomsky, 'The responsibility of intellectuals', *New York Review of Books*, 23 February 1967, available at: https://chomsky.info/19670223/ [accessed 6 June 2021].

41 Webb, 'Bolt-holes'.

42 Osuna, 'Class suicide'.

43 Harney and Moten, *The Undercommons*, p. 26.

Notes

44 Choudry, 'Reflections on academia, activism', p. 34.

45 Baldwin, 'Reparations in higher education'.

46 Resistance Lab is an ongoing collaboration between tech experts and scholars, activists, and grassroots community groups working to confront state violence in Greater Manchester (see resistancelab.network).

47 Northern Police Monitoring Project (NPMP) is an independent grassroots organisation working to build community resistance in Greater Manchester to police harassment, violence, and racism. Whilst providing support to over-policed communities in the immediate term, NPMP is committed to abolitionism (see npolicemonitor.co.uk).

48 Whilst this may be true, it is also important to note the ways in which university spaces are saturated in racialised and classed meanings and, though in different ways, are therefore themselves not neutral.

49 Clennon, 'Scholar-activism as a nexus', p. 53.

50 Ibid.

51 Pierre Bourdieu, *Distinction: A Social Critique of the Judgement of Taste* (Cambridge, MA: Harvard University Press, 1984).

52 These tensions and contradictions are evident in Pulido's writing. She reflects, with regret, on not 'utilizing [her] legitimacy as a university professor' to leverage power for communities of resistance, due to her desire to reject the 'model of the academic "expert"'; see Pulido, 'Frequently (un)asked questions', p. 356.

53 Chomsky, 'The responsibility of intellectuals'.

54 See Osuna, 'Class suicide'.

55 Harney and Moten, *The Undercommons*, p. 26.

56 Collins, *Black Feminist Thought*.

57 Clarke, Chadwick, and Williams, 'Critical social research'.

58 Phil Scraton, 'Bearing witness to the "pain of others": Researching power, violence and resistance in a women's prison', *International Journal for Crime, Justice and Social Democracy*, 5:1 (2016), 5–20.

59 Cornel West, *Black Prophetic Fire* (Boston: Beacon Press, 2014), p. 64.

60 Bhattacharyya, 'How can we live with ourselves?', pp. 1419–1420; also see Michael Keith, 'Public sociology? Between heroic immersion and critical distance: personal reflections on academic engagement with political life', *Critical Social Policy*, 28:3 (2008), 320–334.

61 Harney and Moten, *The Undercommons*.

62 Eschle and Maiguashca, 'Bridging the academic/activist divide'.

63 Harney and Moten, *The Undercommons*.

Chapter 4 – Backlash: opposition to anti-racist scholar-activism within the academy

1   Eric Herring, 'Remaking the mainstream: The case for activist IR scholarship', *Millennium: Journal of International Studies*, 35:1 (2006), 105–118, p. 117.

2   Harney and Moten, *The Undercommons*, p. 26.

3   Suzuki and Mayorga, 'Scholar-activism: A twice told tale', p. 19.

4   In this chapter, we do not focus on the backlash that occurs outside of the academy. It is, however, worth noting that some academics who might be understood as anti-racist scholar-activists have been subjected to mainstream and social media backlash, including Kehinde Andrews and Adam Elliott-Cooper (both frequent targets of the *Daily Mail*), and Priyamvada Gopal. As we will discuss, George Yancy is a particularly pertinent example in the United States.

5   Nayak, '"White English ethnicities"'; Yancy, *Backlash*; Bonnett, *Anti-Racism*; Keith Aoki, 'The scholarship of reconstruction and the politics of backlash', *Iowa Law Review*, 81:5 (1995), 1467–1488.

6   Collins, *Black Feminist Thought*.

7   Aoki, 'Politics of backlash', p. 1468.

8   Mirza, 'Racism in higher education'; Sian, *Navigating Institutional Racism*; Katy Sian, 'Being black in a white world: Understanding racism in British universities', *Papeles del CEIC: International Journal on Collective Identity Research*, 2:176 (2017), 1–26; Rollock, *Staying Power*; Shirley Anne Tate and Paul Bagguley, 'Building the anti-racist university: Next steps', *Race, Ethnicity and Education*, 20:3 (2017), 289–299; Remi Joseph-Salisbury, 'Institutionalised whiteness, racial microaggressions and black bodies out of place in higher education', *Whiteness and Education*, 4:1 (2019), 1–17; Jason Arday and Heidi Safia Mirza (eds), *Dismantling Race in Higher Education* (London: Palgrave, 2018).

9   Nirmal Puwar, *Space Invaders: Race, Gender and Bodies Out of Place* (Oxford: Berg, 2004).

10 In *Empire's Endgame*, Bhattacharyya and colleagues unpack the limits of such representational politics, not least for the presupposition of the value of calls for increased representation (or diversity) in institutions, in this case the university; see Bhattacharyya et al., *Empire's Endgame*.

11 Karis Campion, 'Universities must not forget about BAME students during this crisis', *WONKHE*, 15 May 2020, available at: https://wonkhe.com/blogs/universities-must-not-forget-about-bame-students-during-this-crisis/#:~:

Notes

text=Evidence%20shows%20that%20while%20othere,students%20is%2013.4%20
percentage%20points [accessed 7 June 2021].

12   Puwar, *Space Invaders*, p. 8.

13   Ibid.

14   Faludi in Aoki, 'Politics of backlash'.

15   Bonnett, *Anti-Racism*; Nayak, '"White English ethnicities"'. It is worth noting
here that *anti-anti-racist backlash* comes in a range of forms, with a range of
motivations, and from a range of actors across the political spectrum – that
is, it is not the preserve of the political Right.

16   George Yancy, 'Dear White America', *The New York Times: Opinionator*, 24
December 2015, available at: https://opinionator.blogs.nytimes.com/2015/12/24/
dear-white-america/ [accessed 7 June 2021].

17   Yancy, *Backlash*.

18   Ibid.

19   Kalwant Bhopal, *White Privilege – The Myth of a Post-Racial Society* (Bristol:
Bristol University Press, 2018); Shirley Anne Tate, '"I can't quite put my finger
on it": Racism's touch', *Ethnicities*, 16:1 (2016), 68–85.

20   Ahmed, *Feminist Life*.

21   Patricia Hill Collins, 'Learning from the outsider within: The sociological
significance of black feminist thought', *Social Problems*, 33:6 (1986), S14–S32.

22   Remi Joseph-Salisbury, Claire Alexander, Stephen Ashe, and Karis Campion,
'Race and ethnicity in British sociology', *British Sociological Association*,
available at: https://britsoc.co.uk/publications/race-and-ethnicity-in-british-
sociology/ [accessed 7 June 2021]; Aldon Morris, *The Scholar Denied: W.E.B.
Du Bois and the Birth of Modern Sociology* (Oakland, CA: University of
California Press, 2015).

23   Judith Butler, *Gender Trouble: Feminism and the Subversion of Identity* (London:
Routledge, 1999), p. xxvvi.

24   Sara Ahmed, 'Being in trouble: In the company of Judith Butler', *Lambda
Nordica*, 2:3 (2015), 179–189, p. 180.

25   Kimberlé Crenshaw, 'Demarginalizing the intersection of race and sex: A
black feminist critique of antidiscrimination doctrine, feminist theory and
antiracist politics', *University of Chicago Legal Forum*, 1:8 (1989), 139–167, p.
140.

26   Hazel Carby, 'White woman listen! Black feminism and the boundaries of
sisterhood', in *The Empire Strikes Back*, ed. by Centre for Contemporary
Cultural Studies (London: Hutchinson and CCCS, 1982), 212–236; Valerie
Amos and Pratibha Parmar, 'Challenging imperial feminism', *Feminist Review*,
17 (1984), 3–19; Phipps, *Me, Not You*.

Notes

27 Natalie Thomlinson, *Race, Ethnicity and the Women's Movement in England, 1968–1993* (Basingstoke: Palgrave, 2015).

28 This is an issue in activism more widely. For example, Adam Elliott-Cooper notes that 'Women lead almost every campaign against a black death in police custody in post-2011 England'; see Elliott-Cooper, '"Our life is a struggle"', p. 539.

29 Barbara Applebaum, *Being White, Being Good: White Complicity, White Moral Responsibility, and Social Justice Pedagogy* (New York: Lexington Books, 2010).

30 Anne duCille, 'The occult of true black womanhood: Critical demeanor and black feminist studies', *Signs*, 19:3 (1994), 591–629, p. 623.

31 Collins, 'Learning from the outsider within'.

32 Reynolds, Block, and Bradley, 'Food justice scholar-activism'.

33 Collins, *On Intellectual Activism*, p. 147.

34 Work that, to some extent, is not counter-hegemonic acts to solidify the status quo. As Howard Zinn puts it, you can't be neutral on a moving train; see Howard Zinn, *You Can't be Neutral on a Moving Train: A Personal History of Our Times* (Boston, MA: Beacon Press, 2018).

35 Henry Giroux, *Neoliberalism's War on Higher Education* (Chicago, IL: Haymarket Books, 2014).

36 Charles R. Hale, 'Introduction', in *Engaging Contradictions: Theory, Politics and Methods of Activist Scholarship*, ed. by Charles R. Hale (London: University of California Press, 2008), 1–28, p. 3.

37 Lennox and Yildiz, 'Activist scholarship in human rights'.

38 William Shankley and Patrick Williams, 'Minority ethnic groups, policing and criminal justice', in *Ethnicity, Race and Inequality in the UK: The State of the Nation*, ed. by Bridget Byrne, Claire Alexander, Omar Khan, James Nazroo, and William Shankley (Bristol: Policy Press, 2020), 51–72.

39 Flood, Martin, and Dreher, 'Combining academia and activism', p. 20.

40 la paperson, *A Third University*.

41 Clarke, Chadwick, and Williams, 'Critical social research'.

42 Sudbury and Okazawa-Rey, 'Activist scholarship and the neoliberal university'.

43 Puwar, *Space Invaders*, p. 8.

44 Joseph-Salisbury, 'Institutionalised whiteness'.

45 Patricia Hill Collins, 'The social construction of black feminist thought', *Signs*, 14:4 (1989), 745–773; Suryia Nayak, *Race, Gender and the Activism of Black Feminist Theory* (London: Routledge, 2015); bell hooks, *Talking Back: Thinking Feminist, Thinking Black* (Boston, MA: South End Press, 1989); Akwugo Emejulu and Francesca Sobande (eds) *Black Feminism in Europe* (London: Pluto Press, 2019).

46 Quaye, Shaw, and Hill, 'Blending scholar and activist', p. 393.

47 As a woman of colour, Ereene embodies the excess that Bill Ashcroft describes: 'Too much, too long, too many, too subversive, too voluble, too insistent, too loud, too strident, too much-too-much, too complex, too hybrid, too convoluted, too disrespectful, too antagonistic, too insistent, too insistent, too insistent, too repetitive, too paranoid, too … excessive' (ellipsis in original); see Bill Ashcroft, 'Excess: Post-colonialism and the verandahs of meaning', in *De-Scribing Empire: Post-Colonialism and Textuality*, ed. by Chris Tiffin and Alan Lawson (London: Routledge, 1994), 33–44, p. 33.

48 Sara Ahmed, 'Rocking the boat: Women of colour as diversity workers', in *Dismantling Race in Higher Education: Racism, Whiteness and Decolonising the Academy*, ed. by Jason Arday and Heidi Safia Mirza (London: Palgrave, 2018), 331–348, p. 334.

49 Claire Alexander and William Shankley, 'Ethnic inequalities in the state education system in England', in *Ethnicity, Race and Inequality in the UK: The State of the Nation*, ed. by Bridget Byrne, Claire Alexander, Omar Khan, James Nazroo, and William Shankley (Bristol: Policy Press, 2020), 93–126; see note 34 of the Introduction for a description of Prevent.

50 Anna Fazackerley, '"Xenophobia in the system": University staff launch fightback against hostile environment', *Guardian*, 26 November 2019, available at: www.theguardian.com/education/2019/nov/26/university-staff-launch-fightback-against-hostile-environment [accessed 7 June 2021]; Lennox and Yildiz, 'Activist scholarship in human rights'.

51 Universities UK International, *International Facts and Figures 2019*, available at: www.universitiesuk.ac.uk/policy-and-analysis/reports/Pages/Intl-facts-figs-19.aspx [accessed 7 June 2021].

52 International and Broke Campaign, 'The "hostile environment" in British universities', *USS Briefs*, 20 June 2018, available at: https://medium.com/ussbriefs/the-hostile-environment-in-british-universities-c8d2c04da064 [accessed 7 June 2021]; see note 33 in the Introduction for a brief description of the hostile environment.

53 Joseph-Salisbury, 'Does anybody really care?'

54 Harney and Moten, *The Undercommons*.

55 hampton, *Black Racialization and Resistance*.

56 Frances Fox Piven, 'Reflections on scholarship and activism', *Antipode*, 42:4 (2010), 806–810, pp. 809–810.

57 Joseph-Salisbury et al., 'Race and ethnicity in British sociology'.

58 UCU, *The Experiences of Black and Minority Ethnic Staff in Further and Higher Education* (London: UCU, 2016), available at: www.ucu.org.uk/media/7861/

The-experiences-of-black-and-minority-ethnic-staff-in-further-and-higher-education-Feb-16/pdf/BME_survey_report_Feb161.pdf [accessed 7 June 2021].
59 bell hooks, 'Sisterhood: Political solidarity between women', *Feminist Review*, 23 (1986), 125–138, p. 125.
60 Pulido, 'Frequently (un)asked questions'.

Chapter 5 – Struggle where you are: resistance within and against the university

1   la paperson, *A Third University*.
2   The UCU is a British trade union for further and higher education; it is the foremost of its kind, with over 130,000 members. UCU has taken industrial action at several points over the last few years – often against pay and pensions, but also in response to precarity, and issues of race and gender inequality.
3   Discussed briefly in Chapter 4, Rhodes Must Fall was a campaign initiated in South Africa, which was taken up at the University of Oxford in the UK. Although the campaign is understood to have focused primarily on demands for the removal of the statue of Cecil Rhodes, it also made wider interventions calling for institutional change; see Joseph-Salisbury, 'Institutionalised whiteness'.
4   Why is my Curriculum White? was a UK-based campaign emerging in 2014 at University College London, and lasting for several years across several campuses. The campaign drew attention to the whiteness of university curricula, amongst other issues; see UCL, *Why is My Curriculum White?* (2014), available at: www.youtube.com/watch?v=Dscx4h2l-Pk [accessed 7 June 2021].
5   Cited by Gillborn, 'White lies', unpag.
6   Ibid., unpag.
7   Rodney, *Walter Rodney Speaks*, p. 113.
8   Cited by Gillborn, 'White lies', unpag.
9   Davis, *Freedom is a Constant Struggle*.
10 Chantal Mouffe, *For a Left Populism* (London: Verso, 2018), p. 61.
11 Davis, *Freedom is a Constant Struggle*, p. 1.
12 Ibid., p. 2.
13 Michael W. Apple, *Education and Power*, 2nd ed. (London: Routledge, 1995); Johnson, 'An academic witness'; Smith, *Decolonizing Methodologies*.
14 Cabral, *Unity and Struggle*; Fanon, *The Wretched*; Rodney, *Walter Rodney Speaks*; Robinson, *Black Marxism*; Osuna, 'Class suicide'.

Notes

15 Sara Ahmed, *On Being Included: Racism and Diversity in Institutional Life* (London: Duke University Press, 2012); Les Back, 'Ivory towers? The academy and racism', in *Institutional Racism in Higher Education*, ed. by Ian Law, Deborah Phillips, and Laura Turney (Stoke on Trent: Trentham Books, 2004), 1–6; hampton, *Black Radicalization and Resistance*; Tate, '"I can't quite put my finger on it"'.

16 Ahmed, 'The non-performativity of anti-racism', p. 111.

17 Back, 'Ivory towers?', p. 4.

18 hampton, *Black Radicalization and Resistance*.

19 Esther Stanford-Xosei, 'Universities and reparative justice', *INOSAAR Roundtable* (2020), available at: www.facebook.com/INOSAAR/videos/3222009504575075 [accessed 7 June 2021].

20 Webb, 'Bolt-holes', p. 108.

21 Rodney, *Walter Rodney Speaks*, p. 113.

22 Castle and McDonald, 'Intellectual activism and public engagement'; Cann and DeMeulenaere, *The Activist Academic*; Lennox and Yildiz, 'Activist scholarship in human rights'; Sudbury and Okazawa-Rey, 'Activist scholarship and the neoliberal university'.

23 William V. D'Antonio, 'Academic man: Scholar or activist?', *Sociological Focus*, 2:4 (1969), 1–25, p. 16.

24 Freire, *Pedagogy of the Oppressed*.

25 Mary Breuing, 'Problematizing critical pedagogy', *International Journal of Critical Pedagogy*, 3:3 (2011), 2–23.

26 H. James Garrett, *Learning to be in the World with Others: Difficult Knowledge and Social Studies Education* (New York: Peter Lang, 2017).

27 Henry Giroux, *On Critical Pedagogy* (London: Bloomsbury, 2020); bell hooks, *Teaching Community: A Pedagogy of Hope* (London: Routledge, 2003); Freire, *Pedagogy of the Oppressed*.

28 Cann and DeMeulenaere, *The Activist Academic*, p. 92; also see Ricky L. Allen, 'The race problem in the critical pedagogy community', in *Reinventing Critical Pedagogy*, ed. by César A. Rossatto, Ricky L. Allen, and Marc Pruyn (Plymouth: Rowman & Littlefield, 2006), 3–20.

29 Cann and DeMeulenaere, *The Activist Academic*, p. 92; also see Marvin Lynn, Michael E. Jennings, and Sherick Hughes, 'Critical race pedagogy 2.0: Lessons from Derrick Bell', *Race Ethnicity and Education*, 16:4 (2013), 603–628; Daniel G. Solórzano and Tara J. Yosso, 'Toward a critical race theory of Chicana and Chicano education', in *Charting New Terrains of Chicana(o)/ Latina(o) Education*, ed. by Carlos Tejada, Corinne Martinez, and Zeus Leonardo (Cresskill, NJ: Hampton Press, 2000), 35–65.

Notes

30 Freire, *Pedagogy of the Oppressed*.

31 Henry Giroux and Peter McLaren, 'Radical pedagogy as cultural politics: Beyond the discourse of critique and anti-utopianism', in *Theory/Pedagogy/Politics: Texts for Change*, ed. by Donald E. Morton and Mas'ud Zavarzadeh (Urbana, IL: University of Illinois Press, 1991), 152–186, p. 160.

32 Ibid.; Freire, *Pedagogy of the Oppressed*; Lynn, Jennings, and Hughes, 'Critical race pedagogy'; Peter Mayo, *Hegemony and Education Under Neoliberalism: Insights from Gramsci* (London: Routledge, 2016); Peter Mayo, *Higher Education in a Globalising World: Community Engagement and Lifelong Learning* (Manchester: Manchester University Press, 2019).

33 Freire, *Pedagogy of the Oppressed*.

34 Rodney, *Walter Rodney Speaks*.

35 Freire, *Pedagogy of the Oppressed*, p. 35.

36 Alexis Jemal, 'Critical consciousness: A critique and critical analysis of the literature', *Urban Review*, 49:4 (2017), 602–626.

37 Collins, *Black Feminist Thought*.

38 Cann and DeMeulenaere, *The Activist Academic*, p. 96.

39 Rodney, *Walter Rodney Speaks*, p. 113.

40 Gerardo del Cerro Santamaría, 'Challenges and drawbacks in the marketisation of higher education within neoliberalism', *Review of European Studies*, 12:1 (2020), 22–38; Rille Raaper and Mark Olssen, 'Mark Olssen on neoliberalisation of higher education and academic lives: An interview', *Policy Futures in Education*, 14:2 (2015), 147–163; Pat Young, 'Out of balance: Lecturers' perceptions of differential status and rewards in relation to teaching and research', *Teaching in Higher Education*, 11:2 (2006), 191–202.

41 Feldman and Sandoval, 'Metric power and the academic self'.

42 Sanders-McDonagh and Davis, 'Resisting neoliberal policies'.

43 Henry Giroux, 'The curse of totalitarianism and the challenge of critical pedagogy', *Philosophers for Change*, 13 October 2015, available at: https://philosophersforchange.org/2015/10/13/the-curse-of-totalitarianism-and-the-challenge-of-critical-pedagogy/ [accessed 7 June 2021], unpag.

44 In the UK, key 'student-centred' (or consumer-centred) performance metrics include the National Student Survey and the Teaching Excellence Framework. For a critique of metrics, see Stephen J. Ball and Antonio Olmedo, 'Care of the self, resistance and subjectivity under neoliberal governmentalities', *Critical Studies in Education*, 54:1 (2013), 85–96; Sanders-McDonagh and Davis, 'Resisting neoliberal policies'.

45 Webb, 'Bolt-holes', p. 100.

Notes

46 Laura Connelly and Remi Joseph-Salisbury, 'Teaching Grenfell: The role of emotion in teaching and learning for social change', *Sociology*, 53:6 (2019), 1026–1042.

47 For a discussion of the tower block fire which caused seventy-two deaths and numerous injuries, see Dan Bulley, Jenny Edkins, and Nadine El-Enany, *After Grenfell: Violence, Resistance and Response* (London: Pluto Press, 2019); Remi Joseph-Salisbury and Laura Connelly, 'Grenfell was the result of a campaign of racial terror', *Novara Media*, 17 June 2018, available at: https:// novaramedia.com/2018/06/17/grenfell-one-year-on-an-unatoned-act-of-racial-terror/ [accessed 7 June 2021].

48 Connelly and Joseph-Salisbury, 'Teaching Grenfell', p. 1037.

49 Sarah Finn, 'Writing for social action: Affect, activism, and the composition classroom'. PhD thesis, University of Massachusetts, 2013, available at: https:// scholarworks.umass.edu/open_access_dissertations/791/ [accessed 11 June 2021].

50 Freire, *Pedagogy of the Oppressed*.

51 Kelley, *Freedom Dreams*.

52 Heather W. Hackman, 'Five essential components for social justice education', *Excellence and Equity in Education*, 38:2 (2005), 103–109, p. 103; also see hooks, *Teaching Community*.

53 Stanley Aronowitz and Henry Giroux, *Education Under Siege* (South Hadley, MA: Bergin and Garvey, 1985), p. 37.

54 Castle and McDonald, 'Intellectual activism and public engagement', p. 130.

55 Rodney, *Walter Rodney Speaks*, p. 113.

56 Collins, *On Intellectual Activism*, p. 153.

57 Harney and Moten, *The Undercommons*.

58 Webb, 'Bolt-holes', p. 100.

59 Ball and Olmedo, 'Care of the self, resistance and subjectivity'; Sanders-McDonagh and Davis, 'Resisting neoliberal policies'.

60 Webb, 'Bolt-holes', p. 100.

61 The 'flipped classroom' describes an approach to teaching that purportedly attempts to decentre the 'teacher', and requires students to complete reading and preparations before entering the classroom in order to increase student engagement and participation. There is evidence to suggest, however, that the flipped classroom is driven by neoliberalisation and profit interests, and 'offers no additional benefits to student learning over a nonflipped, active-learning approach'; see Jamie Jensen, Tyler Kummer, and Patricia Godoy, 'Improvements from a flipped classroom may simply be the fruits of active learning', *CBE—Life Sciences Education*, 14:1 (2015), ar5–ar12; Matthew Evans,

Notes

'Navigating the neoliberal university: Reflecting on teaching practice as a teacher-researcher-trade unionist', *British Journal of Sociology of Education*, 41:2 (2020), 574–590.

62 Sara Ahmed, *The Cultural Politics of Emotion* (London: Routledge, 2004), p. 3; also see Audrey Bryan, 'The sociology classroom as a pedagogical site of discomfort: Difficult knowledge and the emotional dynamics of teaching and learning', *Irish Journal of Sociology*, 24:1 (2016), 7–33.

63 Connelly and Joseph-Salisbury, 'Teaching Grenfell'; Dan Bousfield, Heather L. Johnson, and Jean M. Montison, 'Racialized hearts and minds: Emotional labor and affective leadership in the teaching/learning of IR', *International Studies Perspectives*, 20:2 (2019), 170–187.

64 Ahmed, *The Cultural Politics of Emotion*.

65 Megan Boler and Michalinos Zembylas, 'Discomforting truths: The emotional terrain of understanding differences', in *Pedagogies of Difference: Rethinking Education for Social Justice*, ed. by Peter P. Trifonas (New York: Routledge, 2003), 110–136; Michalinos Zembylas, 'Pedagogy of discomfort and its ethical implications: The tensions of ethical violence in social justice education', *Ethics and Education*, 10:2 (2015), 163–174.

66 See note 34 of the Introduction for a description of Prevent.

67 Joseph-Salisbury et al., 'Race and ethnicity in British sociology'.

68 Martin Oppenheimer and George Lakey, *A Manual For Direct Action: Strategy and Tactics for Civil Rights and All Other Nonviolent Protest Movements* (Chicago, IL: Quadrangle Books, 1965); Joshua K. Russell, 'Blockade', in *Beautiful Trouble: A Toolbox for Revolution*, ed. by Andrew Boyd and Dave O. Mitchell (London: OR Books, 2013), 14–17.

69 Joseph-Salisbury et al., 'Race and ethnicity in British sociology'.

70 Alexander and Shankley, 'Ethnic inequalities in the state education system'.

71 Mirrlees and Alvi, *EdTech Inc.*

72 Ibid., p. 5.

73 Webb, 'Bolt-holes', p. 102.

74 Collins, *On Intellectual Activism*, p. 129.

75 Henry Giroux, *Theory and Resistance in Education: Towards a Pedagogy for the Opposition* (London: Bergin and Garvey, 2001), p. xxvi.

76 Joseph-Salisbury et al., 'Race and ethnicity in British sociology'.

77 Gilmore, 'Public enemies and private intellectuals', p. 71.

78 hampton, *Black Radicalization and Resistance*, p. 139.

79 Ibid., p. 142.

80 Webb, 'Bolt-holes'.

81 Ahmed, *On Being Included*.

Notes

82 Azeezat Johnson and Remi Joseph-Salisbury, '"Are you supposed to be in here?" Racial microaggressions and knowledge production in higher education', in *Dismantling Race in Higher Education*, ed. by Jason Arday and Heidi Safia Mirza (Basingstoke: Palgrave Macmillan, 2018), 143–160.

83 hampton, *Black Radicalization and Resistance*, p. 146.

84 An example here would be the role that Suhraiya Jivraj and Dave Thomas, as well as Sheree Palmer, played in supporting Decolonise UKC at the University of Kent, UK; see *Decolonise UKC*, available at: https://decoloniseukc.org/ [accessed 7 June 2021] and Decolonise University of Kent Collective, *Towards Decolonising the University: A Kaleidoscope for Empowered Action*, ed. by Dave Thomas and Suhraiya Jivraj (Oxford: Counter Press, 2020).

85 Ahmed, *Feminist Life*, p. 37.

86 Collins, *On Intellectual Activism*, p. 38.

87 In Janice M. McCabe, 'Activism and the academy', *Contexts*, 17:3 (2018), 10–11.

88 Collins, *On Intellectual Activism*, p. 38.

89 Mumia Abu-Jamal, 'Intellectuals and the gallows', in *Imprisoned Intellectuals: Political Prisoners Write on Life, Liberation and Rebellion*, ed. by Joy James (New York: Rowman & Littlefield, 2003), 179–189, p. 179.

90 Heidi Safia Mirza, 'Racism in higher education', p. 11.

91 Harney and Moten, *The Undercommons*; Webb, 'Bolt-holes'.

92 Virasami, *How to Change it*; hampton, *Black Radicalization and Resistance*.

93 Kelley, *Freedom Dreams*; Bettina L. Love, *We Want to Do More Than Survive: Abolitionist Teaching and the Pursuit of Educational Freedom* (Boston, MA: Beacon Press, 2020); Virasami, *How to Change it*.

94 UCU, 'University staff balloting for pension strikes £240,000 worse off as costs rise and benefits cut', *UCU* website, 3 September 2019, available at: www.ucu.org.uk/article/10269/University-staff-balloting-for-pension-strikes-240000-worse-off-as-costs-rise-and-benefits-cut?list=1676 [accessed 7 June 2021].

95 Paul Gilroy, 'Steppin out of Babylon – race, class and autonomy', in *The Empire Strikes Back*, ed. by Centre for Contemporary Cultural Studies (London: Hutchinson, 1982), 275–314; Ambalavaner Sivanandan, 'The liberation of the black intellectual', *Race and Class*, 18:4 (1977), 329–343.

96 Satnam Virdee, 'A Marxist critique of Black Radical theories of trade-union racism', *Sociology*, 34:3 (2000), 545–565.

97 Wilf Sullivan, 'Race and trade unions', *Britain at Work: Voices from the Workplace 1945–1995*, London Metropolitan University website, available at: www.unionhistory.info/britainatwork/narrativedisplay.php?type=raceandtradeunions [accessed 7 June 2021].

98   Stephen Ashe, 'The 2018 university strike, the Tuc's racism at work survey and hegemony in higher education', *The Sociological Review*, 28 March 2019, available at: www.thesociologicalreview.com/the-2018-university-strike-the-tucs-racism-at-work-survey-and-hegemony-in-higher-education/ [accessed 7 June 2021]; Stephen Ashe, 'Why I'm talking to white trade unionists about racism', *Open Democracy*, 6 September 2019, available at: www.opendemocracy.net/en/opendemocracyuk/why-im-talking-white-trade-unionists-about-racism/ [accessed 7 June 2021]; Stephen Ashe, Magda Borkowska, and James Nazroo, *Racism Ruins Lives: An analysis of the 2016–2017 Trade Union Congress Racism at Work Survey* (Manchester: Centre on Dynamics of Ethnicity, 2019).

99   Brenden McGeever, 'Rethinking collective action: The 2018 university strike', *Discover Society*, 1 March 2018, available at: https://discoversociety.org/2018/03/01/rethinking-collective-action-the-2018-university-strike/ [accessed 7 June 2021]; Isabelle Rahman, 'Report on TUC Black Workers' Conference 2019', *UCU* website, 30 April 2019, available at: www.ucu.org.uk/article/10060/Report-on-TUC-Black-Workers-Conference-2019?list=8182 [accessed 7 June 2021].

100   Harney and Moten, *The Undercommons*.

101   Tanzil Chowdhury, 'Temporalities of the neoliberal university and resistance', *Legal Form*, 8 September 2020, available at: https://legalform.blog/2020/09/08/temporalities-of-the-neoliberal-university-and-resistance-tanzil-chowdhury/ [accessed 7 June 2021], unpag.

102   Gilmore, 'Public enemies and private intellectuals', p. 71.

103   Giroux, *Theory and Resistance in Education*, p. xxv.

104   Castle and McDonald, 'Intellectual activism and public engagement'.

105   Malia Bouattia, 'Pandemic redundancies speak volumes about the real state of progress for women of colour', *The New Arab*, 13 November 2020, available at: https://english.alaraby.co.uk/english/comment/2020/11/13/pandemic-redundancies-speak-volumes-about-real-state-of-progress [accessed 7 June 2021].

106   Castle and McDonald, 'Intellectual activism and public engagement', p. 130.

107   Madeleine Metcalf, 'Future of Goldsmiths: Staff and students hold virtual picket', *East London Lines*, 7 March 2021, available at: www.eastlondonlines.co.uk/2021/03/future-of-goldsmiths-staff-and-students-join-virtual-picket/ [accessed 7 June 2021].

108   Ashe, 'The 2018 university strike'; Ashe, 'Why I'm talking to white trade unionists about racism'; Ashe, Borkowska, and Nazroo, *Racism Ruins Lives*; UCU, *Witness: The Lived Experience of UCU Black Members* (London: UCU, 2017).

109   Kelley, *Freedom Dreams*.

110   Gilmore, 'Public enemies and private intellectuals', p. 71.

111   Webb, 'Bolt-holes', p. 99.

Chapter 6 – Uncomfortable truths, reflexivity, and a constructive complicity

1   Chandra T. Mohanty, 'US empire and the project of women's studies: Stories of citizenship, complicity and dissent', *Gender, Place and Culture*, 13:1 (2006), 7–20, p. 13.

2   Spivak, *Critique of Postcolonial Reason*.

3   Ibid.; also see Sara de Jong, 'Constructive complicity enacted? The reflections of women NGO and IGO workers on their practices', *Journal of Intercultural Studies*, 30:4 (2009), 387–402.

4   Back, 'Ivory towers?'

5   Johnson, 'An academic witness'; Zeus Leonardo, 'Through the multicultural glass: Althusser, ideology and race relations in post-civil rights America', *Policy Futures in Education*, 3:4 (2005), 400–412.

6   Kelley, *Freedom Dreams*.

7   Abu-Jamal, 'Intellectuals and the gallows', p. 179.

8   Webb, 'bolt-holes'.

9   Elliot Murphy, *Arms in Academia: The Political Economy of the Modern UK Defence Industry* (London: Routledge, 2020).

10   Maryam Jameela, 'Academics and police tied together with a £10m fund', *The Canary*, 15 January 2021, available at: www.thecanary.co/uk/2021/01/15/academics-and-police-tied-together-with-a-10m-fund/ [accessed 7 June 2021].

11   See note 33 in the Introduction for a brief description of the hostile environment, and note 34 in the Introduction on Prevent.

12   Jason Arday, 'Understanding racism within the academy: The persistence of racism within higher education', in *The Fire Now: Anti-Racist Scholarship in Times of Explicit Racial Violence*, ed. by Azeezat Johnson, Remi Joseph-Salisbury, and Beth Kamunge (London: Zed Books, 2018), 26–37; Rollock, *Staying Power*; Sian, *Navigating Institutional Racism*.

13   See note 119 in the Introduction for an explanation of what is meant by the 'awarding gap'.

14   Sven Beckert, Gill Balraj, Jim Henle, and Katherine Stevens, 'Harvard and slavery', *Transition*, 122 (2017), 201–205; Stephen Mullen and Simon Newman, 'Slavery, abolition and the University of Glasgow', *University of Glasgow* (2018), available at: www.gla.ac.uk/media/Media_607547_smxx.pdf [accessed 7 June

2021]; Lindsey K. Walters, 'Slavery and the American university: Discourses of retrospective justice at Harvard and Brown', *A Journal of Slave and Post-Slave Studies*, 38:4 (2017), 719–744.

15   Mohanty, 'US empire and the project of women's studies'.

16   De Jong, 'Constructive complicity enacted?', p. 391.

17   Beginning in the 1970s, the reflexive turn has transcended disciplinary boundaries to become one of few topics in which a consensus exists; see Douglas Macbeth, 'On reflexivity in qualitative research: Two readings, and a third', *Qualitative Inquiry*, 7:1 (2001), 35–68.

18   Newman, *Working the Spaces of Power*, p. 130.

19   Ahmed, 'Declarations of whiteness', unpag.

20   Spivak, *Critique of Postcolonial Reason*, pp. 3–4.

21   De Jong, 'Constructive complicity enacted?'

22   Osuna, 'Class suicide'.

23   Abu-Jamal, 'Intellectuals and the gallows'.

24   As we have noted in earlier chapters, capacity to engage in such work is always mediated by a range of factors, including our positionality in relation to structures of inequality (racism, heteropatriarchy, disablism, classism etc.). Our employment status and our standing within our place of work will also have an impact.

25   Abu-Jamal, 'Intellectuals and the gallows'.

26   Mirza, 'Racism in higher education'; Sian, *Navigating Institutional Racism*.

27   Spivak, *Critique of Postcolonial Reason*, pp. 3–4.

28   Boler and Zembylas, 'Discomforting truths'; Connelly and Joseph-Salisbury, 'Teaching Grenfell'.

29   Ahmed, 'Declarations of whiteness', unpag.

30   Harney and Moten, *The Undercommons*.

31   Nayak, *Race, Gender and the Activism of Black Feminist Theory*, p. 30.

32   Freire, *Pedagogy of the Oppressed*, p. 51.

33   Harney and Moten, *The Undercommons*.

34   Kelley, *Freedom Dreams*; Lipsitz, 'What is this black in the Black Radical tradition?', p. 109; also see Virasami, *How to Change it*.

35   Such spaces are often based on a radical vision of community, cooperation, and education for liberation. Drawing inspiration from the 1968 Anti-university and the Tent City University of the Occupy Movement, Free University Brighton offers a good example of this kind of work (see freeuniversitybrighton.org). Whilst other examples abound, The Free Black University is a particularly ambitious project (see freeblackuni.com). See Jakobsen for more information on the Anti-university and Walker for more information on Tent City: Jakob

Notes

Jakobsen, 'The Anti-university of London', *Libertarian Education*, 27 July 2015, available at: www.libed.org.uk/index.php/articles/515-the-antiuniversity-of-london [accessed 7 June 2021]; Peter Walker, 'Tent City University – one of the most remarkable aspects of Occupy London', *Guardian*, 19 January 2012, available at: www.theguardian.com/uk/2012/jan/19/occupy-london-tent-city-university [accessed 7 June 2021].

36 Some examples include the excellent *Surviving Society* podcasts – hosted by Chantelle Lewis and Tissot Regis, and produced by George Ofori-Addo – which aim to open up sociological knowledge (see soundcloud.com/user-622675754); the *Global Social Theory* website – a free online resource, organised by Gurminder K. Bhambra, that seeks to move beyond parochial social theory to more global perspectives (see globalsocialtheory.org/); and *Connected Sociologies*, also directed by Gurminder K. Bhambra, which provides free resources for those interested in decolonising education (see connectedsociologies.org).

37 Though there are many other informal groups, the work of Abolitionist Futures offers a great example here: https://abolitionistfutures.com/reading-groups [accessed 11 June 2021].

38 Mark Coté, Richard Day, and Greig de Peuter, 'Utopian pedagogy: Creating radical alternatives in the neoliberal age', *The Review of Education, Pedagogy, and Cultural Studies*, 29:4 (2007), 317–336.

39 Alexander Vasudeven, *The Autonomous City: A History of Urban Squatting* (London: Verso, 2017).

40 Kelley, *Freedom Dreams*; Coté, Day, and de Peuter, 'Utopian pedagogy'.

41 Pierre Bourdieu, *Language and Symbolic Power*, ed. by John B. Thompson, and trans. by Gino Raymond and Matthew Adamson (Cambridge: Polity, 1991).

42 Audre Lorde, *Sister Outsider: Essays and Speeches* (Berkeley, CA: Ten Speed Press, 1984).

43 Paulo Freire, 'On the right and duty to change the world', *Counterpoints*, 422 (2012), 45–52.

44 Mouffe, *For a Left Populism*, p. 6.

45 In Chapter 1, Dez made this point more explicitly when he warned about intellectual vanguardism. There are clear echoes, in Dez's accounts, of the Black Radical tradition that Osuna traces through Frantz Fanon, Walter Rodney, Amílcar Cabral, and Cedric Robinson. Each of these thinkers emphasises the importance of 'petit bourgeois intellectuals' betraying their class interests, in order to work in service to communities of resistance, but are deliberate and explicit in noting that struggle must be led by those at the

coalface (the colonised, or formerly colonised, proletariat); see Osuna, 'Class suicide'.

46 Andrews, *Back to Black*; Joseph-Salisbury, 'Institutional whiteness'; Sian, *Navigating Institutional Racism*.

47 Back, *Academic Diary*.

48 Alison Mountz, Anne Bonds, Becky Mansfield, Jenna Loyd, Jennifer Hyndman, Margaret Walton-Roberts, Ranu Basu, Rias Whitson, Roberta Hawkins, Trina Hamilton, and Winifred Curran, 'For slow scholarship: A feminist politics of resistance through collective action in the neoliberal university', *ACME: An International Journal for Critical Geographies*, 14:4 (2015), 1235–1259.

49 David W. Orr, 'Slow knowledge', *Conservation Biology*, 10:3 (1996), 699–702.

50 Clennon, 'Scholar activism as a nexus'.

51 Harney and Moten, *The Undercommons*.

52 The university is made up of contradictions and competing forces. As such, whilst working under the radar can be necessary and productive, as we have shown elsewhere in this book, there are also (limited and precarious) pockets of opportunity to work in ways that are more visible. In some cases, such work may even be celebrated.

53 See Sojoyner for a discussion of how struggles over time can be a feature of the Black Radical tradition; Damian M. Sojoyner, 'Dissonance in time: (Un)making and (re)mapping of blackness', in *Futures of Black Radicalism*, ed. by Gaye T. Johnson and A. Lubin (London: Verso, 2017), 59–71.

54 André Gorz, *A Strategy for Labor* (Boston, MA: Beacon Press, 1967).

55 Angela Y. Davis, *Are Prions Obsolete?* (New York: Seven Stories Press, 2011 [2002]).

56 Lopes and Dewan, 'Precarious pedagogies?'; UCU, *Precarious work in Higher Education*.

57 David Graeber, *Bullshit Jobs* (London: Simon & Schuster, 2018).

58 Kelley, *Freedom Dreams*.

59 This raises questions about how we support students in mobilising for free education, and whether such work – as well as building community education alternatives – is a way that we can mitigate our complicity.

60 Matthew Bolton, *How to Resist: Turn Protest to Power* (London: Bloomsbury, 2017).

61 De Jong, 'Constructive complicity enacted?'

62 Several of our participants noted that such recognition was often superficial and did not reflect meaningful engagement with the more radical or oppositional aspects of the research, or that such recognition was given at the

Notes

same time that the institution pursued interests that were directly antithetical to the work that had been recognised for its impact.

63 Bhattacharyya, 'How can we live with ourselves?', p. 1424.
64 Ahmed, 'Declarations of whiteness', unpag.
65 See note 47 in Chapter 3 for a short description of the Northern Police Monitoring Project.
66 Spivak, *Critique of Postcolonial Reason*.
67 Mohanty, 'US empire and the project of women's studies'.
68 Ahmed, 'Declarations of whiteness', unpag.
69 Abu-Jamal, 'Intellectuals and the gallows'.
70 Kelley, *Freedom Dreams*.

A manifesto for anti-racist scholar-activism

1   Back, *Academic Diary*, p. 21.
2   Derrick Bell, *Faces at the Bottom of the Well* (New York: Basic Books, 1992), p. 198.
3   Ruth Wilson Gilmore, 'Fatal couplings of power and difference: Notes of racism and geography', *The Professional Geographer*, 54:1 (2002), 15–25, p. 21.
4   Whilst remembering, as we argued in the book's Introduction, there is more to anti-racism than the inverse of racism.
5   Alana Lentin, 'Racism in public or public racism: Doing anti-racism in "post-racial" times', *Ethnic and Racial Studies*, 39:1 (2016), 33–48; Goldberg, *Are We All Postracial Yet?*
6   Avery F. Gordon, 'On "lived theory": An interview with A. Sivanandan', *Race & Class*, 55:4 (2014), 1–7, p. 3.
7   Gargi Bhattacharyya, 'Gargi Bhattacharyya on racial capitalism', *Our Voices, Open Democracy* (2020), available at: www.opendemocracy.net/en/oureconomy/gargi-bhattacharyya-racism-state-sponsored-predilection-early-death/ [accessed 11 June 2021].
8   Angela Y. Davis, *Women, Culture and Politics* (New York: Vintage Books, 1984), p. 14.
9   Collins, *Black Feminist Thought*.
10 Gilmore, 'Public enemies and private intellectuals', p. 72.
11 Mohanty, 'US empire and the project of women's studies'.
12 Sivanandan, *Communities of Resistance*.
13 Bakan, 'Marxism, feminism, and epistemological dissonance'; Bobel, '"I'm not an activist"'.

Notes

14 Clennon, 'Scholar activism as a nexus'.

15 Johnson, 'An academic witness'; Smith, *Decolonizing Methodologies*.

16 Reynolds, Block, and Bradley, 'Food justice scholar-activism'.

17 Virasami, *How to Change it*; Aziz Choudry, *Learning Activism: The Intellectual Life of Contemporary Social Movements* (Toronto: Toronto University Press, 2015).

18 Ture, *Stokely Speaks*, p. 185.

19 Gilmore, 'Public enemies and private intellectuals', p. 71.

20 Ahmed, *On Being Included*; Bhambra, Nişancıoğlu, and Gebrial, 'Decolonising the university in 2020'; Dar, Dy, and Rodriguez, *Is Decolonizing the New Black?*

21 Choudry, 'Reflections on academia, activism'.

22 Davis, *Freedom is a Constant Struggle*.

23 De Sousa Santos, *Epistemologies of the South*.

24 Although the similarities and overlaps are significant, these different configurations may reflect different power balances and emphases between activism and scholarship, as well as reflecting the space from which one operates.

25 Ambalavaner Sivanandan, 'All that melts into air is solid: The hokum of New Times', *Race & Class*, 31:3 (1990), 1–30; Sivanandan, 'Catching history on the wing'; Sivanandan, *Communities of Resistance*.

26 Osuna, 'Class suicide'.

27 Collins, *On Intellectual Activism*.

28 See, for example, Choudry, 'Reflections on academia, activism'; Clarke, Chadwick, and Williams, 'Critical social research'; Huerta, 'Viva the scholar-activist'.

29 We use 'study' here in Harney and Moten's sense; see Harney and Moten, *The Undercommons*.

30 Ibid., p. 26.

31 As Campt puts it, '"practicing refusal" names the urgency of rethinking the time, space, and fundamental vocabulary of what constitutes politics, activism, and theory, as well as what it means to refuse the terms given to us to name these struggles'. It may involve, therefore, refusing the institution; see Tina Marie Campt, 'Black visuality and the practice of refusal', *Women & Performance: A Journal of Feminist Theory*, 29:1 (2019), 79–87, p. 80.

32 Kelley, *Freedom Dreams*.

33 Clarke, Chadwick, and Williams, 'Critical social research', p. 261.

34 Derek H. Alderman and Joshua F.J. Inwood, 'The need for public intellectuals in the Trump era and beyond: Strategies for communication, engagement, and advocacy', *The Professional Geographer*, 71:1 (2019), 145–151; Derickson and Routledge, 'Resourcing scholar-activism'.

Notes

35 Julius Lester, 'James Baldwin: Reflections of a Maverick', *New York Times*, 27 May 1984; Phil Scraton, 'Bearing witness'.

36 Harney and Moten, *The Undercommons*.

37 Ibid.

38 Rodney, *Walter Rodney Speaks*.

39 Harney and Moten, *The Undercommons*, p. 26.

40 la paperson, *A Third University*.

41 Mullen and Newman, 'Slavery, abolition and the University of Glasgow'; Walters, 'Slavery and the American university'.

42 Sian, *Navigating Institutional Racism*.

43 Noting the 'long and varied history' of the struggle for reparations, as well as the need for a 'multidirectional and multidimensional definition of reparations', INOSAAR offer a useful definition: 'Reparations are not simply a long-overdue "pay cheque" but a call for holistic repairs that seek to heal those within the black and Afrikan communities, guarantee the equal participation of all members of the human race (for example, through self-determination), eradicate the effects of Afrikan enslavement and the subsequent histories of colonialism and racial oppression, and find ways to rebuild respectful and egalitarian relations between all communities through the recognition of responsibility for the wrong committed and the harm inflicted'; see INOSAAR, *Global Report*, p. 14.

44 Harney and Moten, *The Undercommons*.

45 INOSAAR, *Global Report*.

46 Rodney, *Walter Rodney Speaks*, p. 113.

47 Freire, *Pedagogy of the Oppressed*; hooks, *Teaching to Transgress*; hooks, *Teaching Community*; Giroux, 'The curse of totalitarianism'; Giroux, *On Critical Pedagogy*.

48 Webb, 'Bolt-holes'.

49 Karl Marx, 'Theses on Feuerbach', *Marx/Engles Internet Archive*, available at: www.marxists.org/archive/marx/works/1845/theses/theses.htm [accessed 7 June 2021].

50 As discussed in Chapter 5, we offer the concept of the *classroom-to-activism pipeline* to refer to the ways in which we can set up our classrooms, and our pedagogical praxis, to encourage and enable students to engage in activism beyond the classroom – that is, the task of ensuring our teaching is nurturing future and emerging anti-racist scholar-activists.

51 Feldman and Sandoval, 'Metric power and the academic self'.

52 Antonia Darder, 'Imagining justice in a culture of terror: Pedagogy, politics, and dissent', in *Critical Pedagogy in Uncertain Times*, ed. by Sheila Macrine (Basingstoke: Palgrave Macmillan, 2009), p. 151–166.

Notes

53 Choudry, 'Reflections on academia, activism'; hampton, *Black Racialization and Resistance*.

54 Virasami, *How to Change it*.

55 Cann and DeMeulenaere, *The Activist Academic*, p. 35.

56 Freire, *Pedagogy of the Oppressed*.

57 Ahmed, 'Declarations of whiteness', unpag; also see Azeezat Johnson, 'Throwing our bodies against the white background of academia', *AREA: Ethics in/of Geographical Research*, 52:1 (2020), 89–96.

58 Joseph-Salisbury, 'Confronting my duty', p. 52.

59 Cornel West, 'The betrayal of the black elite, *The Real News*, available at: www.youtube.com/watch?v=CA7NA2TgXBQ [accessed 7 June 2021], unpag.

60 Cann and DeMeulenaere, *The Activist Academic*, p. 13.

61 Campt, 'Black visuality'.

62 Kelley, *Freedom Dreams*.

Index

Index